A Season of Opera: From Orpheus to Ariadne

A Season of Opera: From Orpheus to Ariadne

M. OWEN LEE

UNIVERSITY OF TORONTO PRESS
Toronto Buffalo London

© University of Toronto Press Incorporated 1998
Toronto Buffalo London
Printed in Canada

Reprinted 1998

ISBN 0-8020-4296-1

Printed on acid-free paper

Canadian Cataloguing in Publication Data

Lee, M. Owen, 1930–
A season of opera : from Orpheus to Ariadne

Includes index.
ISBN 0-8020-4296-1

1. Operas – Analysis, appreciation.   I. Title.

MT95.L483 1998   782.1015   C97-932460-2

Musical excerpts from *Salome* © Copyright 1905 by Adolph Furstner.
U.S. Copyright Renewed. Copyright assigned 1943 to Hawkes & Son (London)
Ltd. (a Boosey & Hawkes company) for the world excluding Germany, Italy,
Portugal, and the Former Territories of the U.S.S.R. (excluding Estonia, Latvia,
and Lithuania). Reproduced by permission of Boosey & Hawkes.

University of Toronto Press acknowledges the financial assistance to its publishing
program of the Canada Council for the Arts and the Ontario Arts Council.

for
Dr Bill Lonsdale

Contents

Preface   ix

1 The Birth of Opera from the Spirit of Orpheus   3

2 Du Musst dein Leben Ändern: *Orfeo ed Euridice*   13

3 The Opera of All Operas: *Don Giovanni*   19

4 The Music of Intuitive Angels: *The Magic Flute*   27

5 Music to Set the Spirit Free: *Fidelio*   41

6 Show Business Sense: *L'Elisir d'Amore*   54

7 Oh, Sweet Music of Donizetti! *Lucia di Lammermoor*   60

8 Elemental, Furious, Wholly True: *Il Trovatore*   67

9 The Requisite Miracle: *La Traviata*   78

10 The Whole Checkered Play of Life: *La Forza del Destino*   84

11 Melt Egypt into Nile: *Aida*   90

12 A Figure as Old as Comedy: *Falstaff*   97

13 The Exasperated Eagle and the Stoic Saint: *Les Troyens*   101

14 The Sins of Wagner's Youth: *Rienzi*   111

15 Long Day's Journey into Night: *Tristan und Isolde*   118

16 The Making of a Musical Legend: *Palestrina*   139

17 The Moon Is Like the Moon: *Salome*   147

18 Genius and *Morbidezza*: *Manon Lescaut*   153

19 Mists, Sails, Sounds, and Impressions: *Pelléas et Mélisande*   158

20 It Is Your Turn to Speak: *Dialogues des Carmélites*   170

21 An Opera Made of Songs: *Porgy and Bess*   182

22 The Music Wrote Itself: *Oklahoma!*   191

23 HURRY UP PLEASE ITS TIME   197

Further Reading   217

Recordings and Videos   221

Index   231

Preface

Poscimur. The Roman poet Horace began one of his odes with that one word, which in English must be expanded to six: 'I am asked for a song.' With that same word I, who have taught Horace for thirty-five years, would like to preface this collection of pieces on opera. Its chapters were written for and requested of me by an audience generally acquainted with the operatic canon of the past four centuries (as Horace's was acquainted with the centuries-old Greek lyrics he took for his themes). And my audience has also been interested (as his was) in seeing the familiar works of the past through a contemporary sensibility.

This book is called *A Season of Opera* because, in discussing a score or more operas ranging from the seventeenth to the twentieth centuries, it represents something like a season's repertory. (The Metropolitan Opera stages some two dozen operas per season. The Vienna Staatsoper may stage a dozen more. Düsseldorf's Deutsche Opera am Rhein, in its heyday in the seventies, staged as many as sixty, in a repertory that reached, as this volume does, from Monteverdi to Gershwin.)

I have added the subtitle *From Orpheus to Ariadne* because myth has been the stuff of opera for most of its history and is likely to be a vital part of its future. Much of the writing here has an eye on the future as well as the past. And as the myth of Orpheus presided over the birth of opera, so, some four centuries later, an opera on Ariadne looks forward to opera's future.

This volume is to some extent intended to complete two previous publications, *Wagner's Ring: Turning the Sky Round* and *First Intermissions.* Those volumes took their inception from commentaries I gave during the intervals of the Saturday afternoon radio broadcasts from the Metropolitan Opera in New York; the present collection gathers together most of the other occasional pieces I have written on opera over the past three decades. The individual chapters here vary considerably in approach and in length. The chapter on *Tristan und Isolde*, the longest in the book, is an only slightly condensed version of a lecture given several times to Wagner Societies in Canada, the United States, and the United Kingdom. Since only two of Wagner's works are represented here, as against five of Verdi's, I thought that a balance might be struck by making *Tristan* the imposing centrepiece of the collection. Many of those who have heard the *Tristan* lecture over the years have asked that someday it be published complete, and that has almost been done here.

All of the pieces reappear in rewritten and updated form, and paragraphs that were once edited out for reasons of space (or, on the Met broadcasts, for reasons of time) have been restored. The author would, accordingly, like to thank the editors of *The Opera Quarterly* (which first published the pieces on *Il Trovatore*, *Les Troyens*, *Palestrina*, and on opera in the twentieth century), the editors of *Opera News* (where some of the material on *Orfeo ed Euridice*, *Die Zauberflöte*, *Fidelio*, *L'Elisir d'Amore*, *Aida*, *Tristan und Isolde*, *Salome*, and *Manon Lescaut* first appeared), the San Francisco Opera (whose magazine first printed some of this volume's discussion of *Dialogues des Carmélites*), and the Los Angeles Opera (which actually mounted a production of *Oklahoma!* and 'asked for a song' about it).

I should also like to thank Texaco, the sponsors of the Metropolitan Opera broadcasts, and Michael Bronson, producer of the broadcast intermissions on which I first delivered the pieces on *Lucia di Lammermoor*, *La Traviata*, and *Falstaff*. Very special thanks are due to Paul Gruber, producer for the Metropolitan Opera Guild of the series 'Talking About Opera,' for permission to publish here, in shorter form, my commentaries on *Don Giovanni*, *Die Zauberflöte*, *Fidelio*, and *Pelléas et Mélisande*. Anyone who enjoys this volume's discussions of those four works will find a good deal more commentary, illustrated from the best available recordings, on Mr Gruber's very successful ninety-minute cassettes and seventy-minute CDs, available from the Metropolitan Opera Guild.

Finally, I must thank the University of Toronto Press and its editors Suzanne Rancourt, Barbara Porter, and John St James, and, for help given in various ways, William Ashbrook, Edward Downes, James K. Farge, Michael Keenan, Richard Mohr, Iain Scott, Brian Shanley, Irene Sloan, Sherwin Sloan, Mark Yenson, and the Paulist Fathers of New York.

I have, in keeping with the practice observed in my previous volumes, dispensed with the footnotes which some of the journals that first published the material rightly expected. I should, however, say that the translations from Berlioz in the chapter on *Les Troyens* are from David Cairns's invaluable *The Memoirs of Hector Berlioz* (London: Victor Gollancz, 1969), and that in writing the pieces I sometimes drew on the books listed in the 'Further Reading' sections of this and my two previous volumes on opera.

Horace, to come again to him, wrote his odes for various occasions, and finally gathered them together, juxtaposing the long and inspired flights with the shorter, quieter, more playful pieces, at a time when his Rome and the world at large were poised to enter into what eventually came to be called the first millennium. It is my hope that these varied chapters, written for diverse occasions and gathered together as we look forward to a third millennium, may be read as a journey through the four hundred years of opera's existence. They reflect only one man's sensibility. Perhaps it should be said at the start that that sensibility is a religious one. The book is not, however, intended to make converts, except possibly to opera. It is offered with the hope that its chapters will, each in its own way, deepen understanding of some of the major events in the evolutionary history of a splendid art form, born from the spirit of Orpheus.

M. Owen Lee
St Michael's College
University of Toronto
1998

A Season of Opera

1

The Birth of Opera
from the Spirit of Orpheus

How does a new art form come to be?

If we think of myth as the basic stuff of art, we may say that it happens in this way. In the beginning there is a myth, some fanciful tale embodying a truth about man and the universe, often told perhaps, but still waiting for full expression. And there is a poet who has not yet found his theme. The poet woos the myth. And the myth is so potent, so imaginative, so beautiful that it makes new demands on the poet. It invites him to step beyond the limits he knows, to experiment in new ways of expression. Thus it may have been that, in the dark age of Greece, a myth – perhaps first the vast, burgeoning story of the Trojan War – demanded a new artistic form of unprecedented scope. And myth begot the epic. Or again, a myth was being sung – perhaps the story of Dionysus torn limb from limb by the Titans – and it cried out for dialogue. And myth begot the drama. If at the source of every performing art there lies a myth, then surely at the source of opera lies the myth of Orpheus.

The birth of opera from the spirit of Orpheus – this Nietzschean event can actually be documented, for it took place not in some early age we know nothing of but, in a succession of evolutionary phases, in the full light of the Italian Renaissance.

Some twenty years before Columbus landed at San Salvador, an entertainment was commissioned to mark the return of Cardinal Francesco Gonzaga to Mantua. It was to be ready in two days, and the unenviable task of creating and presenting it fell to Angelo Ambrogini di Montepulciano, known as Angiolo Poliziano or, in plain English, Politian. Best known today as a Latin humanist, Politian would have been only seventeen years old in 1472 (if indeed that was the date). He was immensely talented, eager to innovate, eager to pass beyond the drama of his day, liturgical drama, and to provide for his worldly, aristocratic audience something of the new secular spirit of the Renaissance. He found in pagan mythology a subject which fitted neatly into formulae of the *sacre rappresentazione* his audience was familiar with – the myth of Orpheus.

As Ovid told the story in his *Metamorphoses*, Orpheus was a Thracian lyre player whose song could charm rivers, trees, animals, and all of nature. Heavenly messengers graced his wedding to the lovely nymph Eurydice. But the omens were bad, and Eurydice died, before she and Orpheus could come together, of the bite of a poisonous serpent. Orpheus, disconsolate, descended lyre in hand to the world of the dead, where he sang and played so sweetly for the gods below that they gave him back his Eurydice, on condition that he not look on her face till he reached with her the world above. But, afraid that she might lose her way, Orpheus did look back, on the very brink of light, and suddenly Eurydice was gliding back into the darkness. He held out his hands to her, but the last, lonely 'Vale' that she gave him already echoed in the depths of Avernus, and infernal spirits came between them. Orpheus mourned this second loss so intensely, forswearing the love of woman that had brought him so much pain, that Bacchic Maenads attacked him in anger and tore him limb from limb. At this, the trees in sorrow dropped their leaves, and the rivers welled up tears. But Orpheus's lyre still sang, and drifted down the river to the open sea (so stringed instruments made their way from West to East), and Phoebus Apollo, in tribute to Orpheus, who was his son, placed the singing instrument among the stars.

All of this Politian read in Ovid. And in addition he knew from Virgil's *Georgics* that this was a story that should be told by shepherds, that Eurydice was fleeing the advances of the shepherd god Aristaeus when she was bit by the serpent, and above all that Orpheus could be a compelling symbol for the artist whose work interprets, as Virgil's did, a whole culture.

Here was a story that allowed young Politian to put on the stage what his audience had always seen in its musical dramas – shepherd prologue, serpent devil, heaven opening, hell yawning, the hero martyred – but with all the important meanings changed. In outline it was still sacred drama; in spirit it was pagan and secular. Orpheus descending to hell, Orpheus martyred and immortalized is not a saint but an artist, a civilizer, a lover. (He even becomes, as he forswears the love of women, an advocate of homosexual love.)

Politian called his new entertainment *La Favola d'Orfeo* – for though he had his hero sing lines from Ovid in Latin, he wrote most of his play not in Latin but in Italian. His *Orfeo* was, so far as we know, Europe's first secular drama sung in a modern language.

Is it also the first opera? The music has not survived, and we are not even sure who composed it. But that does not really affect our considerations here. The important fact is that the Orpheus myth *demanded* music, once it was put on the stage, and music that was not incidental but essential to playing out the story: Orpheus must sing to lament the death of his Eurydice, to persuade the gods below to restore her to life, to mourn her second loss, and to precipitate his own death at the hands of the Bacchantes.

Politian later regarded the little work as a youthful indiscretion, as a child he would have preferred to expose. But in the history of culture it may be more important than any of his scholarly enterprises. It is, if not the first opera, at the very least a forerunner of opera, and for two reasons. It uses music to tell its story, and it is wholly secular in spirit. Opera has always been both of these things. No opera has succeeded unless the real drama lay in the music. And, as it evolved, opera was always a secular entertainment, antithetic to sacred drama, the oratorio, and the musical setting of the Mass. What religious subjects opera has touched on in the four centuries of its history have been sensationalized (in, for example, Meyerbeer), or sentimentalized (in Massenet), or conflated with para-religious ideas (in Wagner). Poulenc, as we shall see, is an exception.

Why then did opera not follow immediately from this archetypal *Orfeo*? Because Politian's era was immediately succeeded by a golden age of polyphony, and it is hard to imagine any music less suited to dramatic purposes than that of Palestrina and his contemporaries, music elaborately written for four or more voices singing simultaneously. Some attempts were made to adapt polyphony to the stage, with each actor mouthing words sung by a multi-voiced chorus in the wings. But these madrigal-dramas were short-lived. No polyphony, however intense or expressive, could delineate character or develop a situation. To fit music to drama something closer to ordinary speech was needed.

The solution came almost exactly one century after Politian's *Orfeo*, in 1597, and again the impulse came from men who were not primarily musicians or dramatists, but scholars and humanists – a group of Florentines called the Camerata, from the vaulted chamber in the house of Giovanni Bardi, where they first held their meetings. Among their number were the foremost Florentine patron of the arts, Jacopo Corsi, and that amateur musicologist Vincenzo Galilei, father of the astronomer. (Corsi eventually moved the meetings to his palazzo, while Galilei's treatise *Dialogo della Musica Antica e Moderna* preserved for the group the four fragmentary hymns of Mesomedes that were for more than a century the only known examples of the music of antiquity.)

The not-always-amicable poets and scholars of the Camerata were at least in agreement that something beautiful could be built on the ideal, if not on the actual remains, of Greek music, and they drew their principles from what they knew about the musical settings of Greek tragedy – that the dialogues and choruses were sung in a simple, monophonic style, with equally simple instrumental accompaniment. One of the musicians in their midst, Jacopo Peri, was persuaded to try his hand at dramatizing Greek myth (Corsi helped him at the task), and a poet, Ottavio Rinuccini, undertook to provide the text. When the experiment was unveiled in the Camera, it was nothing so ambitious as *Agamemnon* or *Oedipus* or *Medea*. Aeschylus, Sophocles, and Euripides were bypassed for the classical author still best known and loved in Europe, Ovid. The story of Apollo and Daphne was adapted from the *Metamorphoses*.

The audience was reportedly delighted with Peri's *Dafne*, which it took to be an authentic reconstruction of Greek tragedy, and the piece was repeated on several occasions. But this 'first opera' is for us little more than a statistic, as its music, save for a few fragments, has been lost.

The score of the Camerata's second experiment, however, survives complete. This time Peri may have remembered Politian's century-old *Orfeo*, for he based his new effort on the myth of Orpheus, and called it *Euridice*. The text, again by Rinuccini, dispenses with the backward glance of Orpheus; the hero successfully brings his Eurydice back from the underworld to the rejoicing of Arcadian shepherds and nymphs. Peri set the text to the simple yet flexible monophonic music (the Camerata called it *recitar cantando*) that he seems to have used in *Dafne*, and he sang the role of Orpheus himself when the piece was first performed, at the Pitti Palace in 1600, to celebrate the marriage, by proxy, of Henri IV of France and Maria de' Medici. The production was modest and the orchestra small. Corsi accompanied the singing at the harpsicord. And a rival of Peri's, Giulio Caccini, succeeded in getting some of his own music – still monophonic but less austere than the rest of the score – sung at the performance. Within a year, Caccini had completed his own *Euridice* to the same text Peri had used, hurried it into publication, and claimed the invention of the new monophonic style as his own.

So it was that a group of humanists, using the Orpheus myth, restored to drama the monophonic music that was essential to the creation of opera. Peri, in the preface to his *Euridice*, claimed that 'forsaking every other means of singing heard so far,' he had found the only style that could effectively adapt Greek myths for the stage – though he rather graciously acknowledged a debt to Emilio de' Cavalieri, who had incorporated the new monophonic vocal style into the then richer musical traditions of sacred drama. In fact, the declamatory speech-song and the musically jejune 'choral odes' in Peri and Caccini must have seemed painfully thin to audiences who could hear Cavalieri or Palestrina when they went to church. The *Euridices* of the Camerata were not Greek drama, nor yet quite opera. They were experiments, attempts at Greek drama that, rightly and fortunately for opera, restored monophonic music to the stage.

At this point a genius appeared, 'one of those extraordinary individuals,' says Paul Henry Lang, 'who create and organize a new form of art, and whose advent into the domain of thought is analogous to the appearance of a superior species in nature, after a series of unfruitful attempts.' Claudio Monteverdi, a master of polyphony, was encouraged to experiment with the new monophony, and undertook to write a music drama. He knew where he should start. He chose for his subject the myth of Orpheus, and his *Orfeo* was produced in 1607 in Mantua, at the very court where the myth had first been dramatized by Politian a century before.

A good many composers have derived inspiration from their libretti. But with Monteverdi's *Orfeo* it was more than that. It was a case of the Orpheus myth suggesting the groundwork for opera itself. Monteverdi realized that, if Orpheus's story was to be dramatized, it would require monophonic solo voices. The Camerata had been right in this particular, though for the wrong reason. It was not the historical fact that Greek tragedy had been sung monophonically, but the dramatic exigency that his Orpheus must voice an individual grief that prompted Monteverdi to set aside, for the moment, the polyphonic style that was his specialty. Nor would the pseudo-Greek phrases of the Camerata do. Monteverdi realized that, if Orpheus is a singer capable of moving heaven and hell, and a lover grieved enough to face death, he must express himself in more compelling strains. Madrigalist though he was, Monteverdi evolved for opera a marvellously expressive single vocal line, approximating human speech but with a musical intensity, a daring chromaticism, that went beyond speech. As his Orpheus pleaded with Charon to ferry him across the river Styx, declamation became, for the first time, operatic aria.

So Monteverdi began by adapting and expanding the experiments of the Camerata. But he ended by blending the styles of a century of other Renaissance music to tell the Orpheus myth. The story is set in Arcadia: let there be the music of the *pastorale*, old as Politian. Orpheus descends to hell: let the instrumentation be ecclesiastical and solemn, as in the sacred drama. Apollo takes Orpheus to the stars: let their voices blend in a truly operatic duet. The chorus comments on Orpheus's joy and sorrow, his tragedy and final apotheosis: let there be the flaming trumpets of the *trionfi* and *tornei*, the tender melody of the *intermedi*, the splendor of the *mascherata*, above all the intense expressiveness of Monteverdi's beloved *madrigale*. The Orpheus myth is a glorification of music, and the librettist Alessandro Striggio brings Musica herself on stage at crucial moments of the action: let her pervading presence be expressed by repeating her *ritornello* at each of those moments.

Monteverdi's *Orfeo* thus synthesizes all the musical forms, from the tourney to the experiments of the Camerata, which could contribute to the effective dramatization of its subject. It looks backward over a century of Renaissance music, and forward across the whole history of opera, for it contains in embryonic form all the major traditions that still govern operatic composition – recitative, aria, duet, choral and dance interludes, musical characterization, and continuity by leitmotif.

The wonder is that these traditions were, in large part, suggested by the Orpheus myth, the pregnant material already used in every operatic experiment. Other stories, most of them from Greek antiquity, had been presented before 1607, and often – as tragedies with incidental music, as mimes, masques, pastorals, and ballets. But it was Orpheus's story that effected the new art form in the making; it alone required that, for each of its dramatic climaxes, music be put in the mouth of its hero. In Monteverdi, the myth met its poet at last. And opera was born.

At least fifty more operas on Orpheus followed Monteverdi's. Domenico Belli's *Il Pianto d'Orfeo* (1616) was set to another Camerata text. Stephano Landi's *Morte d'Orfeo* (1619) was the first opera for which the composer wrote his own libretto. Luigi Rossi's *Le Mariage d'Orphée et Euridice* (1647) was the first opera produced in Paris, and the first of the French theatre's many elaborate 'machine plays.' Lully's sons, Louis and Jean-Baptiste, produced an *Orphée* in 1690. Campra's *Orfeo al Inferno* was a one-act opera set within his larger entertainment *Le Carnaval de Venise* (1699).

As seventeenth-century Europe went opera-mad, other myths surpassed that of Orpheus in popularity. Musical speech became credible in the mouths of Ariadne and Iphigeneia, of Jason and Perseus, of Hercules and Adonis. Figures from Greek and Roman history also took the stage, in thousands of works. In the eighteenth century a single classicizing libretto by the elegant poet Metastasio could be set to music by as many as fifty different composers. Eventually, a separate kind of opera, *opera buffa* – dealing with lighter, more amusing, more contemporary subjects –

established itself. But everyone knew what real opera, *opera seria*, was. It was big, elaborately staged, sung in Italian, and its subject was Greek myth, or at the very least some story from antiquity.

Most of this long period of mythological *opere serie* is uncharted territory today, partly because, while the libretti have survived, the scores were often performed only once and then discarded, and partly because the heroic roles were usually sung by castrati, and are now virtually unsingable.

Then, halfway through the eighteenth century, the whole concept of opera was reconsidered and reshaped. Handel's Julius Caesar, a castrato hero bestriding the world, yielded the stage to Mozart's Count Almaviva – only a baritone, only a nobleman, and at that a nobleman the lower classes get the better of.

This reform of opera began with Christoph Willibald von Gluck, a German (the reformers of Italian institutions seem invariably to be Germans). As a composer Gluck had his limitations. But he was an intelligent man, in touch with the intellectual currents of his day – with the French Encyclopedists, with Rousseau, and with Winckelmann's return to classic Greece to find the truest impulse for artistic expression. Gluck knew that opera was in trouble. It was cliché-ridden, undramatic, dominated by vain, posturing singers in love with their voices. And most damning of all, in its excesses it claimed to represent the spirit of ancient Greece. Gluck undertook to reform opera. And he chose as his subject the myth of Orpheus. Why should he not? It was clearly the archetypal opera story.

Gluck's *Orfeo ed Euridice* was carefully mapped out by the composer and his equally idealistic librettist Ranieri de' Calzabigi. Each was convinced that the drama must come first, that the music was to be the means through which the drama was realized. Gluck immersed himself in the myth of Orpheus, and said that in setting it to music he tried to forget he was an opera composer. The myth, in turn, began to speak.

When Gluck's opera was first presented, at the Hofburg in Vienna in 1762, it made some unfortunate concessions to contemporary tastes. Orpheus was sung, still, by a castrato; instead of Hermes as messenger of death, a soprano Cupid was substituted; and after the backward glance of Orpheus, Eurydice was restored a second time to life. But despite the *lieto finale* and some occasional rococo prettiness, the new *Orfeo* was worthy of its creators' classic ideal. Gluck had tried to write only what the myth demanded, and what resulted had the effect of moving an audience as no work in memory had moved them.

Gluck expanded his *Orfeo ed Euridice* for Paris in 1774, rewriting the part of Orpheus for tenor and adding the incredibly beautiful flute solo for the scene where his hero enters the Elysian Fields – perhaps the loveliest music ever inspired by Greek myth. He continued his reform with works on Alcestis, Iphigeneia, Orestes, and Helen of Troy. Then, ironically enough, in the great period of opera that followed there were next to no operas on classical subjects. These were associated with the declining baroque, its excesses, its castrati. Composers turned to new themes. Haydn told the story of Orpheus in an opera titled *L'Anima del Filosofo*, but it was never performed in his lifetime. *Opera seria* was dying. Mozart wrote, out of Greek myth and Roman history, the last great examples of the genre (*Idomeneo* and *La Clemenza di Tito*), but between them he fashioned the operas for which he is best remembered, wonderful mixtures of the *seria* and the *buffa*, in which matters of the heart are set against class struggles in a changing Europe.

And opera changed as society did. With the rise of nationalism in the new century, Verdi wrote passionate dramas of patriotism and familial love in his Italy (though the setting may have been Spain or France or even Egypt, it was always of Italy he was singing). Wagner wrote passionately about, and learned from, Greek theatre but dramatized the ancestral myths of his Germans, in an all-out attempt to reshape his nation's consciousness. Both of them thought of their art as a vehicle for ideas – contemporary, even revolutionary ideas – and Greek myth simply did not suit their purposes. When a nineteenth-century genius did use the classics, when Hector Berlioz wrote an immense opera on Virgil's *Aeneid*, he couldn't get it on the stage. Classical heroes became figures of fun, as Offenbach demonstrated with lively spoofs of the Trojan War and – it is no surprise to discover – the myth of Orpheus. (His *Orphée aux Enfers* might be said to have begot that minor art form, the Offenbachiade.)

Serious mythological opera reclaimed the stage in our century, as Richard Strauss found inspiration in the myths of Daphne, Helen, Midas, and, most notably, Ariadne. Puccini on the other hand never chose, among the many subjects he considered, a classical myth as an operatic subject; he had an acute awareness of what he could and couldn't do. As our century nears its end, there is a feeling, voiced more often by the public than by musical critics, that operatic composition is in decline. Art forms do not last forever. The lifespan of opera as we know it today, from Gluck to Richard Strauss, from Orpheus to Ariadne, has been twice that of classic Greek theatre, but the gods have given us no guarantee that it will last forever. Tragic writing in Greece virtually died with the death of Sophocles, even though Greek culture – and great tragic performances – continued apace for several more centuries. Similarly, in the twenty-first century we may with confidence look forward to great operatic performances. But will we see new works of stature?

How does one halt the decline of an art form? Was Euripides trying to save Greek tragedy from decline when, at the end of his life, he returned to its sources and wrote a play about Dionysus, out of whose myths came the birth of tragedy?

If my observations here are even partly correct, the vitality of opera has something to do with opera's own myth. Perhaps that is why, throughout the decline in the twentieth century, serious composers began experimenting again with the Orpheus myth – among them Elliott Carter and Harrison Birtwistle and, before them, Stravinsky, Krenek, Milhaud, Malipiero, Casella (with a new setting of Politian's text), and (with three separate versions of Monteverdi) that influential educator and back-to-basics composer, Carl Orff.

Perhaps those composers knew that, through its long history and prehistory, opera had depended on and been revitalized at critical moments by one classic myth: Politian's *Orfeo* was Europe's first secular music drama, Peri's *Euridice* the earliest surviving attempt at opera, Monteverdi's *Orfeo* the work that began the major traditions of operatic composition, and, after a century and a half of excess, Gluck's *Orfeo ed Euridice* the work that began the reform of opera, shaping it to what it has been ever since. Greek myths have always had a special fascination for artists, but here it is as if one myth, in four clear stages, suggested, attempted, evolved, and perfected an art form of its own – as perhaps the myth of Troy evolved the epic, and the myths of Dionysus the drama.

I would like to go further than that, because I can see Orphean themes, only slightly transmuted, in my favourite operas. In nineteenth-century Germany, Orpheus became, along with Apollo and Dionysus, a powerful symbol, though his influence on such poets as Novalis and Hölderlin was as subtle as it was profound, and it has only recently been documented. Perhaps this influence on Wagner was only subconscious, but the German master surely touches on the themes of the Orpheus myth – the all-compelling power of music, the renunciation of love, the attempt of love to triumph over death. He finds these themes in German mythology. Tannhäuser is the German Orpheus who descends to an underworld. Elsa is the German heroine undone by a condition put on her love. Tristan, reversing the path of Orpheus, leaves his unconscious world of night to summon Isolde from the light of day. And in Wagner's operatic manifesto, Orpheus is reincarnated both in young Walther (who sees

Nuremberg's pedants advancing 'like evil spirits' to carry Eva away) and in Hans Sachs (who must renounce his love for Eva before he can win the true reward of his art). Even the unsympathetic Joseph Kerman sees *Die Meistersinger* as an 'operatic metamorphosis of the Orpheus idea.' To this sympathetic listener Wagner's great comedy reads like a medieval allegory of the Orpheus myth.

Beethoven's Leonore also descends (in the third of her overtures and in Act II of *Fidelio*) to bring her husband up from the darkness, and her death-braving spirit transfigures other altogether unmythic characters. But most striking of all is Mozart's Prince Tamino, who like Orpheus charms the animals with his music, who is commanded to observe a reverent silence if he is to rescue his Pamina, and who eventually leads her safely, by the power of his music, through an inferno of fire and water.

Orpheus is opera's myth.

2

Du Musst dein Leben Ändern
Orfeo ed Euridice

Gluck's *Orfeo ed Euridice* is invariably cited as the work which reformed opera in the eighteenth century, spearheading a reaction against complicated Metastasian plots and extravagant Neopolitan vocalizing. Every history of musical drama notes the twofold reform: Gluck's librettist Calzabigi reduced the Orpheus myth to its simplest elements, and Gluck wrote for it music that was almost austere and always a faithful illustration of the text. Later writings of both librettist and composer, especially Gluck's preface to *Alceste*, are often used to support these observations.

But it can be misleading, even damaging, to see Gluck's *Orfeo ed Euridice* only, or even primarily, as a revolutionary manifesto.

For one thing, Gluck began his career as a practitioner of the very baroque opera he was destined to destroy, and he passed through a rococo phase before reaching, in *Orfeo*, what we might call his neoclassic style. Accordingly, some features of his reform opera are still baroque (a castrato Orpheus) and rococo (a soprano Cupid). Even when, in modern productions, Orpheus is sung by a mezzo-soprano, a tenor, or a baritone, Gluck's *Orfeo* does not adhere completely to the tenets he was to lay down in the preface to his *Alceste*; its overture is neither musically nor dramatically equal to what follows, and its happy ending – a concession to imperial taste in Vienna in 1761 – is wholly out of spirit with what has gone before.

All of this might imply that *Orfeo ed Euridice* is only a transitional work, that the real reform came with *Alceste*. But even after *Alceste* Gluck occasionally embarrassed his followers by relapsing into previous styles.

Gluck's *Orfeo* really is the work that reformed eighteenth-century opera, but in affirming this we must understand more in the term reform than is usually implied, and we must look beyond the writings of Gluck and Calzabigi. Like those other German reformers, Luther and Wagner, Gluck did not bind himself to his theories. In fact, the writings of all three Germans are partial, overemphatic, and of far less value than the spiritual force that prompted them. And as no one today has experienced *opera seria* in the fullness of its extravagant baroquery – strutting male castratos confronting mechanical monsters with da capo arias and flying to the rescue of shipwrecked sopranos with coloratura capable of reducing trumpeters to despair – we cannot hope to have any more than a textbook appreciation of Gluck's practical reforms. What we can hope to respond to today is his music, which speaks to all times, and in a language that is not so much reformatory as ever new.

Gluck the reformer is famous; Gluck the composer has sometimes been regarded with undeserved condescension. Verdi, for example, complained that Gluck had never mastered some elementary techniques of composition, and Handel remarked, 'He knows no more counterpoint than my cook.' Actually, those judgments tell us more about Verdi (who fought his way to technical mastery) and Handel (who was a superb contrapuntalist) and even, according to Sir Donald Tovey, about Handel's cook (who sang small bass roles in the master's operas) than they tell us about Gluck. Composers have always tended to miss or find in Gluck what they find or miss in themselves.

The exception to this is Berlioz. That most sensitive of all orchestral painters acknowledged and praised Gluck's skill with instrumental colours. Speaking of the special tone quality of the flute, Berlioz said, 'Only one master seems to have known how to avail himself of this pale colouring, and he is Gluck.' The flute Gluck wrote for may have been different from the flute Berlioz knew, but the Frenchman nonetheless praises, as an example of what the instrument can do, the extended solo in the second act of *Orfeo ed Euridice*, where the flute's silvery tone floats above a gently swaying accompaniment of strings:

Musically, this is something more than reform. It is discovery. Many composers before Gluck had written beautiful music for the flute, but no one, not even Bach, had written a melody so perfectly adapted to the instrument's special colouring. And, as we expect from Gluck, both melody and instrumentation serve a dramatic purpose: the restless chromatic convolutions of the melody indicate that the spirits in the Elysian Fields are still, as Berlioz notes, 'imbued with the passions of earthly life,' but the pure, passionless sound of the instrument suffuses the melody with a feeling of resignation and ineffable peace. In Gluck's silver-grey paradise, passion is not spent but sublimated. (The contrast to the preceding scene with the Furies – fluteless, and filled with swirling strings and dark-coloured trombones – could not be greater.)

The sequence in the Elysian Fields is one of the marvels in all music. Yet, as Handel and Verdi would very likely point out, the means used are astonishingly simple. An F-major melody, a sort of disembodied minuet, opens the scene:

This gentle dance both precedes and follows the famous flute solo and serves as a musical and emotional frame for it: in the minuet, flutes conspire *with* the strings to shape the contour of the melody, and all is suspended, unearthly and passionless, while in the solo, the flute is set *against* the strings, and the melody, turned from major to minor, is 'imbued with the passions of earthy life.' Then, when the minuet returns in all its sweetness and serene assurance, the effect is supremely beautiful – and out of all proportion to the musical means used. Gluck was blessed with a dramatic instinct that expressed itself naturally in musical terms. When it was operating, he hardly needed counterpoint or conservatory training.

As the scene in the Elysian Fields continues, one clear, calm, geometrically proportioned melody follows another. This should by all odds be wearying. But such is not the case. A spell is cast in which we come to accept Gluck's neoclassic heaven as we do the medieval ones of Dante and Fra Angelico. Part of this effect is achieved by a careful arrangement of key relationships: from the becalmed F-major opening, the listener is wafted to more emotional melodies in the related tonalities of D minor, C major, and B-flat major, always to return between each of these to placid choruses in the initially established and therefore emotionally satisfying key of F major. But even more of the effect comes from a kind of alternating design in the melodic lines. One of the F-major choruses flows in almost circular 6/8 patterns:

This is followed by the long horizontal of a 4/4 oboe solo with forward-moving accompaniment, signalling the approach of Orpheus. It is in effect not circular, but linear:

The aria that follows is another case of musical effects making the most delicate dramatic points. For all the mood established in the scene up to now, there has been nothing we could call pictorial in the music – only the suggestion of an infinite expanse of radiance and peace. Now, as Orpheus walks through paradise and the horns and lower strings provide an insistent, steadily moving beat, we hear in the first violins the sound of a brook:

And in the second violins, alternating with the flutes and constantly modulating, we hear a gentle wind in the trees:

So Gluck implies that before mortal eye beheld the scene there was only clear, limitless space. Then his Orpheus, like Rilke's two centuries later, calls up 'a tree in the ear' and 'a breath around nothingness.' For all his technical inadequacy, Gluck has, with attention to key relationships and instrumental colours, contrived to depict those Virgilian 'summers in the snakeless meadow' we must have in the music if we are to believe in his classic Elysium.

Almost every scene in *Orfeo ed Euridice* is a carefully wrought architectural structure built around recurring movements and tonalities. The sequence at the entrance to Hades is the most famous: Orpheus's solos alternate with the Furies' dances and choruses as the tonality shifts in clear stages from C minor to F major. But equally effective, in their quieter ways, are the two laments sung by Orpheus – the opening 'Ah! se intorno,' with its alternating chorus and recitative, and the famous 'Che farò,' with its rondo-like structure. In the course of these, every anticipated return of the melody brings subtle variations in figuration and instrumentation – to increasingly moving effect.

All of this deliberate austerity, this slightly asymmetrical proportion, this passion achieved by the simplest means, suggests that *Orfeo ed Euridice* is more than a mere reaction against the excesses of *opera seria*. We should look elsewhere for the formative impulse behind it. And we might begin our search with a famous criticism levelled against the opera's most celebrated number, 'Che farò.' Romantic critics were unable to understand why Gluck wrote a broad, serene C-major melody to express the grief of Orpheus at this tragic moment. Hanslick even said that the melody might just as easily express a completely opposite meaning to that intended.

It is best to meet this nineteenth-century objection with an eighteenth-century answer – not from Gluck himself, for he admitted that 'one false nuance' could destroy the piece, but from the one man whose vision of antiquity affected every artist of the day, Johann Joachim Winckelmann. More than the French Encyclopedists, more than Gluck's librettist Calzabigi or any of the musical theorists, Winckelmann opposed the senseless ostentation, the melodramatic overstatement, of baroque art. He rejected in particular its claim to represent the spirit of ancient Greece. 'The universal dominant characteristic of Greek masterpieces,' the archaeologist said, 'is noble simplicity and serene greatness … The depths of the sea are always calm. however wild and stormy the surface; and in the same way the expression in Greek figures reveals greatness and composure of soul in the throes of whatever passions.'

As with Winckelmann's suffering Laocoön, so with Gluck's bereaved Orpheus. By Act III Gluck's hero has reached a point beyond human feeling. The grief in 'Che farò' is, and must be, different from that expressed in the Act I lament, the C-minor 'Ah! se intorno.' There, Orpheus had lost Eurydice as any lover might lose his beloved; here, he has destroyed her despite his harrowing of hell and the persuasive power of his art. For this superhuman grief Gluck writes C-major music, a melody beyond grief, full of 'noble simplicity and serene greatness.'

So, while Peri and Monteverdi in their seventeenth-century operas treated the myth of Orpheus according to the ideas then prevalent about Greek drama, Gluck's *Orfeo* seems to owe more to eighteenth-century notions about Greek sculpture. A practised ear can hear in Gluck's music a Winckelmannian serenity and simplicity, and perhaps even something of *contrapposto*, that carefully balanced asymmetry that brings a classic statue to life.

In these last days of our century, when Gluck and Greek sculpture can seem about equally remote, this listener trained in the classics often feels, in the presence of Gluck's melodies, as that Orphic poet Rainer Maria Rilke felt before the 'archaic torso of Apollo' in one of his famous sonnets. That Greek torso, in its serenity and simplicity, in its carefully balanced asymmetry, told Rilke, in the piercing last line of the poem, that he had to change his life: Du musst dein Leben ändern. Gluck's music once inspired the Abbé François Arnaud to say, 'With that one might found a new religion.'

Du musst dein Leben ändern. It is part of the greatness of great art and music that they prompt us to re-examine and re-evaluate all of living. That is reform in its deepest sense, and that is why Gluck's *Orfeo* still speaks to us.

3

The Opera of All Operas
Don Giovanni

One of the best stories ever written about a famous composer, a story to tease us out of thought, is Eduard Mörike's *Mozart auf der Reise nach Prag – Mozart on the Journey to Prague*. The young composer is writing *Don Giovanni*, hastily, for its première in Prague just a few days away. The Bohemian capital has gone wild over his *Marriage of Figaro*, a comedy about the ironies and ecstasies of love, and has called for more of the same. So Mozart's new opera will, like *Figaro*, concern itself with the many guises of love, and with the most famous of all lovers, Don Juan. Some of the new music will remind us of the innocence of childhood – Mozart's own childhood memories of the sea at Naples, where youths and maidens in bright little boats tossed golden balls like oranges back and forth in a stylized kind of love game. But other pages of music will be terrifying, and bring us face to face with death. We will watch a man defying eternal laws, and we will share his agony as he destroys himself.

Mozart's carriage halts. He wanders down the road to an Italian-style castle. There are orange trees. A splashing fountain. For just once in his life the innocent but tormented young genius, soon to burn himself out in the flames of his own inspiration, experiences a moment of pure repose. Remembering his childhood he plucks an orange, like Adam from the tree of the knowledge of good and evil, or like Apollo from the tree of the muses. The golden ball comes gently in his hand. He cuts it in half with a little silver knife, and admires the perfect inner surfaces. He joins them gently, very gently, then separates them, then joins them again. We know that he soon will die.

The audience at Prague didn't expect to hear so serious a strain from its favourite composer.

Mörike is not alone in seeing larger issues in *Don Giovanni*. Mozart's opera, more than any other save perhaps only *Tristan und Isolde,* has caught the imagination of artists, composers, poets, philosophers, psychologists, men of letters, and music lovers. Rossini, when the great singer Pauline Viardot showed him the autograph score, fell to his knees weeping, kissed the music, and exclaimed of its composer, 'He was God himself.' Goethe thought that only the man who had written *Don Giovanni* could set his masterpiece, *Faust,* to music. Gounod, a composer who did set *Faust* to music – lovely music, but more sentimental than Mozart would have written – said of *Don Giovanni,* 'It has been a revelation all my life. For me it is a kind of incarnation of dramatic and musical perfection.' Wagner asked, 'Is it possible to find anything more perfect than every piece in *Don Giovanni?* Where else has music individualized and characterized so surely?' Tchaikovsky's famous comment is, 'Through that work I have come to know what music is.' Bruno Walter confessed, 'I discovered beneath the playfulness a dramatist's inexorable seriousness and wealth of characterization. I recognized in Mozart the Shakespeare of opera.' Shaw thought the fine workmanship he found in *Don Giovanni* 'the most important part of my education.' Kierkegaard exclaimed, 'Immortal Mozart, you to whom I owe it that I have not gone through this life without being profoundly moved.' E.T.A. Hoffmann, he of the tales, called *Don Giovanni* 'the opera of all operas.' And for some two centuries Mozart's opera has pretty well kept that title unchallenged.

And yet *Don Giovanni* is a work full of contradictions. Robert Craft, for example, says that, while the music is 'some of Mozart's greatest,' the opera itself is 'imperfect in conception, a miscarriage as drama,' that the libretto is 'disjointed, marred by implausible incidents, peopled mainly with one-dimensional figures, and confused in its moral position.'

The truth is, we have never been able to form an adequate idea of what *Don Giovanni* is. It defies classification. Its librettist, that witty rascal Lorenzo Da Ponte, wanted it to be an out-and-out comedy, with the *vis comica,* the comic force, of the old Roman clown Plautus – at least that's what he told his doctor years later, adding that it was Mozart who was set on making it serious. Da Ponte may, for once, have been telling the truth. We know that Mozart always took a hand in the shaping of his librettos, and that in the course of writing *Don Giovanni* he also wrote the poignant string quintets in C minor and G minor, and had lost the father who had loved and bullied him all his life. Something of this seriousness is in *Don Giovanni,* which begins with the death of a father, in a scene with a special poignancy in the string writing. All the same, Mozart entered *Don Giovanni* in his personal catalogue as an *opera buffa* – the standard name, for a hundred years, for comic opera. How seriously are we to take it? It is called, on the title page, a *dramma giocoso* – a humorous drama – a designation that, despite the ink spilt over it, solves no problems of interpretation.

Perhaps then we should say first that *Don Giovanni* is built from elements of medieval morality plays, those allegorical struggles between good and evil, and also from the Punch and Judy farces, the carnival puppet shows, the presentations of strolling players in which the Don Juan myth seems first to have surfaced. (In Vienna there had been All Souls Day performances of 'Don Juan, the dissolute man punished' for as long as anyone in Mozart's day could remember.)

Some of the Don Juan myth may have grown too out of the escapades of a seventeenth-century historical figure, Don Juan de Tassis, Count of Villamediana. And the opera owes much as well to a literary tradition: a play by the Spanish monk Tirso de Molina (a remarkable piece in which almost all of Da Ponte's elements are already present) and other dramas – by Molière in France, Shadwell in England, Goldoni in Italy. Through all of these one can sense the old morality play turning rationalistic. Don Juan was becoming less a dissolute sinner punished and more a hero in revolt against conventional morality. A new treatment of the story by Giovanni Bertati, with music by Giuseppe Gazzaniga, opened in Venice shortly before Da Ponte and Mozart set to work, and both of them, Da Ponte especially, seemed to have known and borrowed from it without scruple. But then the whole Don Juan tradition is a succession of borrowings.

Musically, *Don Giovanni* draws equally on two quite separate traditions – *opera buffa* (a popular genre fast coming into prominence) and *opera seria* (an aristocratic tradition fast becoming obsolete). Mozart had already combined the two in *The Marriage of Figaro*, where the *opera buffa* figures of the servants interact with the *opera seria* figures of the count and countess. But in *Figaro*, based on a solid, stageworthy play by Beaumarchais, the two elements are under much firmer control. In *Don Giovanni* they run riot, so much so that *Don Giovanni* soon came to mean something different wherever it was shown. In the Latin countries it was a comedy, thrown slightly out of whack by its composer's insistence on empathizing with his characters. In the Germanic countries it was a tragedy, in which a hero like a force of nature – a demonic, even satanic force – rises heroically to challenge God himself. By the nineteenth century the opera's hero had become a kind of Hamlet or Faust, an inexhaustible figure – which certainly would have surprised Da Ponte, who never gave his hero a moment's pause for reflection, and sketched him in conversation with a thoroughly exhausted Don Juan of his day, the notorious Casanova. Then, at the beginning of our century, in Bernard Shaw's *Man and Superman*, Don Giovanni became the incarnation of an evolutionary 'life force' – which would have surprised Mozart, who gave his hero mostly low *opera buffa* music to sing.

Today we are even more at a loss to interpret Mozart's opera. Our trendy directors see its hero, not as a swashbuckler intent on his pleasures, but as a perpetual adolescent needing instant gratification, or as a latent homosexual who actually hates women, or as an anti-hero intent on evil, or as an Oedipus-figure, slaying an interfering father and seducing one unsatisfactory mother after another. All of that, I'm sure, would have surprised both Da Ponte and Mozart. But our century's critics go even farther. Winthrop Sargeant, in the pages of *Opera News*, argued, not unconvincingly, that Mozart's hero was a fertility god, and that to attend *Don Giovanni* was to participate in the celebration, not of a performance, but of a ritual. Wagner never claimed any more for *Parsifal*.

Don Giovanni is at least the partial embodiment of *all* the many theories about it. The opera's ambiguities have been its glory. After Mozart other versions of the Don Juan myth continued to pour forth, from the likes of Byron and Baudelaire, de Musset and Mérimée, Pushkin and Tolstoy. But there was never any question that the great treatment of the subject was Mozart's opera. There is scarcely a number in the score that is not referred to in the art, music, and literature that followed upon it. The first music we hear after the overture, Leporello's 'Notte e giorno faticar' ('Night and day I'm worked to death') was used by Beethoven in his Diabelli Variations as a jibe at the publishers who never allowed him to rest, and by Offenbach at the start of *The Tales of Hoffmann*, to indicate that the whole of that work is, on one level, an exegesis of Mozart's opera. A few pages later in Mozart's score comes the poignant passage where the Commendatore dies. It was copied out by, again, Beethoven, and remembered by him when he wrote his 'Moonlight Sonata,' though Beethoven's triplets shape a romantic landscape for piano and Mozart's underlie a sinister trio for dark male voices.

And the famous pages continue: the supreme challenge for light tenor voice, Don Ottavio's aria 'Il mio tesoro,' became one of the most admired single recordings in the history of the phonograph when John McCormack recorded its aristocratic phrases with effortless ease – though there will always be connoisseurs who will raise, without recorded evidence, the name of Rubini (who trilled a high A and B-flat that Mozart never wrote), or compare the recorded evidence of the splendid versions by Richard Tauber and Léopold Simoneau.

But perhaps the most famous number in the score is the little love duet, 'Là ci darem la mano.' Both Beethoven and Chopin wrote variations on it, and Liszt worked it prominently into his 'Don Juan' fantasy. It is what Dorian Grey, in the film version, cannot miss hearing at the opera the night after his first seduction. And in James Joyce's *Ulysses* it haunts the cuckolded Leopold Bloom – for his wife sings it for her lover, and they carry it to its physical conclusion. It is not just the music of the piece that has given it this literary life. It is the ambivalence. By the time Giovanni sings it with the pretty peasant girl Zerlina, we have seen him revealed as a deceiver, a rapist, and a murderer. We really should hate him. And yet for the moment we do not, we can not, so artlessly does Mozart combine the man's aristocratic bearing and the girl's pastoral shyness in his charming duettino.

One of the questions often asked at performances of *Don Giovanni* is 'Who is the leading lady?' In the eighteenth century, Mozart's century, it was assumed that the feminine lead was the adorable Zerlina, a figure straight out of *opera buffa*. In Mörike's story, where Mozart is still in the process of composing *Don Giovanni*, the music that comes into his head as he plucks that symbolic orange is music for Zerlina and her swain Masetto, for the orange calls to mind the Italian girls and boys he saw at their love games. It is only right that the leading lady in an *opera buffa* should be the light and lovely Zerlina.

But in the nineteenth century, there was no question that the leading lady in *Don Giovanni* was the *opera seria* figure Donna Anna – especially after E.T.A. Hoffmann told one of his spookiest tales about her, and audiences wondered whether Giovanni had had his way with Anna, whether she fought him or yielded to him willingly. Anna made the opera dark and Romantic, and her aria 'Or sai chi l'onore' showed her the equal of any of the spirits of *opera seria* past. You can see why Hoffmann in his tale called her 'a divine woman, over whose pure spirit evil is powerless.'

All the same, in our century we have come to think that the most important of the three ladies is Donna Elvira, for she represents in her one person the true ambivalence of the work – the conflicting claims of the comic and the serious. Elvira is what Mozart called *mezza carattere*, a character midway between *opera buffa* and *opera seria*, a woman gone slightly dotty and at the same time a grieving, avenging angel, by turns comic and serious, and sometimes both at once. In a puppet play, we might laugh at her, but in Mozart our feelings for her are complex. Molière, who invented the character, made it clear that she had been a nun. In Da Ponte there are indications that Giovanni actually married her to have his way with her. If we take her plight seriously, Edward Dent says, 'Elvira's degradation is horrible.' The laws of comedy would insist we not take her seriously. But Mozart will not have it that way. Before the opera is over, his musical portrait of Elvira, delicately balanced between acute observation and sympathy, makes our finest critic, Andrew Porter, weep for her – weep, he says, 'while around me some of the audience is laughing.' Of such ambivalences is *Don Giovanni* made.

What the tragicomic Elvira is the opera itself becomes in its celebrated ensembles. Here we can mark the immense difference between the operas of Mozart and those of his predecessors. In the greatest of those, Handel, the characters are defined by long solo arias, and rarely if ever combine their voices. In Mozart, solo arias also define the characters, but we learn at least as much about them in the ensembles, where each character is further defined in terms of the others. In the second act sextet, as six different voices weave their separate lines like six instruments in chamber music, the feeling is both comic and serious at once – for each separate personage remains completely in comic or serious character, colouring and coloured by the others.

Another striking difference between *Don Giovanni* and the older Handelian *opera seria* is that, while Mozart's satellite characters are, like Handel's, given large-scale, introspective, self-revealing arias to sing, Don Giovanni himself gets only the slightest of pieces, each barely a minute long. He is almost opaque, a hero defined, not by himself, but by those he pursues and is pursued by. And that may be one reason why Mozart's opera exerts such a disconcerting power. Its hero, whom we are never allowed really to know, seems to know us. Or at least he knows something vulnerable about all the characters that confront him. He senses that vulnerability, and exploits it, in the men as well as the women. They are all humbled, reduced to fixed attitudes, lost in wonder about what he makes them feel. In this he is a real seducer. He makes the other characters see themselves in their weaknesses. They call one another cruel. But he is the cruel one. He seems to see unflinchingly into their souls. No wonder they pursue him.

There is a moment in Act I of the opera when trumpets and drums announce the arrival inside Giovanni's castle of three masked aristocrats. Don Giovanni shouts 'Viva la libertà!' and all the characters on stage repeat that phrase in a series of remarkable flourishes. For Giovanni 'liberty' means, of course, licence, his freedom to have his way with all the peasant women and to dupe all the peasant men he has tricked into coming to his castle. For Leporello, 'liberty' means the freedom to cavort as freely as his master. For the captive Zerlina, it means the freedom, if she dares, to give herself to a seigneur who might raise her to his station. For Masetto it means the freedom to fight for what is rightly his. For the three mysterious newcomers, Elvira, Anna, and Ottavio, it means the freedom their masks have given them to enter this den of iniquity and unmask the seducer and murderer. 'Viva la libertà!' they sing. But it is the man they are advancing against who has prompted them to sing that ringing phrase. He is the only one in their world who can give them a proper sense of their own individualities.

Such ambiguities, and the interlaying of comic and tragic, pervade the opera right to the final scene, where the statue of the dead father bursts open Giovanni's castle doors, and Elvira flees, and Leporello hides under the table, and Giovanni will not repent of his dissolute life even when the threatening statue grips his hand and flames rise up around him. It is a moment that splendidly combines both *buffa* and *seria* styles, and its D-minor music – even to ears that have heard Wagner and Strauss and Schönberg – is genuinely frightening. In Mörike's story, Mozart tells his listeners that only when he had finished composing this scene did he realize that his candle had burnt out in his hand, leaving it coated with wax. He entertained for a chilling moment the idea of his own death.

But that is, again, a serious nineteenth-century view of *Don Giovanni*. The eighteenth century did not end the opera there. It wanted the vaudeville Mozart appended to that death scene – the charming ending wherein life returns to normal for the other characters, who advance in turn to the footlights and speak to the audience directly. And we today want it too, for we have come to see this mercurial drama, with its vivid yet elusive characters, as something more than the story of Don Giovanni alone, and perhaps as something more than its creators, its performers, its past admirers, and its few present detractors have been able singly to say.

Because its roots are in the puppet theatre, the opera's characters are to some extent puppets, yet Mozart makes the puppets sing music to break the heart. Because it is part morality play, it is clearly about sin, yet there is a strange innocence and an even stranger intimation of wisdom about it. Because its hero is promiscuous, treacherous, and murderous, he comes to represent what is most dangerously attractive in a man to three very different kinds of women, but perhaps too what every man would like to be if only he dared. For those ambiguities, and for the almost existential perception that a human being is defined not so much by what he is himself as by his constantly shifting relationships with others, for the sense that man, fatally flawed, is most a man when, like Hamlet or Faust, he confronts boldly whatever power it is that moves the world beyond him – for all of these in *Don Giovanni* it is Mozart's music, ever shifting from mysteriously serious to joyously comic, that is responsible.

That music tells us, with sometimes cruel but cleansing insight, not about its hero, but about ourselves. In a past age, a Romantic poet like de Musset could call the opera's protagonist 'a marvellous symbol of man on earth.' In our more existentialist age, none of us can really see, or would want to see, ourselves as that hero. None of us has been blessed or cursed with his superabundant sexuality. But creatures of flesh we none the less are, driven by that irrational force he represents. So today we tend to see ourselves as the other figures in the opera, those pathetic figures the hero leads on and unmasks and reveals in all their vulnerability. We human beings are after all comic and tragic at once in our utter dependence on love. Our predicament would be comic, did we not suffer so much pain from our fleshly yearning. So Mozart's prismatic opera keeps to the simple lesson of the old cautionary tale about the wages of sin, but shifts the emphasis from the sinner to the sinned against. Written in the Age of Reason, it tempers its rationalism with that truest of insights, compassion. Mozart, lavishing on his characters music of unparalleled understanding and sensitivity, comes at last to seem a kind of omniscient Prospero. Or, as some of our best thinkers have not hesitated to say, a kind of God.

That's a view of this 'opera of all operas' that we owe to Rossini and Kierkegaard and that tale of E.T. Amadeus Hoffmann. But I'd like to end with the words Eduard Mörike uses in his story, as Mozart, 'on the journey to Prague,' sits poised to play for the people at the orangery the climax of his new opera. The manuscript lies open on the piano, the candles burning. The men and women sit breathlessly waiting for the composer to begin the scene where the statue appears. At such times, Mörike says, 'a person longs to be lifted out of his ordinary self, and yet he is afraid. He has the feeling that infinity will touch him and draw his soul unto itself. That exaltation,' Mörike says, 'experiencing a miracle that is of God, yet somehow also a part of oneself – that is perhaps the happiest and purest feeling any one of us can ever know.'

Then, in the story, Mozart plays the D-minor music from *Don Giovanni*, and his listeners know that infinity has touched them.

4

The Music of Intuitive Angels
The Magic Flute

A quarter of a century ago, I went to Vienna for the first time. Of all the cities in the world, Vienna calls music most to mind. Many of the great composers of the eighteenth and nineteenth centuries lived and worked in its graceful environs. The central cemetery contains, with a million and a half other graves, those of Gluck, Beethoven, Schubert, Brahms, and the two Johann Strausses. And although Mozart was from Salzburg and had his best successes in Prague, and travelled as far as Naples and Paris and London in his young days as a child prodigy, it was in Vienna that he lived and worked and suffered most. And it was there he died. It was in Vienna that he was laid in a common grave.

It's a curious story. Not a single mourner stood by when the young composer's remains were disposed of, not in the great central Friedhof, but in a little suburban cemetery.

On that first trip to Vienna, I found Rauhensteingasse 8, the address where Wolfgang Amadeus Mozart died, almost in the shadow of St Stephen's Cathedral. A 'Mozart Court' stood on the site, half-demolished, with stone images of Gluck and Cherubini, Beethoven and Haydn staring into space, as if overawed by the Mozart who, when he lived here, wrote such strange and difficult music.

Behind the façade of Rauhensteingasse 8 there was nothing to interest me. The house where Mozart lived through his last months was no more. A few blocks away, Vienna had preserved another house, the place where, in a happier day, Mozart had composed that most vivacious, profound, and revolutionary opera, *The Marriage of Figaro.* Perhaps it was better to preserve the memory of that triumph – and not the memory of the death here in the Rauhensteingasse.

As Mozart lay on his death bed, another opera of his was running nightly in a people's theatre beyond the old walls. That was *The Magic Flute*. Everyone loved it – little children, young lovers, shopkeepers, professors from the university. The two hundred ducats Mozart was paid to write it wasn't enough even to cover his debts, while the joy and beauty he gave to all who came to see it were altogether immeasureable.

Night after night, lying in the house in the Rauhensteingasse in a fever, he would follow in his imagination the performance of *The Magic Flute* across the city. He would look at his watch and say, 'Ah, now they are all laughing at the bird-catcher's song. Now they are hearing how man and wife together can reach to godliness. Now the Prince and Princess are passing unharmed through the fire and water.' Then, if his strength held out, he would work some more on a Requiem Mass. He was never to finish it.

I am a Catholic priest, and I have stood at the bedsides of more than a few dying people. I have seen them fevered, confused, dying before they could provide for their families, dying too young to have realized their potential. But I know of no death like Mozart's. Not one with so many unanswered questions.

He wasn't afraid of death. His Freemasonry had taught him to think of death as a friend. But toward the end, he suffered under a peculiar illusion. His last work, a Mass for the Dead, had been commissioned by an anonymous messenger who one day appeared unannounced before him, dressed in grey. Mozart was to write a Requiem Mass, quickly, and he was to tell no one, nor ever try to find out whence the commission came. He started writing, observing the secrecy imposed on him. And when he turned to another assignment, when he hurried off to Prague, planning en route to complete an opera the court there had commissioned, the grey stranger reappeared to warn him that the time for the Requiem was running out.

His health began to fail – so fast that he was sure he was poisoned. And his letters, too, grew feverish: 'I cannot rid myself of the sight of that strange man. I see him constantly entreating me, impatiently demanding the work ... and I know from what I suffer that my hour is come. I am at the point of death.'

Actually the sinister-looking stranger was only a servant sent by a rich Viennese nobleman who was in the habit of commissioning works from professional composers and passing them off as his own. But to the fevered Mozart the stranger was an emissary from another world. The death he was writing a Requiem for was, he began to believe, his own.

He was in fact working on the Requiem the day he died. He lay in bed and some of the singers from *The Magic Flute* came to see him and, at his request, sang the pages he had just written. 'Lacrimosa dies illa' – that day of tears. After a few measures, Mozart wept so fitfully they had to stop. Later he sank into a delirium, during which he kept trying to complete the Requiem. As always, he had it fully composed in his head. But there wasn't time to get it down on paper. Shortly after midnight, he died.

As I stood there, twenty-five years ago, at Rauhensteingasse 8, shut out by that irrelevant stone façade, I wanted, somehow, to make amends. They had sent for a priest that night. Mozart's wife, Constanze, ill herself, asked her sister to go to the Peterskirche and plead with one to come. I know pretty well the reply she got: 'This Mozart has turned Freemason. And besides, it is well known he has displeased His Grace the Archbishop in Salzburg.' That worldly and unworthy ecclesiastic once paid Mozart less than the valets and cooks he made him eat with, treated him always with contempt, and finally had him thrown bodily from his presence. In any event, a priest finally came to the composer's bedside.

I walked to that symbol of Vienna, St Stephen's Cathedral. Here, a wealthy Freemason had arranged for Mozart's funeral – but for the least expensive funeral available. There was no Mass. A solitary priest blessed Mozart's corpse before only a few mourners. Constanze had been taken away by friends.

Then, the accounts say, the funeral party was proceeding to the little cemetery of St Marx when a sudden storm sent them all scurrying to their homes. One lone gravedigger saw the body into the earth.

A sudden, blustery storm. So we are told. It makes a romantic story. Actually, records indicate that 6 December 1791 was a mild, misty, windless day in Vienna. Why, then, did the mourners all leave? Why was the coffin abandoned? Why, when Constanze finally visited the cemetery and asked to see the grave, could no one tell her where it was? In my ministry, and earlier when I had helped my grandfather digging graves in a little German town in Michigan, I had laid to rest some unfortunate men – poor, disinherited, imprisoned, crazed. But none had gone so unattended as had this man, perhaps the greatest natural genius known to humankind.

I made the two-mile walk from St Stephen's to the cemetery of St Marx, a tiny place now half-hidden in a subsection of Vienna. Old people were sitting there in the sunlight. I didn't know if I would find any grave supposed to be Mozart's. But I hoped at least to find the pauper's section.

'Mozart?' I asked.

'Mozart.' An old woman responded. 'Da – hinter den Bäumen.'

And there, behind the trees, was a broken column. A desolate stone angel. And the name in small letters. It was touchingly modest and nicely tended. But the real grave? No one now can say where it is.

What did it all mean? This man's genius was, for some, sufficient of itself to demonstrate the existence of God. Yet God left him with us to witness to that truth for so short a time – and silenced him before we could hear all there was to know. It seemed at once a demonstration and a refutation of Providence. I left the cemetery full of emotion but without understanding.

These melancholy considerations are a part of any Mozart-lover's response to *The Magic Flute*, even though *The Magic Flute*, or *Die Zauberflöte* as Mozart called it, is mostly a happy work, at times a radiantly beautiful work, a fairy tale. A fairy tale that raises still more questions about life and death.

Its main conflict is between the star-flaming Queen of the Night and the sun-lit Egyptian wise man, Sarastro. The Queen is one of a long line of ambivalent matriarchs in the history of literature and the history of religions. She has been compared to Isis and Ishtar and Astarte and Cybele and Demeter and Juno – grieving and sympathetic at first, then turning savage, vindictive, and destructive. The Sarastro who opposes her is, as his name indicates, akin to the Persian Zoroaster, a Zarathustra almost a century before Nietzsche. He heralds the destruction of one era and the dawn of a new one. Does that make him good or evil? Neither, completely. We eventually see that he is as ambivalent as the Queen he confronts, though at first, when we hear from the Queen that he has abducted her daughter, Pamina, we think Sarastro must be evil. So does the Prince who travels to Sarastro's realm to rescue Pamina. But once there he is told differently. He wonders, 'O everlasting night, when will you end?' And mysterious voices answer, 'Soon, soon, young man, or never.' It's a moment that Ingmar Bergman made much of in his film *The Hour of the Wolf* – and later he said, to the surprise of many of his public, 'Those measures are to me the center of all of Mozart and also of the whole history of civilization.'

Bergman's is a welcome comment, for among opera-goers outside of German-speaking lands it is more or less received wisdom that, while *The Magic Flute* contains a lot of charming and often sublime music, it is saddled with the most nonsensical libretto this side of *Il Trovatore*. I am of the opinion that *The Magic Flute* and *Il Trovatore* have two of the best librettos ever set to music. In a subsequent chapter I hope to defend Verdi's masterpiece. In defence of Mozart's, let me say first that to be convinced of the worth of the libretto of *The Magic Flute* one has only to see the opera in a city where German is spoken. Where it was an instant success and has been one of the most popular operas in the repertory for two centuries. Where its characters' names have become household words. Where one of the greatest of all intellects, Goethe, was so taken with it he began work on a sequel. Where both philosophers and those humble people the poet calls the 'best philosophers' – children – still watch it with equal amounts of levity and gravity, laughing at the bird-man Papageno, who claims to have slain a dragon, and wondering what the three ladies and the three boys mean, and the three temples, and the three initial chords, and all the music in three flats.

How did this strange opera come to be? Mozart's librettist, Emanuel Schikaneder, wanted for his popular theatre outside the old city walls a typical Viennese fairy-tale pantomime – a magic opera with plenty of spoken dialogue between the songs, plenty of scope for crowd-pleasing stage machinery, and, he hoped, a big fat part for himself. The basis of the new opera was a story from a book of oriental genie-tales collected by the poet Christoph Martin Wieland. But this was soon conflated with Masonic elements derived largely from a novel by the Abbé Jean Terrasson called *Sethos*.

Both Mozart and Schikaneder were Freemasons. Schikaneder, something of a philanderer, was not always a Mason in good standing, and seems actually to have been expelled for loose conduct from the lodge at Regensburg. But Mozart, in his last years, was more and more convinced of the secret society's high ethical aims, had written music in a new style for its ceremonies, and seemed determined to express something of its mysteries in his last opera. The symbolism in *The Magic Flute* is, then, bound to remain obscure to those of us who are non-initiates. But most people who write about the work today, including those who are initiates, will say that the Masonic element can be, and usually has been, over-emphasized, and that dealing with it requires considerable delicacy. Many allegorizing commentators have gone too far. If Sarastro, who sings 'Within this sacred masonry' in Mozart's new Masonic style, represents Freemasonry, then the Queen, who first appears as a *mater dolorosa* and then turns vindictive and evil, must, they say, represent Catholicism. Or, more specifically, Sarastro must be the Masonic scientist Ignaz von Born, an expert on the myths of Greece and Egypt, and the Queen of the Night must be the empress Maria Theresa, intent on suppressing Masonry throughout Austria. Some commentators have gone further. Pamina represents Austria itself, rescued from a benighted Mother Church by an enlightened Freemasonry. Prince Tamino represents Crown Prince

Joseph, who had succeeded his mother and introduced radical reforms. The Moor Monostatos represents the black-robed clergy, secretly aiding the church by joining the Masons and working against them from within. Or else Monostatos represents those black-souled initiates in the Viennese lodges who denounced their fellow Masons to the police as dangerous anti-monarchists.

Not all of this is satisfactory, or even acceptable. Maria Theresa, for one thing, was a far more benevolent and beloved ruler than ever was her son Joseph II, and it was *his* successor, the new emperor in Mozart's day, Leopold II, who was the real anti-Freemason. Further, Ignaz von Born, the supposed Sarastro, had parted with the Masons several years before *The Magic Flute* was written.

But some of this commentary is almost certainly right. *The Magic Flute* is, on one level, an allegory celebrating the conflict of the Enlightenment, and particularly Masonic enlightenment, with what was perceived as reactionary Catholic baroquery. *The Magic Flute* is a very personal, psychobiographical statement by a still young Catholic composer who turned in his last years to Freemasonry to find strength and inspiration.

But to stop at a level of Masonic symbolism is to limit a universal opera severely to its own period. It is to make a mere allegory, only partly true, out of what is, in the end, a universal and profoundly true mythic statement. *The Magic Flute* is more than the struggle between Counter-Reformation and Enlightenment. It has much more to do with the universals of myth than with the particulars of history. Its meanings, like its music, are prismatic. And if Ingmar Bergman and many others are right, *The Magic Flute* is about more than any one of us. It is about the whole history of civilization.

George Bernard Shaw once said that Sarastro's was the only music that would not sound blasphemous coming from the mouth of God. He might have added, however, that it is hardly music that the Judaeo-Christian God would be likely to sing. Sarastro invokes the Egyptian divinities Isis and Osiris, important figures in rituals connected with the dead. Isis was in fact believed to have brought her lover Osiris back from the dead. Isis and Osiris are rhyming gods who symbolize rebirth, and embody the union of the female and male principles that, in the rhyming persons of Pamina and Tamino, *The Magic Flute* is very much about.

In the climactic scene in the opera, we are in a mountainous landscape where two men in armour stand guard on either side of a pyramid with a mysterious inscription. The orchestra twice strikes three chords in Mozart's Masonic idiom, in the three-flat key of C minor. Then the strings play the Kyrie of a Catholic Mass popular in Mozart's day. Over the Kyrie the two armed men sing a Lutheran chorale. But the words they sing are not Christian. They are a translation of the inscription on the pyramid: 'He who wanders through these terrifying paths will be purified by fire and water, earth and air. If he overcomes the fear of death, he will mount from earth to sky. He will be filled with light, and worthy to consecrate himself to the mysteries of Isis.' The mixture of Catholic and Protestant music reminds us of the Credo of Bach's B Minor Mass, which also combines ecumenically the two quite distinct liturgical idioms. But the additional overlay here of Masonic words and symbols, of the myths of Egypt and, a minute later, of the myths of the Greeks and the Germans – all this is utterly new with *The Magic Flute*.

In this mountainous landscape where all civilizations come together, Pamina and Tamino meet and, at last, speak. And they speak in matching musical phrases, complementing each other like Isis and Osiris. If he must face death, she will undergo his trial with him. In fact, she says that she will lead him. But he must play on the magic flute that her mother gave to him and her father carved long ago from a primeval oak tree. It will keep them safe. It is a talisman like the Golden Bough that gives Virgil's hero Aeneas safe passage through the world of the dead. So Tamino and Pamina begin their perilous journey together. They pass into the pyramid and thence through the first mountain's cavern of swirling fire, then through the second mountain's cavern of rushing water, he playing all the while on her ancestral flute. Mozart wrote a quiet, unearthly march for this, with mysterious kettledrum footbeats. It is like putting footprints down in space. The lovers emerge from the trial unscathed, successful where Orpheus and Eurydice had failed. The mysterious voices of Act I proclaim that together they have passed their supreme test.

Purification by fire and water is a ritual in many religions. In the Catholic Easter vigil, the Church passes through the night, purifying itself by lighting new fire and blessing new water. The readings are from *Genesis*: 'Let there be light' and 'The Spirit of God moved over the water.' The night is hymned: 'O truly blessed night, when heaven is wedded to earth.' And at the door of the church, before the celebrant enters to say the Easter Mass, the lit candle is plunged three times into the Easter water, fructifying it: '*Descendat in hanc plenitudinem fontis ...*' Fire, the archetypal symbol of the male, impregnates the archetypally female water. And the Church is reborn.

Well, that's one shiveringly beautiful formulation (and peoples of other beliefs will have their own formulations) of what Mozart, from many different traditions, gives us here – renewal, rebirth, and regeneration. Isis and Osiris.

It seems best, then, to approach *The Magic Flute*, not as an allegory of the struggle between the Counter-Reformation and the Enlightenment, but as something much older and more important, as an allegory of mankind's progression from nature to culture, from unreason to reason, and from matriarchy to patriarchy – and of its creative fusion of those opposites.

Man's first deities, so far as we can tell, were not father-gods but mother-goddesses. In our oldest mythologies, mother earth antedates father sky. Gaia is older than Uranus. The first social groups were familial and tribal. Taboos, spells, and magic were important for them. Only when, inevitably, there was contact and conflict with outsiders was there a slow, painful movement towards larger communities. Magic then was succeeded by ritual. Taboo gave way to morality. The family circle recognized the rights of a wider civilization. And the mother-goddess yielded to a father.

This may be thought to be one of the great evolutionary moments in the prehistory of the race. The memory of it was preserved for us, not by historians, but by myth-makers. Later, it was dramatized for us in one of the great periods of civilization, in classic Athens, by Aeschylus in his *Oresteia*, and by Sophocles in his *Antigone*. If we scale this down to fantasy level, we have a surprisingly workable analysis of Mozart's opera. When Tamino first hears the magic voices in Sarastro's kingdom, they instruct him to move back from the temples of Nature and Reason. He has to enter the central temple, that of Wisdom, first – so he will realize that he is making a journey from natural mother to reasoning father. This is the hero-myth found in all civilizations, a study fashionable again thanks to the popular TV conversations between Joseph Campbell and Bill Moyers and the renewed interest in the writings of Carl Jung.

The mythic hero of Campbell and Jung goes on a quest for his father, which is ultimately the male's quest for his own self. On his way, if he is fortunate, he first encounters a companion of his own sex but of a different age or race or caste or level of sophistication, who represents everything which the hero himself is not. Jung calls this figure the shadow, potentially dangerous to the psyche of the hero unless won over. But if he is won over, the shadow is helpful to the hero, as Tonto is to the Lone Ranger, or Jim to Huck Finn, or Sancho Panza to Don Quixote, or Pylades to Orestes, or Patroclus to Achilles, or Enkidu to Gilgamesh.

The hero then must meet the feminine. Initially she is fearsome, and often represented in the figure of the dragon. But if the hero, like the knight of old, can defeat the potentially destructive aspect of the feminine (slay the dragon) he will release the feminine's creative potential (free the maiden in distress). Jung calls this feminine archetype the anima – potentially destructive, potentially creative, ever ambivalent.

The hero then encounters his masculine archetype, a father figure which Jung calls the Wise Old Man. He usually appears in bright sunlight, and gives the hero a pattern for living his life.

Finally, the hero achieves maturity when he integrates all of these experiences, especially what he has learned of his feminine and masculine, around some centripetal circular pattern, which Jung calls the Self.

Well, think of Tamino as your archetypal male hero, befriending his opposite in Papageno, encountering the anima in the Queen of the Night (who obligingly has the dragon slain for him and then expects him to free her daughter from distress), discovering the Wise Old Man in Sarastro, integrating the experiences by passing with his princess through fire (the archetypal male symbol) and water (the archetypal female symbol), and finally finding the completion of his Self in that figure around which the three boys, the two lovers, and the two bird-people are grouped at the end – the sevenfold circle of the sun. It's all in Jung. And most of it works, two centuries before Jung – in Mozart.

Or you can take all this mythologizing more personally. Think of Pamina as a child maturing. Before birth, a child and its mother are one. Then, after the physical sundering at birth, a process of spiritual separation begins. The child learns to speak, to experience, to find other relationships – most importantly, with a new, commanding figure, the father. Psychologists distinguish between mother and father principles. The mother, physical source of being, is nature. The father, a new and separate influence, is culture, discipline, and law. The mother's love is typically protective and lavished unconditionally on the child. The father's is won through obedience to commandments. The child normally progresses from the mother to the father and reaches maturing when he – or she – achieves a synthesis of maternal intuition and paternal reason in himself – or herself.

Seen this way, the Queen of the Night is not, however she may appear to some of the characters on stage, a personification of evil. She is a personification of the dark unconscious, where intuition reigns and reason is unknown; of nature, which nurtures and also destroys; of the closed family or tribal circle, which guards its own traditions in the face of change; of motherhood, which wants to but cannot (however much the child might wish it) be indulgent and protective forever. The ambivalent Queen is served by three ambivalent ladies who bestow magical, intuitive gifts. Together they represent a never-never land which children are delighted and contented with, but must outgrow.

On the other hand, Sarastro is not a personification of good. He is that bright consciousness which is the beginning of reason, which builds cities and civilizations, and is associated archetypally with the father. He too is ambivalent, however, abducting those he would purify, subjecting them to cruel and horrendous ordeals, yet behind the frightening exterior benevolent and ultimately just. He is served by an ambivalent villain, symbolically dark-skinned because he is a shadow figure who, like the satans of literature (Lucifer in *Paradise Lost*, Caliban in *The Tempest*, Mephistopheles in *Faust*) is not so much evil as the unwitting instrument of good.

Tamino moves from the mother's natural paradise, where flowers grow in rocks and beautiful ladies baby him, to the father's civilized kingdom, where the emphasis is on striving, virtue, and achievement. Like the heroes in epic (like Homer's Achilles and Virgil's Aeneas), he is at first mother-bound, but comes eventually to see that he must listen to the wisdom of the father.

Papageno too begins in a blissful state of irresponsibility. He calls himself a 'child of nature.' His peccadillos are punished in childish, gamelike ways. He has no worries except that he cannot find a mate. (It is of course his prolonged service to the mother-goddess that has kept him infantile.) With the prince he attempts the journey from nature to culture. Though only half-human, and so not fully equipped to live a life of reason, he is rewarded, as is the prince, with a feminine companion like himself, a counterpart who is a completion and a fulfilment.

The father's kingdom, then, does not so much oppose the mother's as complement it. In fact, the new realm appropriates the intuitive gifts of the old, and restores them: the Queen's flute and bells still work their intuitive magic in Sarastro's land of reason. The three boys, too, move easily from one kingdom to the other. In fact they embody what the myths that make up the opera are all about: they sing with feminine sweetness the ideals of masculine reason. Like the flute and the bells, like all children, the three boys partake of the nature of both kingdoms.

So *The Magic Flute* is about mankind's evolutionary progress from the mother's realm to the father's. But I don't think that, as it dramatizes this journey, it turns into some kind of anti-feminist tract. It tells us in fact that both realms are important. The continuity of the mother's world in the father's is clearly established in Mozart's music. Let me explain.

You often read that each character in *The Magic Flute* lives in a separate musical idiom. That's certainly true. The Queen's high coloratura is ornamentally baroque; Sarastro's low bass solos are in Mozart's new 'Masonic' style; Papageno sings folk tunes; Tamino is, as Edward Dent has observed, 'Italian and classical,' Pamina 'German and almost romantic.' It's all very carefully done. So it is all the more significant that, across the carefully divided musical lines, almost identical melodies sound. The phrase sung in the Queen's realm when Tamino receives his magic flute:

O   Prinz,   nimm dies   Ge - schenk von   mir,

is echoed in Sarastro's realm, as Sarastro prays:

O   I - sis   und   O - si - ris,   schen- ket

Even the words correspond to a degree. And similarly, the Queen's first revelation to Tamino, in her lunar world:

O   zitt- re nicht   mein lie- ber   Sohn

corresponds to the wondering phrase Tamino sings as he lifts his eyes in Sarastro's world:

O   ew'- ge Nacht,   wann wirst du   Schwin- den?

These and other similarities of musical phrase indicate that what takes place in the opera is not so much a conflict of opposing forces as a transition from one experience to another. The older feminine is not entirely destroyed. Its best values (flute and bells, three boys, beautiful princess – that is to say, intuition, incipient wisdom, natural beauty) are assimilated into the new world of Sarastro. When John Updike retold the story of *The Magic Flute* for children, he expressed the belief that even the Queen survived, and married Sarastro, and Tamino played the magic flute at their wedding.

Updike spoke from the wisdom of hindsight. We now know, two centuries later, that what the Queen represents was in fact not destroyed, that the irrational re-emerged, after the eighteenth century's attempt to suppress it, in nineteenth-century Romanticism. Reason alone is never sufficient. Day wanes, the sun sets, civilizations decay, *natura recurret.* Goethe, writing in the Enlightenment but anticipating the inevitable onslaught of Romanticism, wanted to show some of this in a sequel to *The Magic Flute.* It remained a fragment, partly because no composer cared to risk comparison with Mozart by setting it. But it clearly indicates that the greatest intellectual of the century thought that *The Magic Flute* was much more about the cycles of civilization than about contemporary Freemasonry. In Goethe's sequel, the Queen of the Night reappears to claim, not Pamina, but Pamina's infant son – the new century. And Sarastro leaves his masonry to journey across the earth, a nameless wanderer. Goethe is forecasting here the end of his greatest work, *Faust,* where the civilizing masculine is saved by the eternal feminine. He was also pointing, though he could not realize it, to the great musical-mythic work of the upcoming century, Wagner's *Ring,* and the eventual triumph there of the intuitive, the irrational, and the feminine *over* father Wotan the sky god, his city-building schemes, and his misguided hopes for world power. In Wagner's nineteenth-century *Ring,* everything we see in the eighteenth-century *Flute* comes full circle: the father's masonry falls, the hero and heroine die, the mother returns to her eternal dreams, the three maidens regain their intuitive heritage. The Enlightenment is over. Those who strove for conscious power are destroyed. Only nature and the feminine unconscious are left to guide the world.

Is Mozart's opera then incomplete, lacking in vision, naive in its optimism? No, for the movement towards reason and civilization and father-archetype will always begin again. Creation balances destruction, Classic answers Romantic. Perhaps that is why opera-lovers like to hear a little Mozart between their long sessions with Wagner. The balance is important. With Wagner we are plunged into a subconscious world that affirms the reality and exalts the power of unreason. With Mozart we regard the progress toward reason and order with an emotion that is conscious and clearly objectified, and we do not miss the thunder of Wagner.

Perhaps now we can see something of why Mozart, so popular with the public, was slighted in his day by the wealthy, the powerful, and the privileged. His music was more than they could appreciate when, as was their habit, they half-listened. It was well ahead of its time, as only the most perceptive spirits of the day realized. And his operas, which he rightly thought his greatest works, not only blended serious and comic traditions in surprising new ways; they sounded depths of meaning never dreamed of in opera before. It is not at all inconceivable that Mozart should have known and planned much of what we have said. Classic myths were part of an educated person's fund of knowledge in the eighteenth century, and Mozart could easily have discussed both Greek and Egyptian lore with Ignaz von Born, the Freemason scientist he knew for many years. He certainly said about *The Magic Flute* that, while the delight and applause that came from people of all levels of sophistication gratified him, what pleased him most was 'the silent applause.' I take it he meant those silences when people, touched by the music, quietly wondered what it all meant.

Why was Mozart deserted at his death? The cold facts of the case, now thoroughly detailed in recent books by H.C. Robbins Landon and Volkmar Braunbehrens, are that for a few years Joseph II issued strict regulations for burials, for reasons of public health and to relieve poor families of heavy funeral expenses. Last farewells were to be made at the church, and deceased bodies were then quickly buried in sanitary ways. Unmarked, common graves were, for a time, the rule. Mozart's burial was then not dishonourable, or notably different from that of any other bourgeois in 1791. But of course Mozart wasn't just any other bourgeois. His death still seems the classic rejection of genius by a world not yet ready to receive it.

Today, in Vienna, they've pulled down the Mozart Court completely at Rauhensteingasse 8, and replaced it with a delivery entrance to a department store. But Mozart himself is more popular in Vienna, and throughout the world, than ever before. We are more than ever ready to receive *The Magic Flute* as a supremely civilized work of art, blending as it does Italian and German, Classic and Romantic, comic and tragic, reason and unreason, nature and culture, masculine and feminine, Osiris and Isis, sophisticated and unsophisticated, as no other music does. There is a wonderful completeness about it, and a marvellous lightness. Almost any other composer, confronted with the issues in this opera, would have weighted it with Significant Music. With Mozart, even the most sublime moments are luminous and light: especially those moments when the sweet uses of reason are sung by three intuitive angels – the three boys, sailing in their heavenly chariot, leading us onwards.

It was Karl Barth, I believe, who said that when the angels play for God they play Bach, but when they play for themselves, they play Mozart. I like to think that on those occasions God listens in. Secretly.

5

Music to Set the Spirit Free
Fidelio

A few years ago I saw *Fidelio* at the Met, from the top of the Family Circle, where you can see an opera for the price of a movie. Standing room up there is one of the great bargains to be had anywhere. The sound is good in any part of the Met, but up there it's blessedly beautiful.

The best opera fans are up there too. The ones who really know and love, or want to know and come to love, the music. A lot of them are young. There's the Korean girl who's pursuing law studies, and the Puerto Rican boy who's brought his street brothers over from Brooklyn. There's the piano student who wants to hear the bel canto operas that inspired Chopin. Until recently there was Eddie Hughes, a diminutive man in his eighties, who used to come every night and sit on the floor, propped up against the back wall, and dream a little, quietly dozing off with his memories of earlier performances at the old house on Broadway and 39th Street. Eddie claimed that in the glory days in New York he used to visit Joe DiMaggio in his hotel room, and they'd talk baseball. Then he discovered opera and, he told me, nobody was nicer to him than the famous baritone Lawrence Tibbett, except maybe the famous tenor Giovanni Martinelli, who, if Eddie called at the hotel desk, would invite him up for a drink and a discussion of the finer points of his craft. Even if someone were to have given him an expensive ticket, Eddie wouldn't have taken it. There was no place to see opera except 'up top.'

No one knows a great house, the universality of it, the true power of its performances, until he's been up where the sound bounds round the ceiling, where aspiring singers and veteran opera-goers listen in silence and dream their dreams.

The Met introduced *Porgy and Bess* into its repertory a few years ago, and a lot of black people turned out to hear it, liked what they heard, and came back, in ever-increasing numbers, to hear other operas. Nowadays there are always African Americans up top. At that *Fidelio* I couldn't help but notice a black man who looked for all the world like big Dave Henderson of the Oakland A's. He was hunched massively forward. There were tears in his eyes. I asked him after the performance if he was a singer. 'A church singer, yes,' he said quietly. 'But I'm going to sing in this opera someday. I'm going to sing in *Fidelio*. I'm going to be Florestan ...' It was clear that, in the man chained to a prison wall in darkness, this man had found an emblem for the sufferings of his people and for his own brave hopes. *Fidelio* speaks for all members of the human race.

Beethoven is, for many of us, where we started when we came to classical music. And Beethoven, if we are real lovers of music, is the goal towards which we continue to move. In the end, it is Beethoven who takes the listener to areas of experience that are otherwise inaccessible. That happens in his last works – the *Missa Solemnis*, the final piano sonatas, and especially in the extraordinary late string quartets. In those spare, ascetic, pain-filled, strangely ecstatic works we feel we are in a world never touched by other music, or literature or painting or philosophy. It is a realm Meister Eckhard or Juliana of Norwich might have known, a world of mystical experience. It takes years to feel your way, through the late quartets, into that visionary place that Beethoven eventually came to know.

Beethoven's only opera, *Fidelio*, comes much earlier, and is much more accessible. But already there are intimations in it that the young composer will one day lead us to the limits of human experience – through suffering to illumination.

He was an unlikely and to some extent unlikeable young musician, this rebel from the Rhineland with the pock-marked face, the peasant-like figure, and the stubbornly aggressive, uncompromising intelligence. His powerful fingers were virtuosic at the piano keys. He once improvised for an hour at the keyboard while an aristocratic gathering dined in the next room. Called finally to the table, he brusquely but accidentally sent some of his host's most expensive porcelain crashing to the floor. Later the elegant diners discovered that Beethoven, at the piano under the influence of his wild Muse, had broken half of the instrument's strings.

It was a composer, not a performer, that he wanted to be. But when he studied composition, his teachers said, 'He has not learned anything and he never will. He is hopeless.' The truth was that he heard music differently. He was destined to change the way his century would write, and hear, music.

He had to wrestle with music to make it say new things. It wasn't just that Romanticism was coming to birth in Germany, and would soon change the face of European art, music, and poetry. It wasn't just that in him Romanticism would find its most passionate voice. It was that new thoughts beyond any Romantic understanding were stirring in him – thoughts about God and man and suffering – and music was the only way he knew how to express them.

He was, all his life, the very picture of the Romantic artist, with his scowl and his growl and his mass of disorderly hair. In his native Bonn they called him 'the Spaniard,' because of his dark face and his darker temper. There may have been Spanish blood in him: the Beethovens on the male side were Belgians, from Louvain and Antwerp, and Spain had occupied the lowlands and Flanders two centuries before. The 'von' in his name was an affectation, not a sign of property or breeding. His family was lower class, and they knew about suffering. His mother died young, of consumption. Three of her children went before her to their deaths, and it was said of her that no one had ever seen her laugh. Beethoven's father was an impoverished tenor who for a time tried to pass off his unruly boy as a musical prodigy, and then, when the boy attracted little attention, turned alcoholic. At the age of eighteen Beethoven had to assume full responsibility for what was left of the destitute family.

Before that – we don't really know how he got the money – he had gone to Vienna to play for Mozart. Mozart was cool at first. The youth was supposed to be a prodigy, and Mozart had been a prodigy himself, put on display, and knew how such experiences could spoil a young talent. He thought at first that the exercise this Rhinelander had played for him was just a showpiece worked up for the occasion. But then the teenaged Beethoven asked Mozart for something he could improvise on and, when he was given a theme, played with such inspiration that Mozart called his friends into the room and said, 'Watch this young man. One day he will give the world something to talk about.'

When he could, Beethoven moved to Vienna, which became his home for the rest of his life. But Mozart, by then, had died, tragically young. The twenty-two-year-old Beethoven tried to fit into Viennese society, and at first, because his keyboard prowess was so impressive, he was invited everywhere. People with connections were anxious to take lessons from him. But it wasn't long before he withdrew from the social world, wounded and despairing. He had fallen desperately in love with a succession of women but, repulsed by them all in one way or another, was convinced that he could never marry. A bourgeois life, with marriage, children, love, and domesticity, was impossible for him. When his best-known biographer, Thayer, met the niece of a lady to whom Beethoven had proposed marriage, and asked why the lady had refused him, the answer was, with a burst of laughter, 'Because he was so ugly, and half crazy.'

It wasn't only rejection that made him seem mad. He knew, early in his life, that he was going deaf. (The precise cause of this we can no longer determine.) To be close to his doctor, and also for solitude, he spent his thirty-first summer in the village of Heiligenstadt. The village is now, as a result of urban sprawl, a part of Vienna, easily reached by streetcar, and Beethoven's house there is still preserved. But then it was a secluded little village, and Beethoven wrote there what has come to be called his Heiligenstadt Testament, a personal statement addressed to his two surviving brothers, explaining his withdrawal from normal life. 'This affliction,' he wrote, 'is more difficult for a composer than for any other man ... How could I say to my friends, "Speak louder, shout, for I am deaf"? How could I proclaim that I was deficient in that one sense which ought to have been more perfect in me than in others? Now for me there can be no converse in human society, no mutual exchange of thoughts and feelings ... Now I must live like an exile ... A little more and I would have put an end to my life.'

Then we hear in his words the will to live that sounds so clearly in the 'Eroica' and the Fifth symphonies: 'It was only my art that held me back. It is not possible for me to leave the world until I have written all that I feel is within me.' He went on to write those defiant, life-affirming symphonies in the next years. And the opera *Fidelio*.

Three more things we need to say, briefly, before we turn to the opera. First, the frightening Beethoven had his gentler side. 'When my child died,' wrote the Baroness Ertmann, 'it was Beethoven's tenderness that consoled me most.' He wanted and needed the affection of his fellow human beings, and could empty his pockets to help a friend. In his later years he spent himself in misguided attempts to protect his nephew Carl from what he was sure would be a life of vice. They were smothering attempts which resulted in the young man attempting suicide and the composer coming close to madness. Even his gentleness was frightening.

Second, Beethoven was not at all your standard Romantic pantheist or agnostic. Paul Henry Lang, in *Music in Western Civilization*, sees Beethoven's spirituality as squarely in line with the Catholic Enlightenment of the late eighteenth century. His reading – high-minded and humane – ranged from the Greek classics (in German translations) through Goethe, Schiller, Klopstock, and the writers of the *Sturm und Drang* to – this comes as a surprise to many – Thomas à Kempis and other pious writers. He often consulted the parish priest about his nephew. When he set Latin liturgical texts – and his *Missa Solemnis* is one of his greatest works – he had the Latin translated into German to be sure of every theological nuance. And all his life he was astonishingly conservative in his moral outlook.

Third – and this may seem something of a contradiction of what we've just said – Beethoven had decidedly liberal political sympathies. He once met Goethe at the spa in Teplitz, where he had been sent after a breakdown. The old philosopher-poet and the stormy, rebellious composer went on long walks together, though conversation was difficult because the younger man was already so deaf. On one occasion their walk was interrupted by the passage of the empress of Austria and her archdukes. Goethe, the greatest intellect in all of Europe, politely and ceremoniously deferred to royalty, with his hat off and his head bowed as low as possible. But Beethoven, as he records himself, defiantly tilted his hat forward, buttoned up his coat, folded his arms behind him, and walked straight through the procession. Archduke Rudolph doffed his hat to Beethoven, and the Empress too acknowledged him. But that didn't pacify the composer. He reprimanded Goethe afterwards, and without mercy: the truly great men of the world, the artists and intellectuals, ought not to kowtow to those who were merely rich and powerful. Goethe wrote to a friend, 'A completely untamed personality, and at the same time the most sincere artist I have ever met.'

Fidelio, the only opera of that untamed and sincere artist, is more than an opera. It is a personal statement of the things we have spoken of. It is music's supreme expression of the joys of conjugal love, of devout and high-minded feeling, and especially of the human right to personal and political freedom. In Beethoven's day, at the Congress of Vienna, *Fidelio* was taken as a protest against Napoleon. In our violent century, it has come to speak for every victim of oppression, every prisoner of every prison camp.

Famous performances of *Fidelio* have written the moral history of Europe in my lifetime. When Toscanini conducted *Fidelio* in Salzburg in 1937, it was his final affirmation of the dignity of humankind before he left the city in defiance and Hitler sent in his troops. Bruno Walter's 1941 Met performances of *Fidelio* were an Allied expression of solidarity and hope as thousands of refugees, many of them Jews like Walter himself, fled to America. After the war, Furtwängler's new Salzburg *Fidelio* was a passionate declaration that some had practised, under the very shadow of Hitler, the humanity that others had preached from the safety of other shores; it was a plea from a politically naive but brave and humane German genius for understanding and reconciliation as hostilities ended.

The great soprano Kirsten Flagstad, who had left America in 1941 to be with her Quisling husband in occupied Norway, returned ten years later to face the hostile crowds who accused her of collaborating with the Nazis, to sing *Fidelio* at the Met under Bruno Walter (that fellow artist, at least, did not think her a collaborator) and to prove the point that it can be an act of heroism for a woman to stand at her husband's side.

Another woman who stood by her husband's side was Galina Vishnevskaya, who sang in the first *Fidelio* ever staged in the Soviet Union, a year after the death of Stalin, in 1954. The libretto passed every stage of censorship, but 'as the rehearsals went on,' she recalled, 'I realized more and more that this was about *us* in Soviet society. I was calling on the people to release those unjustly imprisoned and punish the wicked. It was a moment that changed my life.' Eventually the feelings *Fidelio* released in her led to her and her husband, Mstislav Rostropovich, being deprived of their citizenship and fleeing the country. But they stayed together. It was the Soviet Union that changed.

The liberation of Vienna and the reopening of its Staatsoper in 1955 were marked, again, by *Fidelio*, conducted by Karl Böhm. That was the now-legendary performance at which several thousand people stood outside the opera house through the afternoon and into the night, listening to the music on loudspeakers. Some Viennese tell how miracles happened that night – the lame walked, the deaf heard. Certainly the spirit soared.

I wasn't in Vienna that night, nor at any of the other famous performances I've just mentioned. But I once attended a *Fidelio* in Berlin just a few blocks from the Wall, and another in Salzburg at which there was a great shout to free Rudolf Hess, and another in Munich where the emphasis was shifted to make the jailer the central figure, a 'good German' won by human feeling to oppose oppression. Not all of these performances were notable in themselves, nor could I subscribe wholeheartedly to every sentiment expressed. But any performance of *Fidelio* near a border where people are still imprisoned for their political views, or in a city that has such an experience in living memory, any performance anywhere that conveys even a fraction of the work's power and passion and profound humanity, is a liberating experience.

Why then is *Fidelio* – the only opera ever written by one of civilization's greatest composers – not the most popular opera in the world? Perhaps because, as an opera, *Fidelio* is far from perfect. Beethoven makes ferocious demands on his singers and on some of his instrumentalists, and moves in the course of the work from one kind of opera to another – from Singspiel to music drama to melodrama to something close to oratorio. And the libretto seems to many people unworthy of the music. Though it is based on an actual incident in the French Revolution that had already been set by other composers, and though the action is not unlike a number of very successful 'rescue plays' of the day, the subject now seems improbable, even contrived. Some of the text comes perilously close to doggerel, and the subplot is, for many people, an embarrassment.

But these fairly obvious faults have been given more than their fair share of attention. What really matters is that Beethoven's mighty spirit was stirred by the libretto's central concept – political oppression overcome by courage. And he was at least as much moved by the idea of a woman's utterly committed love for her husband. Most of all, he was deeply convinced by the idea of a brotherhood of man under the fatherhood of God. He wrote a pride of lion-like music to express these ideas. For years he laboured over *Fidelio*, casting and recasting his thoughts in half-finished Michelangelesque shapes, heaping overture on mighty overture. The music did not come easily. 'Of all my children,' Beethoven said near the end of his life, 'this was born in the greatest labour, and caused me the most sorrow. And for that reason,' he added, 'it is the child most dear to me.' It took Beethoven twelve years, three versions, four overtures, and three hundred and forty-six pages of sketchbook to bring *Fidelio* to completion. What remains is like the series of rough-hewn figures that lead the traveller through the Accademia in Florence to the finished David. Like those mighty figures, the opera is craggy and unpolished – and immensely powerful.

If *Fidelio* is still unappreciated today, some of the fault is surely ours. Even in the text there are good things that have been overlooked or misunderstood or unthinkingly condescended to – perhaps because in recent decades our own art has not valued highly such things as sacrifice, marital fidelity, courage, hope, and the commitment to freedom. But now that fewer anti-heroes and opportunists dominate our plays, novels, and films, now that we can see every night on our television screens the sufferings of civilians and the pain of prisoners in this very imperfect world, we may be more ready to respond to what Beethoven found in his libretto.

He certainly responded to the words of the political prisoner who says in his suffering, 'What is asked of me is hard, but God's will is just.' He responded when his heroine Leonore, unable to tell whether the prisoner in solitary is her husband, resolves, 'Whoever you are, I will save you. I swear by God that you shall not die. I will set you free, you poor man.' He responded when the minister of justice proclaims to the released prisoners that he is 'a brother come to his brothers, to help them if he can.' He responded when, finally, Leonore and her husband pray, 'Oh God, your design is just. You try us, but you do not forsake us.' There are a dozen such lines in *Fidelio*'s libretto that cut right to the heart of living.

The text is based on a French drama by Jean-Nicolas Bouilly, done into homely German by Schubert's friend Joseph Sonnleithner, revised by some of Beethoven's friends, and finally whipped into shape by the practical librettist Georg Friedrich Treitschke. Most of the text is primer-simple, as when the rescued husband says to his wife:

'Oh, my Leonore. What have you done for me?'
and she replies:

'It was nothing, my Florestan. Nothing.'
I have heard sophisticates laugh at that exchange. But it can be immensely moving when spoken with conviction in the intervals between the powerful musical statements. I for one have always been impressed by the way certain words – *Freiheit, Pflicht, Leben, Liebe, Augenblick*, and, inevitably, *Gott* (that is to say, freedom, duty, life, love, moment, and, inevitably, God) – run through the libretto with leitmotivic force. In their German form those words have all but become, for me, 'Beethoven words.'

Beethoven certainly responded, too, to the characters in his drama. Leonore was the only heroine who spoke to him from all the many librettos he considered. He thought for a while of setting a classical subject suggested by Emanuel Schikaneder, the librettist of *The Magic Flute*, on the faithfulness of a vestal virgin. He also began sketches for operas on Homer's faithful Penelope and on Gretchen, the seduced girl who finally saves Goethe's Faust. But, of all of these, it was only of Leonore that he sang. She so fired his imagination that for her great aria 'Abscheulicher!' he summoned four obbligato horn voices to surround her as she sees hope rising like a rainbow from the depths of suffering. Leonore digging the grave of the still-living man she feels might be her husband, Leonore throwing herself before his would-be murderer with the cry 'Kill first his wife,' Leonore the eternal feminine of Goethe, the womanly ideal that frees a man from the prison of himself, Leonore the ideal of conjugal love that Beethoven hoped in vain all his life to find – this was the only heroine who really spoke to him. And he makes her speak to us. We know what Lotte Lehmann meant when she wrote, 'What joy to impersonate such a human role! I found in it the most exalted moments of my opera career, and was shaken by it to the depths of my being.'

This radiant character illuminates the bourgeois figures of the jailer Rocco, his daughter Marzelline, and her would-be suitor Jacquino. From the moment of Leonore's entrance, the musical texture is altogether changed. One sometimes hears it said that the quartet 'Mir ist so wunderbar,' however moving it may be as music, is ineffective dramatically, that Beethoven did not think to individuate his four characters with separate melodies as, for example, Verdi was to do in *Rigoletto*. In one sense the criticism is well taken, for the words indicate that each character is caught in a different emotion, and the situation seems intended to be at least partly comic. But in the most important way Beethoven, with his intensely serious music, is right. The words of the quartet are probably the low point of the libretto from a literary and dramatic standpoint. Beethoven, with I think sure dramatic instinct, chooses not to write four separate melodies that will only emphasize the maladroit words, but to set each character singing the same melody, to compose a canon that enables us to see their common humanity. So, as the four stand motionless and each takes up in turn Beethoven's simple but wonderful tune (Jacquino attempting unsuccessfully to counter it), we feel the single-minded hope of Leonore ennoble each of them. This quartet at the beginning of the opera predicts the resolution of the final scene, when Leonore's noble spirit will touch and change Rocco's materialism and timidity and the young couple's superficial notions of love and faithfulness.

So sure is Beethoven's dramatic instinct that he can create unforgettable characters out of a single line of text. One of the prisoners, a young man, tells the others with almost unbearable pathos, 'Let us put our trust in God's help. I still hear Hope saying softly to me, We *will* be free, we will find peace, we will find peace.' Then an older prisoner cautions, 'Speak softly! Get back! We are being watched and overheard!' Both prisoners are indelibly limned in music. Bruno Walter, who knew what it was to suffer under an oppressive regime, always cast the young prisoner with the greatest care and affection, for he gives voice to what Walter called 'the principal issue of our time and the theme of Beethoven's *Fidelio* – freedom.' When Walter fled the Anschluss and came to New York to conduct *Fidelio* at the Metropolitan, he was given Kirsten Flagstad as his

Leonore, but he hastened to ask, 'And who will sing the First Prisoner?'
He knew the importance of that youth's single line of text. He also said
that, all the time he fled the Nazis, the warning of the Second Prisoner,
'Softly – we are being watched and overheard,' sounded over and over in
his head.

The evil Pizarro may be a character of only one dimension. But once
again Beethoven, with swirling, menacing strings, makes that a telling
dimension. And the librettists too know how to characterize their villain:
'What a moment this is! My prisoner thought once he could destroy me.
Now I shall twist the steel in his heart and shout "triumph" in his ear as he
dies.' If this is one-dimensional, it is also uncomfortably close to some of
the sentiments expressed by dictators in our own century. And it is a
dimension an ordinary man might be pressured into. That most ordinary
man, Rocco, shows how he has been made to conform to it when he says
to his young assistant – and it sounds sinister after what we have heard of
prison camps in a more recent Germany – 'That's right, my boy. Your
heart will gradually harden. You'll get used to seeing terrible things.'

In the opera's second act we descend to the lower depths of the prison,
where hardly any light can penetrate. For a long time, in the music, we
seem to be lost in this terrifying place, turning dark corners, crossing
bridges over nothingness. Beethoven leads us onwards with a long orchestral introduction – ominous kettledrum beats, screams of pain from the
winds and brass, compassionate prayers from the string choir. And then a
human voice shouts out in despair, 'Gott! Welch' Dunkel hier!' – 'God!
What darkness here! And what a deadly silence!' It is Florestan, in solitary, chained to the wall. 'From this point on,' says David Cairns, 'the
work has us by the throat.'

Florestan is, for me, the great character in the opera. A just man,
defeated in the springtime of life, his only offence daring to speak the
truth, he faces his fate with words that, without Beethoven's music, might
seem impossibly overstated but, with that music, are altogether convincing, true, and moving. 'I do not complain,' he says to his God. 'The measure of my suffering is in your hands ... My heart is comforted with the
thought that I have done my duty. I accept the pain, I accept dying
here in dishonour.' His response to the unknown figure who brings him
comfort in the darkness ('May you be rewarded in a better world, for
it is heaven itself that has sent you here to me') is as heart-rending as his
accusation flung in the face of death ('A murderer stands before me') is
heroically defiant.

I cannot hear Florestan's music without hearing the words of Beethoven himself: 'Come when thou wilt,' the composer says to death in his Heiligenstadt Testament, 'I shall meet thee bravely.' Beethoven wrote that in the midst of his 'Eroica,' 'Waldstein,' and 'Appassionata' years, when he was thirty-one and, like Florestan, in the springtime of life, and realized that the darkness and stillness were closing in on him. And in the letters he wrote through the various revisions of *Fidelio*, as his deafness increased, we read, over and over, sentiments like those of Florestan in the darkness and stillness: 'I would be happy, perhaps one of the happiest of men, if this demon had not taken possession of my ears. If I had not read somewhere that a man may not voluntarily part with his life so long as a good deed remains for him to perform, I should long ago have been no more – and indeed by my own hand.'

And again, on the realization that he would never share his life with a woman who loved him, Beethoven says to himself, 'Submission, absolute submission to your fate – only this can make you capable of the sacrifice duty demands of you. *O harter Kampf* – Oh, hard struggle!' Florestan sings: '*O schwere Prüfung* – Oh, heavy trial! And yet God's will is just.'

Fidelio marks a midpoint in what J.W.N. Sullivan calls Beethoven's spiritual development; it comes between the early symphonies, where the composer finds the meaning of life in achievement 'in spite of suffering,' and the last quartets, where he finds that the highest achievement is reached 'through suffering.' At the end, Beethoven accepted suffering almost as a blessing. But in his middle period, when he wrote *Fidelio*, his reponse to suffering was simple submission. That is the note Florestan sounds, unforgettably. In the Heiligenstadt Testament, Beethoven wrote, 'O Providence, grant me but one day of pure joy. It is so long since real joy echoed in my heart. O when, O when, my God, shall I feel it again. Never? Oh, that would be too hard ...' In the opera Florestan is assured by his wife – and many a great Leonore has found her most memorable spoken moment here – 'Whatever happens, remember that Providence directs our course. *Ja, es gibt eine Vorsehung!* Yes, there is a Providence!'

A dozen or so years ago, the Christian theologian Hamish F. Swanston, in his book *In Defense of Opera*, suggested that Beethoven meant the sounding of the trumpet above Pizarro's prison, at the moment of rescue, as a symbol for the trumpet of the Last Judgment. Similarly, the Jewish composer Ernst Bloch heard in the trumpet at the top of the castle a *tuba mirum spargens sonum*, the trumpet that the 'Dies Irae' in the Requiem Mass says will sound on the last day. A close inspection of the text will support these apocalyptic readings: at the sound of that trumpet from above, Florestan and Leonore acknowledge an intervention of heaven, Pizarro

exclaims at the closeness of hell, Rocco sings that God is coming in judgment. It is all there in the words, as much as it is in the music.

We can go further. Leonore touches on the theological when she says:
'Whatever happens, remember that there *is* a supreme Providence.' And
the final scene, the liberation scene that follows on the trumpet call to
Judgment, is clearly a symbolic re-enactment of Judgment Day itself:
Leonore is hailed by the people, over and over, as 'Retterin' (saviour).
God, in his human agent Don Fernando, dispenses justice and mercy.
What the Bible promises that the Lord in judgment will someday do for
us, Don Fernando does for those freed from their living tombs: he 'wipes
all tears from their eyes.' And in a flood of triumphant music men and
women – one hopes, even the men and women in the theatre – are
strengthened in the symbolic enactment of the scriptural promise that
'Death shall be no more, nor mourning, nor weeping, for the former
things are passed away.'

But the most beautiful of these religious echoes, and one I don't recall
anyone ever remarking on, comes, not on the castle top, but in its depths.
Florestan is about to die. He asks only for water, but Leonore brings him
those sacramental substances, bread and wine. Is there a Eucharistic significance intended? Almost surely, for when Florestan receives the bread
and wine, he sings over and over, 'Dank dir, Dank! O Dank! O Dank!,'
and Beethoven's hymnlike music reminds us that the word Eucharist is
ordinary Greek for that repeated word 'Dank' – 'thank you.' 'Efkaristo,'
perhaps the most familiar word the traveller hears in Greece today, is the
name Christians since the first century have given to the most beautiful of
their rituals, the communion with God in bread and wine. Florestan had
seen Leonore in a vision come to lead him to paradise. When Leonore
actually comes to save him, she gives him the signs of his communion
with the God he prayed to in his suffering.

At that point, this listener at least cannot but remember the words Jesus
promised he would say to those on his right hand on the Day of Judgment: 'I was hungry and you gave me food. I was thirsty and you gave me
drink. I was in prison and you came to me.' And on that day we will
answer him, 'Lord, when, when did we see you hungry and feed you, or
thirsty and give you drink? When did we come to you in prison?' And he
will say, 'As often as you did those things to the lowest of my brothers, you
did them to me.' It was for her husband that Leonore performed those
works of mercy, yes, but she would have done them for any unfortunate.
Before she was certain that the prisoner she saw was her Florestan, she
resolved to risk everything to save him, for no human being should have

to undergo such degradation as he endured. 'Whoever you are,' she sang, 'I will save you. I swear by God, you shall not die. I will loose your chains. I will set you free, *du armer Mann*.'

The greatness of Beethoven's vision is realized in *Fidelio* as surely as it was to be in the *Missa Solemnis* and the last piano sonatas and quartets, works more profound but not more human than this, his only opera. The Ninth Symphony, with its concluding 'Ode to Joy,' reminds us how Beethoven's musical output continues through the years of his life in one consistent onward spiral. Its final, choral movement continually suggests *Fidelio*'s great liberation scene, written years earlier. Even some of Schiller's words in the last movement of the Ninth Symphony were paraphrased in *Fidelio* years before: 'Let him who has found a true wife join us in our joy.'

'Again and again,' says Ernest Newman, Beethoven 'lifts us to a height from which we re-evaluate not only all music, but all life, all emotion, and all thought.' *Fidelio* speaks to and for all of us – the devout African-American at the top of the Met, the Jewish refugee from war-torn Europe, the Russian soprano suddenly realizing that the music was about herself and her society, the German composer coming to terms with the stillness in his ears. Beethoven's music has the power to lift us to where we can survey all of life and what it means, because he was human as we are, but writ ineffably larger. Because he believed mightily in ideals in which we would like mightily to believe – the equality and brotherhood of all humankind, the loving interdependence of man and woman, the just providence of God, and, perhaps above all, the resilience of the human spirit in the face of oppression and tyranny.

I'll close by letting Beethoven speak the farewell he gave his two brothers in the Heiligenstadt Testament – to be read only after his death, but written long before, when he was suffering through the crisis that produced *Fidelio*:

You, my brothers, will be the heirs of my small fortune, if so it can be called. Divide it fairly. Bear with and help each other. It is my wish that you may have a better and a freer life than I have had. Recommend virtue to your children. It alone, not money, can make them happy. I speak from experience. This was what upheld me in my time of despair. Thanks to it, and to my art, I did not end my life by suicide. Farewell and love each other ... Farewell, and do not wholly forget me.

6

Show Business Sense
L'Elisir d'Amore

Every theatrical season the trade papers are filled with details of the try-out afflictions of a new clutch of Broadway-bound musicals. There are rumours of hectic revisions and last-minute replacements, of new songs and new sets, of bad reviews, temper tantrums, and bleeding ulcers. Sometimes there are losses in the millions of dollars. Sometimes there are successes that run for thousands of performances. It's all show business.

Some of this has been true with opera. Verdi seems to have had as much difficulty with his kings and queens as Lerner and Loewe had with their Arthur and Guenevere. But most of Verdi's revisions, and those given *Don Giovanni* and *Tannhäuser* and *Madama Butterfly* by their composers, came in post- rather than pre-première flurries. Very few opera composers ever had the benefit of weeks on the road in try-out towns.

And then there is the case of Donizetti's *L'Elisir d'Amore*. Its composition went like a house on fire from the moment its first note went down on paper. Its composer was nothing if not prolific, and he worked marvellously under pressure. In his comparatively brief lifetime, he composed close to seventy operas, both comic and tragic, and over five hundred other works. When he was told that his friend and rival Rossini had tossed off *The Barber of Seville* in just three weeks, his reply was, 'Well, what do you expect? He was always so lazy.' Donizetti is said to have written *his* comic masterpiece, *Don Pasquale*, in eleven days, and some of his tragedies in a single week. Of course, he didn't always produce first-class music, and some of his best things kept reappearing from work to work. But then Rodgers and Hammerstein transferred *Oklahoma!*'s 'This Was a Real Nice Hayride,' suitably adapted, to *Carousel*, and rewrote *South Pacific*'s original 'Getting to Know You' for *The King and I*. It's all show business. A good melodist isn't going to let a single serviceable semiquaver fall under the table, and Donizetti was not one to do so, even when a new melody was buzzing in his ears.

Such was the case when Milan's Teatro della Canobbiana needed a new opera on the quick – in two weeks. All the details of the situation are not verifiable, and perhaps Donizetti's own penchant for pluming himself on his facility has added an inch or two to the legend. But it seems another composer had failed to come across with a new opera, and the manager of the Canobbiana implored Donizetti to rescue him by rewriting some old score for the promised première. The composer, with an opera behind him to match every one of his thirty-six years, was at first insulted: 'I am not in the habit of patching up my work, or that of other composers.' But with that said, he accepted the challenge instantly: 'All right, now you'll see that I have enough in me to make you an opera in fourteen days. Send me Romani!'

Together with that estimable librettist he set to work. 'We'll see which of the two of us has more guts.' They took a libretto by Scribe (a very good one – its characters were straight out of Plautus and it had already served Auber for his *Le Philtre*), and in two weeks of concentrated labour they had their opera – *L'Elisir d'Amore* – on the stage. Donizetti had reason to be proud. He had suggested major improvements in the text, written all of the music, orchestrated it, and had it copied and into the hands of singers in time to rehearse it with them. (Presumably someone else looked after the scenery and costumes.) And yet, while everyone else was delighted, Donizetti himself thought that the reviewers said 'too many good things – too many, believe me, too many.'

More than a century and a half later, *L'Elisir* still holds the stage, not only for Romani's impeccably paced book and Donizetti's infectious and sweetly melodious score, but for something most Broadway shows fail to capture, despite their months and even years of preparation – a perfect balance of sympathies. An examination of the opera's musical numbers bears out that every step Donizetti and Romani took was the right one.

A prelude sets the tone of the play economically. There is a larghetto for the bittersweetness of passion, and a contrasting allegro almost innocent of passion. When the curtain rises, the allegro becomes the song of Giannetta and the harvesters. Not being in love themselves, they can enjoy the coolness of the trees and flowing stream, while at a distance the solitary Nemorino has no such assurance. He is trembling with emotion:

Quan- to è bel - la,   quan - to è   ca - ra!

Nemorino (his name seems to mean 'little nobody') is mooning over his Adina. But every lady in the audience can take his song as addressed to her personally, for Donizetti, in a master stroke of showmanship, dedicated his opera to 'the fair sex of Milan ... they know best how to distil love's elixir.'

Adina has all the while been reading about the love potion of Tristan and Isolde (a sure-fire touch: the heroine in *Don Pasquale* is similarly discovered reading a romance of old chivalry). Her waltz song is a narrative, and so each stanza keeps almost to a monotone until its break, but we shouldn't miss the repeated half-tones in the violins whereby the potion's magical power is, with tongue-in-cheek artistry, musically suggested:

Enter Sergeant Belcore ('Sergeant Lovelyheart') to a swaggering march that stamps him a *miles gloriosus*, a braggart warrior, as surely as would any quotation from Plautus. In his love song Belcore is quick with classical allusions, to the delight of the bookish Adina and the despair of the unlettered Nemorino. But despite the soldier's supreme self-confidence, we know that the spunky girl is meant for the simple boy. Donizetti indicates this immediately by matching Adina's 'Chiedi all' aura' with Nemorino's 'Chiedi al rio': though she is the changing breeze and he the constant river, the tunes they sing are identical. Like Tristan and Isolde, they are in love without benefit of potions. It's just that Adina hasn't fully sensed it yet.

Now that each of the characters has introduced him- or herself with a cavatina, and Donizetti has involved the chorus in the proceedings, we're ready – as the chorus hurries back onstage – for the climactic introduction of our final character, Dr Dulcamara ('Dr Bittersweet'). Here is another Plautine figure, the quack doctor, instantly individualized by the composer's bubbly rhythms and the librettist's ticklish rhymes. (I first saw the opera in a Metropolitan Opera production that individualized him further by ballooning him onto the scene in the manner of that most spectacular quack, the Wizard of Oz.) I don't suppose Dr Dulcamara has music of quite the quality that Mozart and Rossini gave to Dr Bartolo, but when this doctor's trumpeter takes up his waltz tune and everyone joins in, it's as if the whole stage were swaying:

The ensuing duet between the doctor and Nemorino is all crescendos to churning orchestra in the patented comic style of Rossini. Then, after Nemorino drinks the Doctor's 'magic' elixir, he sings a duet with Adina in which, for all the 'la-la-la's, we catch echoes of Donizetti's tragic style. Suddenly the duped boy's emotions are set to driving three-quarter and triplet rhythms:

E - sul - ti pur la bar - ba- ra per po - coal- le mie pe - ne!

This duet is a Donizetti addition, and we need not seek far for its dramatic purpose in the opera. Nemorino first called himself 'an idiot who knows only how to sigh,' but we are not to be allowed any superior feelings toward him. Donizetti is determined to make us feel for and with Nemorino, while Adina and (in the galloping trio that follows) Belcore still distance us with their comic attitudes.

The finale to Act I is the first point in *L'Elisir* where we feel we are unmistakably in the presence of a master. It begins with a whirling, drunken figure ...

that is tossed from instrument to instrument, stood on its head and played backward, even as poor Nemorino is suddenly confused by the news that his girl is pledged (as almost every girl in Plautus is pledged) to marry a soldier before the day is over. He silences the crowd with an extraordinarily lovely lament ...

A - di - na,   cre - di- mi,   te ne scon - giu - ro

... and again Donizetti's tragic style is upon us. The little aria, which could as well be Edgardo's or Fernando's or Roberto Devereux's, develops into an ensemble with some of the pathos and gravitational pull of Verdi's penultimate finales (one thinks especially of 'Alfredo, Alfredo' in *La Traviata*). We wait for a return of the whirling figure to restore us to the world of comedy, and eventually it does return, to hurry us headlong into a stretto in quick waltz time: the act ends like some mechanical toy that smashes itself by winding up instead of down.

The show business sense operating through all of this is so assured that there was no question, in subsequent performances, of any revisions.

In Act II we are treated to a bumptious, trumpeted wedding song and the famous foot-stomping Barcarole, a grand opportunity for Dulcamara to act the clown and Adina the coquette. Composed in what William Ashbrook calls Donizetti's *popolaresco* style (regular rhythms, symmetrical phrases, unadorned melody), it did indeed become popular. Donizetti sent everyone out of *L'Elisir* whistling it, and saw it go into a French version of his *Anna Bolena* and through several instrumental versions (Glinka made it a galop for piano duet). Nothing helps a show more than a hit tune.

Next is the 'Venti scudi' duet, in which Nemorino and Belcore, the softie and the smoothie, are strongly individualized and contrasted. Less remarkable is the tiptoe chorus for Giannetta and the girls, though it does carry the plot along: we hear that Nemorino has come into a fortune. Then the quartet 'Dell' elisir mirabile' makes the satirical point that for most people the real elixir of love is money, while the duet 'Quanto amore!' makes the dramatic point that the moneyed Adina wants Nemorino for his love alone.

At last, after these comic numbers, 'Una furtiva lagrima' comes like a revelation. Scribe had no such soliloquy in his original, but Donizetti insisted, over Romani's violent objections, on a romanza at this point. His show business instinct was absolutely right. In any work for the stage, the balance of emotions is all-important. 'Una furtiva lagrima' lifts the little comedy above the level of *opera buffa* so carefully maintained till now. We hear a song as beautiful as any ever written, and all the more moving because it is voiced by an innocent, even simple-minded rustic and by that clown among instruments, the bassoon – each pushed to the very limits of feeling. The aria is only a furtive touch in a fast-moving comedy, but with its success the whole opera succeeds, because we come to believe in Nemorino's emotion, even in an atmosphere of artifice, elixirs, and *fioriture.*

Then, in the time-honoured tradition of Italian arias, Adina resists long enough to sing a cavatina of her own ('Prendi per me') and capitulates in a cabaletta ('Il mio rigor'). So a wealthy, pretty, literate young lady gives up everything for a boy who has nothing to offer her but simple and adoring love. It seems fairly clear that, pressed for time though he was, Donizetti was none the less moved by something in this little story. May we see in Nemorino's music something of Donizetti's own devotion to the beautiful Virginia Vasselli, whom he had wooed and wed a few years before? Certainly he worshipped her through the few years they had together, and he never quite recovered from her death, from cholera, three years after *L'Elisir.* The busy composer who introduced such sympathetic touches into his merry comedy was in fact no stranger to grief. The loss of his wife was preceded by the death in infancy of each of their three children and followed in due time by his own heartbreaking end: paralysed and insane at forty-eight, dead at fifty. It is well that he wrote quickly. He had so little time to give the world so much music.

But on the *opera buffa* stage, all ends happily. The lovers are united, Dulcamara does a roaring business with his elixir, and Belcore, equipped with a bottle of it, will doubtless do better next time. Donizetti rings down the curtain not with a new tune but with a quick reprise of his hit song, the Barcarole. Good show business sense, no doubt. But one also has the feeling, as so often with Donizetti, that time was running out. Time to write and time to live.

7

Oh, Sweet Music of Donizetti!
Lucia di Lammermoor

Lucia di Lammermoor, a masterpiece of Italian bel canto based on a novel by Sir Walter Scott, has left its mark on the literatures, including the novels, of many languages. It was at a performance of *Lucia* in Rouen that the passionate Madame Bovary regretted ever marrying her husband, and it was almost certainly at a Moscow performance of *Lucia* in Petersburg that Anna Karenina was moved to flee guiltily from her lover. On the other hand, fictional people without passion seem unable to comprehend Donizetti's famous opera. In E.M. Forster's novel *Where Angels Fear to Tread*, a proper English lady at an Italian provincial performance of *Lucia* is utterly offended by the passion that sweeps across the house. She rises from her seat and says indignantly to her escort, 'Call this classical? It's not even respectable. Take me out at once.' Poor Harriet Herriton had no appreciation of bel canto – beautiful song – and the passions it can unleash in those who surrender to it.

In the United States, a passionate man once surrendered mightily to bel canto opera and described his very physical reactions to it, and the very personal meanings he found in it, in a series of extraordinary poems. Walt Whitman said, in fact, that he never could have written his *Leaves of Grass* if he hadn't gone to the opera. He went almost nightly, a century and a half ago, in Manhattan.

Neither radio nor the Metropolitan Opera had come into existence in Whitman's day, and so he never had an opportunity to speak on New York's famous Texaco broadcasts. But he once wrote a remarkably prophetic newspaper piece in which he described New York opera to people in far-flung parts of North America. He might be Milton Cross or Peter Allen speaking:

'We invite you to spend [a time] with us at the opera ... You there so far from New York, perhaps in Ohio, or Wisconsin, or up toward Canada, or away up northeast or southwest, you need not travel hither; you can stop home and do your day's work ... wash and put on some clean clothes, no matter how coarse, and then eat your supper ... and we will bring the opera to you – even the Italian opera, in full bloom.'

Italian opera first and foremost. Some of Whitman's friends said that *Leaves of Grass* reminded them of Wagner, and indeed Whitman was astonished by Wagner, and liked French opera as well, and hoped for great operas eventually from American composers. But it was Italian opera he loved and learned from and responded to above all others. One of his favourites was *Lucia di Lammermoor*, and it is of *Lucia* I think when I hear Whitman say:

> Ah this indeed is music, this suits me ...
> It glides quickly in through my ears,
> It shakes mad-sweet pangs through my belly and breast.

Whitman felt bel canto melodies deep within him. He thrilled at the excitement of the risks taken by bel canto singers, the triumph of the challenge met, the physical tingle of the sound of it. 'Oh, sweet music of Donizetti,' he exclaimed. There seemed to be a power in the music working with the singer and the orchestra, and it was something more than earthly. It was something cosmic:

> I hear the train'd soprano (what work with hers is this?)
> The orchestra whirls me wider than Uranus flies,
> It wrenches such ardors from me I did not know I possess'd them.

Sometimes Whitman spoke of an operatic experience as exploring the landscape of the soul, sometimes as sailing the seascape of the soul. But more than that he felt at the opera that he was in touch with the central mystery of life itself, though the mystery remained mysterious to him. It may have taken him 'wider than Uranus flies,' but, he wondered, articulating what most of us who love Italian opera wonder, what it *was* that sounded in bel canto song? Why did it give pain as well as pleasure, cause fear as well as exaltation? Why was it close to dying? When, at the end of an aria, the house exploded in shouting and applause, it seemed to be a kind of ritual. But with what, or whom, were we communicating? It was as if we were in touch with something as great as the world itself. So Whitman wrote ...

A tenor large and fresh as the creation fills me,
The orbic flex of his mouth is pouring and filling me full

... and he asserted finally that operatic music not only reached through his body to his soul, but it put the inner world of the soul in touch with – he was emphatic about this – the outer world of the cosmos. He named his operatic poems both 'Song of Myself' and 'Song of the Universal.' Italian opera's wonderful melodies, astonishing cadenzas, sustained high notes, and orchestral surges were paradigms at once of the beauty and power within us and the hurtling and orbiting planets of creation beyond us. That is why we respond. That is why Emma Bovary responded. That is why Whitman wrote, and it might be a description of *Lucia*'s famous sextet:

A tenor, strong, ascending with power and health, with glad notes of daybreak I hear,
A soprano at intervals sailing buoyantly over the tops of immense waves,
A transparent base shuddering lusciously under and through the universe,
The triumphant tutti, the funeral wailings with sweet flutes and violins, all these I fill myself with,
I hear not the volumes of sound merely, I am moved by the exquisite meanings,
I listen to the different voices winding in and out, striving, contending with fiery vehemence to excel each other in emotion.

'Oh, what is it in me,' Whitman wondered, 'that makes me tremble so at voices?' He loved voices. The preachers and orators of his boyhood, the singers of his maturity, thrilled him. The human voice is, after all, the noblest and most wonderful of all musical instruments, capable of more expressiveness than any string or wind or brass instrument. The vibrancy and purity and passion of which a great voice is capable give some sense, in a hushed, humbled theatre, of what life means, how suffering purifies, what it is towards which we aspire, why death is not the end of all. To hear a great singer sing great music is to know perfection as far as it is granted to humankind to know it, and so never to have to despair. At least, Walt Whitman thought so.

He was sometimes so carried out of himself at the opera that he felt close to madness. Often in bel canto operas characters do go mad. In *Lucia* the heroine converses with an unseen solo flute, following it through a maze of high-flying passages, staggering through the wanderings of imagination and memory. The music is a kind of phonographic chart of her mental aberrations. In some productions Lucia covers her ears and flees from the instrument's sound:

Bel canto music seems to express the sadness of all human suffering, our helplessness in the face of adversity. *Lucia* ends with a melody to melt Walt Whitman's heart and brain. When he says,

I hear the violoncello ('tis the young man's heart's complaint)

I can only think of the cello that takes up Edgardo's dying strain:

In one of his great poems, 'Out of the Cradle Endlessly Rocking,' Whitman celebrates the moment he turned from boy to man, listening to the song (he calls it an aria) of a bird mourning the death of its mate. The climax of that poem has always expressed for me what I have felt, leaving the opera house after a great performance:

The aria sinking,
All else continuing, the stars shining ...
The love in the heart long pent, now loose, now at last tumultuously bursting,
The aria's meaning, the ears, the soul ...
The strange tears down the cheeks coursing ...

Much of *Leaves of Grass* seems to describe a listener's response to an evening's performance of *Lucia di Lammermoor*. But one of the poems, 'The Mystic Trumpeter,' is a tribute to all of opera, to the performances that spill across the stage of a great house night after night:

Blow trumpeter free and clear, I follow thee,
While at thy liquid prelude, glad, serene,
The fretting world, the streets, the noisy hours of day withdraw,
A holy calm descends like dew upon me,
I walk in cool refreshing night the walks of Paradise,
I scent the grass, the moist air and the roses;
Thy song expands my numb'd imbonded spirit ...
Blow again, trumpeter! and for my sensuous eyes
Bring the old pageants, show the feudal world.
What charm thy music works! thou makest pass before me
Ladies and cavaliers long dead, barons are in their castle halls, the troubadors
    are singing,
Arm'd knights go forth to redress wrongs, some in quest of the holy Graal;
I see the tournament, I see the contestants incased in heavy armor seated on
    stately champing horses,
I hear the shouts, the sounds of blows and smiting steel;
I see the Crusaders' tumultuous armies – hark, how the cymbals clang,
Lo, where the monks walk in advance, bearing the cross on high.

And of course, for Whitman, the music is an expression of his own self, of his love and hurt and hope and exaltation:

O trumpeter, methinks I am myself the instrument thou playest,
Thou melt'st my heart, my brain – thou movest, drawest, changest them at will.

The music he hears reminds him as well of the terrible war his nation has fought within itself, brother against brother. Whitman, who cared for the war's wounded, weeps now for its woes, and calls on opera's music to help him face the future:

Now trumpeter for thy close,
Vouchsafe a higher strain than any yet,
Sing to my soul, renew its languishing faith and hope,
Rouse up my slow belief, give me some vision of the future,
Give me for once its prophecy and joy.
O glad, exulting, culminating song!
A vigor more than earth's is in thy notes ...

People in Whitman's day objected to such verses as formless. He said, by way of explanation, that he got the form of them, the feel of them, their irresistable bardic surge, from operatic arias – from the freedom of line, the repetition, the sweep and scale of Italian bel canto. His lines may appear to be unmetrical but, as he himself insisted, 'I always had a tune before I began to write.' He meant Bellini, Verdi, Donizetti – the whole repertory he saw in nineteenth-century New York. In the poem 'Proud Music of the Storm' Whitman passes in review the repertory of his day:

I hear the minnesingers singing their lays of love ...
The measureless sweet vocalists of ages,
And for their solvent setting earth's own diapason ...

Across the stage with pallor on her face, yet lurid passion,
Stalks Norma brandishing the dagger in her hand.

I see poor crazed Lucia's eyes' unnatural gleam,
Her hair down her back falls loose and dishevel'd.

I see where Ernani walking the bridal garden
Amid the scent of night-roses, radiant, holding his bride by the hand,
Hears the infernal call, the death-pledge of the horn ...

Awaking from her woes at last retriev'd Amina sings,
Copious as stars and glad as morning light the torrents of her joy ...

The teeming lady comes,
The lustrous orb, Venus contralto, the blooming mother,
Sister of the loftiest gods ...

I hear in the *William Tell* the music of an arous'd and angry people,
I hear Meyerbeer's *Huguenots*, the *Prophet*, or *Robert*,
Gounod's *Faust*, or Mozart's *Don Juan* ...

Finally, Whitman stakes his claim to sing with the rest of them:

> Composers! mighty maestros!
> And you, sweet singers of old lands, soprani, tenori, bassi!
> To you a new bard caroling in the West
> Obeisant sends his love ...

Robert Faner, who wrote a whole book on Walt Whitman and opera, says that the music Whitman heard in the opera house, the emotional experiences of shattering intensity there, awakened him to his poet's destiny: 'In those moments of inexplicable rapture, he came to perceive the meaning of life, and, more important to him, the meaning of death, and of all things bridging the gap from one to the other.' He also articulated what most of us can only feel. To anyone who loves opera, life isn't really thinkable without it. Whitman tells us why: it puts us in touch with feelings deep within us we otherwise would not know, and it aligns those passions with the power that creates worlds:

> Give me to hold all sounds ...
> Fill me with all the voices of the universe,
> Endow me with their throbbings, Nature's also,
> The tempests, waters, winds, [and] operas ...
> I would take them all!

The bard of 'million-footed Manhattan' sang for all of us who listen to and love opera.

8

Elemental, Furious, Wholly True

Il Trovatore

You don't believe that *Il Trovatore* has a good libretto? You say it's crude, confused, ludicrous? How could you have come by such a judgment, when the plot of *Il Trovatore* is so deftly spun out? When the characters not only fill the theatre with passionate song but also point beyond themselves, as characters do in all great dramas, to larger truths? When the whole opera is tightly controlled by a vision of reality that is bold, brave, and, given Verdi's own convictions when he wrote it, searingly beautiful?

You don't think me mad as Azucena? You'll let me go on? Well then, listen and, as the old rhyme has it, I'll 'tell you the story of *Il Trovatore*,' interpreting as I go, following the lead of Ferrando and Leonora and Azucena, who interpret the parts of the story they tell from the stage. Come closer to me, then. *Udite, udite.*

We are in Zaragoza, in Aragon. The Queen and, possibly, the King are in residence at the di Luna fortress of Aljaferia. Huddled around a fire in the courtyard are the soldiers of the young Count di Luna. Their eyelids are heavy, but they must keep watch while the Count passes the night at the windows of the beautiful lady-in-waiting Leonora (and serpents are writhing in the young Count's heart, for he has a rival in a mysterious troubadour who sings by night in the same garden). So, to keep sleep from the soldiers' eyes, Ferrando, captain of the guard, tells them a story they know well already; but then the best stories are the ones we, like children, want to hear over and over, especially at night, and most especially around a fire. It's a horrific story.

When the Count was just a boy (fifteen years before, as we eventually discover), he had a baby brother* named Garzia, whose nurse awoke one

---

* In Verdi's source, *El Trovador* by Antonio García Gutiérrez, the Count is the younger brother – only six months old at the time the two-year-old Manrique

morning at dawn and saw, standing over the cradle, a gypsy hag in sorcerer's robes, fixing her bloodshot eyes on the child. The nurse screamed. The servants came running, and seized the gypsy, who protested that she had only come to tell the baby's fortune. Eventually they let her go. Then little Garzia began to grow pale and feverish. They thought he would die. The di Luna soldiers hunted down the gypsy woman, found her in her own mountains in Biscay, and burned her there at the stake.

But she left a daughter to avenge her, and vengeance came swiftly. Garzia was stolen from his cradle. The di Lunas made a frantic search. All they found was a little half-charred skeleton amid the embers that smouldered on the very spot where the old woman had been burned. The baby's father went to his death soon thereafter, broken-hearted but somehow never really convinced that his infant son was dead. On his deathbed he made his other boy – the present Count – swear that he would never give up searching for his brother.

The gypsy daughter vanished, but Ferrando is sure, even after many years, that he could recognize her if he ever saw her again. Meanwhile, he says, the soul of the mother still appears at night, risen from hell as a screech owl or a raven with blazing eyes. She seems bent on killing those in di Luna's guard who had a hand in her death: one fellow awoke at midnight and looked into her staring eyes ...

Just then midnight strikes in the courtyard – the fastest midnight stroke ever, clanging like a tocsin bell. Around the fire, the soldiers shriek, and we pass beyond the wall they protect to the garden inside.

The moon is obscured. The lady Leonora is on the terrace, heedless even of the reminder from Inez, her attendant, that the Queen of Aragon is within and calling for her. Leonora has another tale to tell us. At a recent tourney an unknown knight in black appeared and won every joust. She crowned him victor that day. Then civil war broke out. He vanished. But one quiet night when the moon showed its full face, she heard a troubadour's song float past her windows, and heard her name invoked, as if in a hymn. She ran to the window, and saw her black knight again. Now she would gladly die for him.

(Manrico) was kidnapped. In Verdi, perhaps because the Count is a baritone, it is always presumed that he is the older brother. As for the ages of the two in the action of the opera, the Count informs us in the first scene of Act III that *tre lustri* (fifteen years?) have passed since the kidnapping. The two brothers in the opera are in any case very young. (Now I hope I haven't spoiled the story. The fact that this information might do so prompted me to drop it into a footnote – the only footnote in this book.)

Inez knows only that all this foretokens sorrow. The ladies retire. The Count di Luna appears in the shadows, and almost instantly the sound of a lute is heard: the troubadour has slipped past the guard. Still unseen, he sings of his loneliness on the face of the earth, of the fate that drives him to war. (We remember that troubadours were outsiders in medieval Europe's closed societies, expressing and disseminating revolutionary and even subversive values, sometimes hounded, in southern France and in Spain, by the Inquisition.)

Leonora rushes into the garden, momentarily mistaking the Count for the troubadour, until the moon comes out from the clouds and the troubadour knight lifts his visor. 'I am Manrico,' he says. The Count identifies him further: 'So it is you! Madman, outlaw, in league with Urgel, with a price on your head! And you dare to invade this palace when royalty is in residence?' (We can now place the black knight in a historical perspective. He is on the rebel side in the civil war. He is one of the disaffected guerrillas from the mountains of Biscay, an insurrectionist fighting for the pretender of Urgel against the Aragonese King Juan I. And the King's forces are led by the very Count di Luna who now opposes this Manrico in love as well as in war. The names of the three personages who form the romantic triangle are attested in the annals of fourteenth-century Spain.) The two men draw their swords. Act I is called 'The Duel.'

Act II, called 'The Gypsy Woman,' takes us to the foothills of the mountains of Biscay at the first ray of dawn. Before another fire, we hear a different version of the story Ferrando told at the opera's start. We hear it now from Azucena, herself a gypsy woman and – we soon realize – the very daughter who disappeared years before. The fire she peers into burns on the very spot where her mother was once executed. And did she really steal little Garzia and throw him into the flames? We listen as, almost in a trance, she relives the terrible moment when she saw her mother burned, heard the shouts of ferocious joy, watched the faces shining sinister around the heaven-reaching flames. The other gypsies, standing at their anvils, listen fascinated. So does Manrico, whom we are startled to see in this company, weak and wounded, contemplating his sword.

When the others have gone to their work, Manrico asks for more of the story. The new revelations are astonishing. First we hear that the old hag that the di Lunas burned was Manrico's grandmother, that he himself is a gypsy – though, when he grew to young manhood, ambition drew him out of their closed society. (His roles as black knight and troubadour must, then, be assumed roles.) Then we hear Azucena say that, on that terrible day they burned her mother, she followed along with her baby in her arms. Though her mother was not allowed to stop and talk to her, she cried out as they bound her to the stake, 'Avenge me!' It was then, Azucena says, that she stole little Garzia away, and came with him to the site of her mother's execution. The fire was still burning. In near-delirium she seemed to hear her mother crying 'Avenge me!' She was also dimly conscious of the baby crying in her arms. Her heart broke for it; but, obeying her mother's dying cry, she flung it into the flames. When the delirium left her she realized that she had flung (who can hear unmoved Verdi's shattering climax at 'Il figlio mio! Il figlio mio!'?) not the di Luna child but her own little son into the fire.

Manrico screams. And after the horror of the moment is gone, he asks his startled questions: 'Am I not your son? Who am I? Who, then?' Azucena hastens to assure him that she has been raving again, that he is her son. Has she not just rescued him by night from among the fallen at the Battle of Pelilla? Has she not, like a mother, tended him back to life?

Manrico is proud of his wounds. In the duel he fought with the young Count after Act I, he was victorious, and spared his opponent. And if, in the subsequent Battle of Pelilla, his army was routed, he at least stood and faced di Luna until he was felled and left for dead. 'Why didn't you kill him first, in the duel?' Azucena asks. Manrico only wonders: 'Some mysterious force stopped my hand. Some voice from heaven seemed to say, "Don't strike!"' (Jolted by the sudden revelations, we wonder, 'Could Manrico actually be Garzia grown now to young manhood? Did Azucena really burn her own baby in her delirium, and raise the di Luna baby as her own? Is that why, intuitively, Manrico shrank from killing di Luna – sensing somehow that his enemy was really his brother?')

Manrico's aide Ruiz sends him word that more than the Count di Luna have given him up for dead. Leonora, too, has heard the report of his death, and will now enter a convent. Though Azucena appeals to Manrico not to risk his life while still weak with his wounds ('Your blood,' she insists, 'is my blood!'), he orders his horse made ready in the valley below and, when the scene changes to the cloister back in Aragon, he appears there – alone, as if risen from the dead – just as the Count and his men are about to carry off Leonora. But it is Manrico who takes the incredulous lady away, for Ruiz and his other followers have run to his aid with swords and the revolutionary cry 'Urgel viva!' The pretender to the throne, Urgel, has secured the castle of Castellor, and given Manrico command of it.

In Act III the scene shifts to the plain before the cliffed (and still standing) Castellor, as di Luna plans to attack it. There di Luna's men find Azucena wandering in search of her son, and Ferrando, as he was sure he would, recognizes her almost instantly as the gypsy who burned the infant Garzia. They bind her with ropes. She cries out, 'Save me, Manrico my son!' The Count realizes that he now has two reasons to burn her. She screams at him to fear the wrath of God.

Above, in Castellor, Manrico is about to wed Leonora when Ruiz brings the news that Azucena has been captured by di Luna's forces below. From the castle window Manrico can see the stake being readied. He is horrified, and rushes off to save the gypsy. 'I am her son,' he shouts to Leonora. Act III is called 'The Gypsy Woman's Son.'

Act IV is, finally, 'The Punishment.' We are back at the palace of Aljaferia, at the far side of the garden, where rises the tower (still standing today) that keeps prisoners of state. Ruiz points it out to Leonora. She glances at a ring on her finger and says she will be safe. The monks are singing the office of the dead, and from the tower we hear Manrico's troubadour voice calling for death and, as before, invoking Leonora's name. Leonora sees death spreading his wings over the tower.

The Count di Luna appears, gives orders that Manrico be led at dawn to the block, his mother to the stake. (So we realize that Manrico arrived on the plain before Castellor in time to save his mother, only to lose the ensuing battle.) The Count muses over his disappointment: when he stormed Castellor, he did not find Leonora within. Just then she steps from the shadows to face him. She pleads for Manrico's life, and finally (in desperation, secretly sipping poison from her ring) offers herself as payment. Di Luna, his passion overriding his sense of honour, accepts.

In the last scene, inside the tower, Azucena is nearly crazed with the thought of being burned alive, remembering her mother's flaming hair, the sparks flying to heaven, the eyes hanging out from their sockets. Her troubadour son tenderly lulls her to sleep with a song of homecoming. Suddenly Leonora is there to set him free. Manrico's honour is offended at the thought of the price she has had to pay – until he sees that she is dying. 'Rather than live for another, I chose to die for you,' she says.

The opera hurries to its end. The Count appears at the door of the cell, and realizes he has been tricked: in a moment, Leonora is dead. Manrico, crying to Azucena, 'Mother, farewell!' goes to the block. The Count drags Azucena to the tower window and forces her to watch. The blade falls. She shrieks, 'He was your brother!' And as the Count exclaims, 'And I still live!' she falls lifeless with the triumphant cry, 'Mother, you are avenged!'

What is there, in this grisly story, that is worthy of commendation? To begin with, there is a cumulative power, a growing sense of wonder and horror about that story – provided we don't approach it with some plot synopsis that provides an account of 'preliminary events' and cues us in, before we hear a note of the music, to what only Azucena knows and only she should reveal, in her penultimate line – that di Luna and Manrico are brothers. Though we might suspect the truth as early as the first scene in Act II, when in an emotional extremity Azucena reveals it to Manrico himself, we cannot be sure of it, nor can he, as she immediately denies it and we conclude, as he does, that she, maddened all her life by the memory of her mother, has been raving.

Actually, that Manrico is Garzia di Luna is only the last of many revelations gradually made about the shadowy young troubadour, each of them made at the moment in the story when it will have maximum impact. In successive moments we discover the *trovatore*'s gypsy name, his revolutionary affiliation, his intuitive sense of affinity with the Count di Luna, and the fact that his mysterious appearances as knight and troubadour are assumed roles while he lives a quite different sort of existence among gypsies. The words that describe him best are the first words he sings: 'Deserto sulla terra.' Manrico is 'alone on the earth,' unknown to others and knowing nothing of himself. 'I am near you,' sings Leonora at the foot of his prison tower, 'and you know it not.' He feels the need, always, to allay his fears about his own identity. 'Who am I, then? Who?' he asks Azucena. He is never so fortunate as that other subversive minstrel-knight from another country but the same period, the outcast Tannhäuser. Verdi's troubadour never achieves, even in death, the self-knowledge eventually granted Wagner's Minnesinger. Manrico / Garzia di Luna goes at the age of seventeen to the executioner's block without ever knowing who he really was.

That knowledge is given, on the last page of the score, to the Count di Luna, whose life's mission it has been to find it. And it would have been better for him had he never found it, for he must live out the rest of his life knowing that he has hated, hounded, and killed – we only discover on that last page – his own brother. Di Luna is the villain of the piece, but how villainous is he? In his own eyes he is justified in sentencing Manrico (as an enemy of state) and Azucena (as the one who, he thinks at the time, killed his brother). His only real fault is his insatiable passion for what he cannot have – a passion that can be gentle (in 'Il balen del suo sorriso') only to turn blasphemously possessive (in 'Per me ora fatale'). That aria and cabaletta show him to be a sensitive but unduly sensual man, raised in chivalry yet – unlike his younger brother, who was not given his advantages – utterly lacking in it. He knows his own weakness and admits it to the faithful Ferrando: 'I am crazed with passion. I have lost every rational instinct.'

Set against him is Leonora, a gentle creature unable to comprehend the violence around her. 'I cannot endure these terrible revelations,' she cries in Castellor. 'It would be better just to die.' She is too noble to play Tosca to di Luna's Scarpia: if she must sacrifice her honour to save her beloved, it is she who will die, not the crazed man she bargains with. The only way she sees out of her extremity is to sacrifice herself; what in her first scene she declares she would do is what in the last scene she actually does do – die for the troubadour. Her resolve to take the veil when she thinks him dead shows the same consistent attitude. Yet all her sacrifices go for nothing: they only implicate her further in actions which, to a woman of her religious faith, must be considered mortally sinful. She knows and affirms that God 'sees [her] whole soul' as she kills herself.

Caught in their fixed attitudes, these characters are not, nor are they meant to be, true to life. They are emotionally charged symbols of life's ironies: Manrico of the inability of a man to know himself; di Luna of the destructiveness of human passion; Leonora of the futility of self-sacrifice. But the central character – Verdi insisted she had to be – is Azucena. 'This woman's two great passions,' he wrote to his librettist Cammarano, 'her love for Manrico and her wild thirst to avenge her mother, must be sustained to the end.' On that last page of the score, Azucena is killed, not by any executioner, but by the convergence of those two powerfully conflicting passions. She had thought, until that moment, that she would die as her mother had died – at the stake. Instead, she is killed by a repetition of the great, irrational moment in her *own* previous experience: ought she to save Manrico again, as once she did in half-consciousness when he was a baby, or ought she to avenge her mother and let him die? At the fire, she killed her real son. At the opera's end, she in effect kills the other who had become a son to her, though at any moment she could have saved him by telling di Luna he was his brother. She is, in fact, only a split second too late for that: 'Oh, stop!' she cries at the window, 'Listen to me!' But it is too late. If we grasp this, we cannot help exclaiming, with di Luna, 'How horrible!' Azucena represents *in excelsis* what the other characters, in their several ways, express: the essential loneliness of every person in this world, the helplessness, destructiveness, and futility of human actions in a universe that is overwhelmingly cruel to its creatures.

Can we justify taking so seriously a plot so often maligned? The composer who brought it to vivid musical life took it seriously, perhaps for more than any other reason because it reflected his own furiously pessimistic view of the world. 'This man,' said Vincent Sheean, 'was angry ... over the Crimean war, the fragmentation of Italy, the status of the holy places in Jerusalem and Bethlehem, the Austrian empire, the survival of the Italian princes and the vicissitudes of Cavour.' Verdi lived in an ugly world – one that cloaked its injustices and cruelty under the promise of progress – and he hated it. He had to set his operas in remote times and places to say what he wanted to say about his own time and place. And while many of his operas before *Il Trovatore* indicate the possibility of a resurgent Italy (and all of them see some redemptive value, at least, in human suffering), with the grim story of Azucena Verdi abandons hope for despair: there is no sense in human striving or human suffering, for life means nothing. Giuseppina Strepponi said Verdi was 'happier believing nothing.' She was in love with him, and they spoke of *Il Trovatore* as their opera, the one they understood, the one that spoke for them. But when, a devout and self-sacrificing woman, she asked him about God, he laughed in her face and said, though he loved her, 'You are mad.' With *Il Trovatore* Verdi was well on his way to Iago's terrible credo, 'After death there is nothing.'

What could have made him so bitter? Events in his life, perhaps, that were not unlike those in *Il Trovatore*. When he was a baby, his mother fled with him in her arms to the village church to escape the sabres of a vindictive Russian regiment venting its hatred of Napoleon by massacring the innocents of Piacenza. While other women and children were slain in the midst of their prayers, Verdi's mother climbed with him to the church tower and escaped the slaughter. Years later, Verdi saw his own two children die of illness within the span of a few months, and fell ill himself, only to lose to death the young wife who had tended him. The year before he wrote *Il Trovatore* his mother died. In the midst of writing *Il Trovatore* his librettist died. When the opera appeared on the stage, Verdi wrote, 'People say that it is too sad, that there are too many deaths in it. But death is all there is in life. What else is there?'

Verdi had no difficulty accepting what strained, and still strains, the belief of the too-sophisticated members of his audience – that a woman could so disregard maternal instinct (even amid the shock and horror Azucena experienced) as mistakenly to kill her own baby. But that, for Verdi, is the terrible heart of the story that had to be 'sustained to the end.' For him it was boldly symbolic of the chaotic cruelty in the universe itself. Instinct is not denied in *Il Trovatore*. It is powerfully at work from first to last: old di Luna goes to his death with a presentiment that his infant son is somehow still alive; Ferrando knows the gypsy daughter will reappear; Inez knows the troubadour will bring sorrows; Manrico is unable to kill di Luna, sensing that there is a kindred bond between them; Leonora rushing from her apartments to meet Manrico, and Azucena wandering across northern Spain in search of him, run into the arms of the one man alive who shares his blood; the young Count's savage hatred for Manrico comes not just from the fact that the troubadour is a political subversive and a rival in love, but (once we sense the ironic undercurrents we can say with some certainty) from sibling jealousy brought on by a father's dying behest. Instinct is alive in the world of *Il Trovatore*, and the terrible truth is that it works chaotically and destructively.

The more one thinks about the story, the more subtleties one can detect. Manrico is associated in Leonora's memory with the moon, and when he first appears and lifts the visor of his helmet, the moon emerges from the clouds to reveal his face – though neither he nor his brother nor Leonora knows that his real name is Garzia di Luna (Garzia of the moon). Has anyone ever suggested about this opera, as they often do about more obviously mythic works, that the moon is an archetypal symbol of the irrational, that it is associated in many works of literature with (remember Azucena) feminine intuition? Has anyone remarked that images of light and darkness are everywhere in the text – in the 'Anvil Chorus,' in the liturgical music of the nuns, in Manrico's 'Mal reggendo' and the Count's 'Il balen'? Has anyone ever remarked that Manrico's tragic fate – that he never be revealed to himself – might have been visited on him by the evil eye of the old gypsy mother bending over his cradle? Has anyone ever remarked that that old gypsy is characterized throughout by the image of staring eyes? Has anyone remarked that *Trovatore*'s musical phrases and rhythms, the narrative strumming:

and the chaotic staggering:

are also found in *Rigoletto* before and *Traviata* after, and may be intentional cross-references, expressing from opera to opera Verdi's emergent pessimism? Has anyone remarked that each of the titles given the acts of the opera are ambiguous? Which 'Duel' – at Aljaferia, where Manrico could have killed his brother, or at Pelilla, where his brother could have killed him? Which 'Gypsy Woman' – the mother or the daughter? Which 'Gypsy Woman's Son' – the one burned or the one saved? Which 'Punishment' – Manrico's, di Luna's, Leonora's, or Azucena's? In a cruel and meaningless universe there is little to distinguish. We are all, regardless of our identities, hurrying toward our respective dooms.

Are these subtleties consciously planned, or are they simply there because instinct was aroused in the creation of this masterpiece – primitive, poetic instinct in the twenty-three-year-old Spaniard who wrote the original play, and profoundly pessimistic, cannily dramatic instinct in the thirty-seven-year-old Italian who wrote the music? The more one sees what appears to be planned, the more one is sure that instinct, not planning, was at work.

All the same, say many opera-goers, *Il Trovatore* is too violent. But is it? In scrupulous observance of classical rules, its violent acts all take place offstage or between scenes. Onstage we only see four characters tensed on the brink of violence. We who watch are left to discover, each time the curtains part, what has happened in the interval, sure only that it will be unexpected and shocking. The opera is compressed from its Spanish original, but, as the best critics keep insisting in the face of the sophisticates, it is not unintelligible. It will reward study, but it actually demands only some understanding of Spanish codes of honour in the Middle Ages, of gypsy codes still observed today, and of Verdi's own deeply felt disaffection with the world as he saw it. People do not laugh at the plot of *Il Trovatore* in Italy, or call it an old warhorse of an opera filled with barrel-organ tunes. The conductor Gianandrea Gavazzeni, who wrote books on Wagner and Mussorgsky, has called *Il Trovatore* 'the Italian St Matthew Passion.'

Il Trovatore is of course full of wonderful music. (If pressed to name the most beautiful tenor and soprano arias this side of Mozart, I would cite 'Ah si, ben mio' and 'D'amor sull' ali rosee.') But the source of the opera's strength lies in more than its melodies. That indefinable source has been best described by Francis Toye: 'Something emerges and hits you, as it were, between the eyes, something elemental, furious, wholly true.'

9

The Requisite Miracle
La Traviata

I once met a priest from a downtown parish in New York. He was of Italian descent, poor, devout, and well read, especially in Dante. Our conversation turned, naturally enough, to Verdi, and eventually to *La Traviata*. About Violetta Valéry, the *traviata* or 'fallen woman' in Verdi's opera, he said, simply, looking me straight in the eye, 'È una santa.' 'She is a saint.'

That was hardly the opinion voiced from pulpits at the time *La Traviata* first appeared. Preachers of all persuasions railed against its immorality. Promiscuous men might be allowed on the stage if, as in Mozart's operas, they repented or were punished. But promiscuous women, especially women who sold themselves for money, were beyond sympathy. They, not the men (married or unmarried) who consorted with them, were to be condemned. Clerics and censors and, perhaps most vociferous of all, music critics were convinced to a man that, if this barrier were not held, society would surely crumble.

I won't say that we are more understanding today. But it is hard to think of a nineteenth-century parish priest who would have said of Verdi's heroine, humbly and plainly, 'Violetta? È una santa.'

What makes a saint? Official canonization requires a careful examination of documents and testimonials to the candidate's steadfast faith and 'heroic practice of virtue,' and the confirmation of this by one or more miracles wrought by God as witness to that heroism. In practice, sainthood implies that the person knew the height and depth and breadth of love, and sacrificed his (or her) own self for others, even to the point of dying if it came to that.

Dying. In the novel on which Verdi's opera is based, *La Dame aux*

Camélias by Alexandre Dumas *fils*, we meet the fallen woman's exhumed corpse before we meet the woman herself. Verdi and his librettist Piave, having to compress the novel into an evening's performance time, dispense with Dumas's macabre scene and plunge into the story's beginning – but not before Verdi has given us a prelude that is something like beginning the story at the end, as in the novel. This opening music for divided strings is also the music of the last act, when Violetta lies dying:

That moving evocation of heroic suffering, and then of striving upwards and falling back to die …

… is followed by a touching melody in the violins, the melody which Violetta will use in Act II when she sings, 'Love me, Alfredo, love me as I love you.' This is the music of – to use a phrase of Verdi's day that we don't use much any more – a beautiful soul:

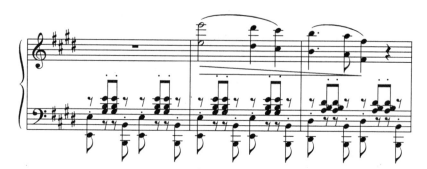

But why is the moving melody introduced with, and accompanied by, an almost crudely lurching waltz rhythm? Why do obsessive waltzes pervade the opera? Why are the closing measures of the opera, again, so lurchingly ugly? Because the woman ennobled by such suffering, capable of such love as the melody expresses, had been a courtesan, an outcast of society. In the prelude, Verdi repeats her expressive melody and surrounds it with skittish, coquettish figures in the violins, to remind us of that blunt fact.

The courtesans of Dumas's Paris, the women of what he was the first to call 'the *demi-monde*,' that half-acknowledged society below respectable society, were numbered in the tens of thousands. They had class systems of their own. In their hectic lives, they could be insolent, venal, and heartless. They were also loveless, abused, and almost invariably cast aside when their charms had faded.

The prototype of Verdi's Violetta, Marie Duplessis, may have been best known for the white camelias she wore at the height of her success, when she numbered Franz Liszt among her patrons, but she had been sold into the *demi-monde* at age fifteen by her own father, and was dead, of consumption, eight years later. Julian Budden explains that 'her disease produced a desire for pleasure which accelerated her decline.'

Near the end of Marie's short life Dumas fell in love with her. In the novel he wrote from her sad story he called her Marguerite Gauthier, and he has her say of the women of the *demi-monde*, without a trace of sentimentality, 'We have no friends. We only have selfish lovers. We no longer belong to ourselves. We are no longer beings, but things.'

Young Dumas, illegitimate himself, son of a famous father and a fallen woman, wrote, 'I was born of an error, and I have errors to fight against.' In his novel he went at some length into the practical business of how much money his courtesan made, and how she made it, so as to show the extent to which she goes when, touched for the first time by the transfiguring power of real love, she gives up everything for it – friends, security, all her defences, even though she is fatally ill.

This was a new figure for literature and, inevitably, for the stage. The play Dumas adapted from his novel was a famous vehicle for Sarah Bernhardt (in three thousand performances), for Eleanore Duse (in storied presentations across the length and breadth of Europe and America), and finally (in an incandescent performance we can still see) for Greta Garbo, on the screen. By 1937 Camille, as she came to be called, was a radiant creature in what MGM clearly thought an old-fashioned story. But film critic Stanley Kauffmann notes that Dumas's original intent was anything but old-fashioned. He wanted 'to face some realities about the exploitation of women by men with the money to do it.'

That was the ugly fact, the contemporary fact, that Verdi was determined to put on the operatic stage. But the censors would not allow it on the stage unless it was set, harmlessly, in an age a hundred years past. When it was finally staged as Verdi intended, in its own period, fifty years had gone by, and that period was itself gone.

So today, we tend to think of *La Traviata*, like Garbo's *Camille*, as a romantic period piece. And thereby we do it, and ourselves, a disservice. Verdi, in mid-career, was determined to use the medium of which he was now a master to arouse sympathy for society's outcasts, the sort of people we might go out of our way to *avoid* on the street – the ugly hunchback, hardened and corrupt (Rigoletto), the old gypsy woman, demented and dangerous (Azucena), and the fallen woman, rejected, impoverished, and ill (Violetta). Three operas on society's cruelties, created in one great arc of intense feeling in little more than two years' time. Three passionate operas about family relationships disrupted by passion. All three of them speak to all times, but only *Traviata* was intended to be set in Verdi's own day. He called it 'a subject of our time.'

Verdi was in love when he wrote the three operas. I don't want to suggest, as some have, that *La Traviata* is an opera explicitly about Verdi and his mistress, later his devoted wife, Giuseppina Strepponi. Though they began to live together in Paris, and saw Dumas's play only a month into its initial run, the opera they always spoke of as their own was not *La Traviata* but *Il Trovatore*. And Giuseppina was no courtesan. A singer and something of a free spirit, she had ruined her voice by working it too hard in a desperate attempt to support her family after the death of her father. In the volatile world of the theatre, she had taken lovers and borne at least four illegitimate children – one stillborn, the others given to charitable institutions. (According to the new Verdi biography by Mary Jane Philips-Matz, Giuseppina may have borne two more children who were put up for adoption and were, very likely, Verdi's.)

Though little of this was known to the respectable people of Verdi's Busseto, they knew, when Giuseppina and Verdi came to live among them, that the two were not married. Giuseppina bore the brunt of the villagers' outraged reactions. Verdi did not marry her till fifteen years had passed. His reluctance to marry a second time (his first marriage had ended with the death of his young wife) remains a mystery to this day. Verdi could be, and often was, extraordinarily generous. He could also be, as anyone reading Mrs Philips-Matz's book will readily see, unexplainably cruel. His was the ambivalence of most great artists.

But there is no question that Verdi saved Giuseppina when she was desperate, and that is the burden of her letters to him, letters that often remind us of *La Traviata*: 'O my Verdi! I am not worthy of you. Keep on loving me. Love me after death, that I may present myself before God's throne of judgment rich in your love and your prayers.' In the opera, Violetta sings – as she makes the great sacrifice of her life and gives up Alfredo without being permitted to say why – 'You do love me, Alfredo, you do love me, isn't it so? I'll always be with you, there among the flowers.' And then, 'Oh, love me, Alfredo. Love me as I love you':

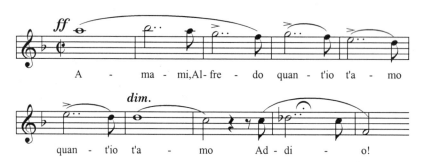

The love in that music, which surely owes something to the love Verdi found in Giuseppina, is so strong, so clear, so true (even if not blessed by the Church) that it touches the heart of that strictest of conventional moralists, Alfredo's father. He becomes more of a father to the courtesan he comes to challenge than to the son for whose sake he intervenes. An honest man, he becomes for a fallen woman the true father she never had. 'Embrace me like a daughter,' she says when she rises to the sacrifice he asks. 'Then I shall be strong.'

Eventually, Verdi's courtesan thinks of everyone but herself. I've always been touched when she promises Alfredo's father, 'He'll be back with you soon, but he'll be terribly hurt. You'll have to comfort him.' The scene between Violetta and Alfredo's father – the courtesan's generous response to the honest plea of bourgeois respectability – is the great heart of Verdi's opera.

Violetta grows so much in the course of the opera that, it is often said, the role requires a different voice for each of the three acts – a coloratura to show Violetta's abandonment to pleasure in Act I, a lyric soprano to show her rising to the sacrifice of Act II, a lirico spinto to ride the tragic force of Act III. But many sopranos make their most lasting impression in a passage that requires only speaking. At the start of Act III, Violetta, after accepting the consolations of religion, and giving what little is left of her money to the poor, reads aloud the letter she has received from Alfredo's father. A solo violin plays the melody of Alfredo's 'Love is the palpitation of the universe, mysterious, ethereal, a crucifixion and a consolation' ...

... as Violetta reads aloud the letter from his father, who finally understands the depth of the sacrifice she has made. He has seen his son disgrace her in public, and heard her say, in forgiveness, 'Alfredo, Alfredo, you can't understand the depth of the love in my heart.' We are not asked, in this opera, to condone. We are asked to understand.

Verdi wrote *La Traviata*, as Dumas wrote the novel on which it was based, in white heat, in little more time than it took to get the notes onto the page. Then he never wrote another opera on a contemporary subject. *La Traviata*, perhaps the first opera set in the time of its audience, was also the first opera to elicit sympathy for a woman rejected by society, and the first to explore to the full the height and breadth and depth of self-sacrificing love. It is indeed some kind of miracle.

It may not be the kind of miracle needed for canonical sainthood. But it is miracle enough for this priest to say – with, I expect, many others – 'Violetta? È una santa.'

10

The Whole Checkered Play of Life
La Forza del Destino

Every commentator on Verdi's *La Forza del Destino* has recourse sooner or later to the same inevitable adjective – 'sprawling.' The adjective is not inappropriate, so long as it is not used pejoratively. But it is inadequate. *Forza* sprawls only as a vast naturalistic canvas by a master painter – by Goya, say, or Velasquez – may be said to sprawl. Verdi's canvas in *Forza* is crowded with varied figures but, as with the great Spanish painters, it uses more than one angle of vision. That is how Velasquez invited his beholder to search for his meanings – through various angles of vision. In the tumultuous work of art that is Verdi's *Forza* there are many conflicting details. But one single idea – a searing, terrifying idea – unifies and gives meaning to all of them.

We do not often think of Verdi as a dramatist of ideas, but as he neared the half-century mark in his life he began to think of himself that way. In fact he called *Forza* his 'opera made of ideas.' He took an angry play by a liberal Spanish nobleman and, far from simplifying it as is the usual case with adaptations of stage plays for operatic purposes, he crowded additional details into it. The melodrama *Don Alvaro, o la Fuerza del Sino* by the Duque de Rivas became in Verdi's hands a complex, ambivalent, ironic vehicle designed to express a single, central idea.

For the better part of a century, *Forza* was thought, despite many fine pages, to have no central idea at all. It was called, not just sprawling, but seriously flawed, incoherent, and unsure in its sense of direction. This was not, at the start, a problem for me. When I first heard the opera, on a Metropolitan Opera broadcast more than fifty years ago, with Ezio Pinza singing Padre Guardiano, Milton Cross told us listeners that Verdi had written *Forza* at the invitation of the Imperial Theatre in St Petersburg. The next time I heard Pinza on a broadcast, he was singing the title role of that greatest of Russian operas, Mussorgsky's *Boris Godunov*. And every-thing about *Forza* seemed to fall into place: Russian opera too was a can-vas crowded with rulers and commoners, with holy and unholy men of the cloth, with great matters of history and religion, with episodes of vast social upheaval juxtaposed with the joys and sorrows of individual lives. Verdi, when he wrote *La Forza del Destino*, was, I thought, simply giving the Russians what they wanted.

Imagine my surprise when I discovered that *Forza*, which premièred in Russia in 1862, actually anticipated *Boris* and the other great Russian pageant-operas by several years. More than that, it appeared on the Rus-sian stage before Tolstoy began, in the second part of *War and Peace*, to expand his historical vistas, and before Dostoevsky wrote those novels obsessed with the idea that Russia's future lay in its common people and its Orthodox faith. Could it be that *Forza* had influenced those essential Russian works? And what about the strange coincidences in Verdi's opera – its characters meeting improbably across vast distances and stretches of time? Didn't that anticipate by almost a century the famous coincidences, the chance meetings from one end of Russia to the other, in Pasternak's *Doctor Zhivago*? Russian opera is properly thought to have begun before *Forza*, with Glinka's pioneering *A Life for the Czar*. But it can also be said that *Forza* – and indeed the very qualities in *Forza* that make it problem-atic – blazed a trail for some of the great Russian art that followed.

But this opera written for Russia is nonetheless a work rooted in the culture of Western Europe. Its structural looseness is not a weakness so much as a manifestation of a new direction that drama began to take in Latin and Germanic countries during the Romantic age. Anselm Ger-hard, writing on another misunderstood and influential Italian opera, Rossini's *La Gazza Ladra*, correctly observed that, in the post-Napoleonic era, the times were inexorably past when an inflexible social order and an unquestioned religion provided easy answers to the greater and smaller events of life. Gone forever were the old certainties. Gone too was the sev-enteenth- and eighteenth-century theory of drama as an art concerned exclusively with the noble and the high-born. Gone for good were the rigid unities of time, place, and action, and the exaggerated notions of what was and what was not in artistic good taste. Above all, coincidence, which before had been used mainly for the purposes of comic intrigue, now became the driving force behind a new kind of drama – a Romantic drama the French called *mélodrame à grand spectacle*, a drama that mixed different genres so as to encompass what A.W. Schlegel called 'the whole checkered play of life.'

That is what Verdi was attempting in *La Forza del Destino*. That is why, powerfully moved though he was by the blows dealt by Fate to the three high-born figures in his source – Donna Leonora, Don Alvaro, and Don Carlo – he insisted to his faithful librettist Piave that the original play had to be expanded, that the three Spanish commoners – the gypsy fortune-teller Preziosilla, the Jewish muleteer-trader Trabuco, and the short-tempered lay brother Melitone – must all appear again when the action moved from Spain to Italy. In fact, Verdi thought the gypsy and the friar the most important characters in the opera, and he borrowed a whole scene, the encampment scene at the end of Act III, from another play, Schiller's *Wallensteins Lager*, so that the gypsy and the muleteer and the friar could turn up, independently of each other, at a place thousands of miles away from where we first met them. They too would be swept along by Fate. They would lend their commoners' dimension to what might be called the Tolstoian vision (some, remembering *Henry V*, have said Shakespearean vision, and others, remembering *Mother Courage*, have said Brechtian vision) of Verdi's new opera.

The three commoners, of course, survive. Preziosilla, Trabuco, and Melitone, committed to no allegiances save their own common-sense existential views of life, are all given scenes in which they demonstrate their survival instincts, their savvy and shrewdness. But the three high-born figures, Alvaro and Carlo and Leonora, with their inflexible codes of honour and their adamant religious faith, are destroyed. They are tragic not because they die but because they are, at the end, more aware than the three commoners of the savage workings of Fate, which in this opera is the only force directing human lives.

And that brings us to Verdi himself. Ultimately, any understanding of *La Forza del Destino* depends on our understanding of its composer. As he neared the age of fifty, Verdi was a man with a fiercely pessimistic view of the world. His Italy had defeated Austria in its Second War of Independence (it is not for nothing that in *Forza* Preziosilla sings 'Death to the Germans'). And as his country moved towards unification, Verdi was elected to the first Italian Parliament. But this was something he undertook from a sense of duty, out of gratitude to Cavour and Garibaldi. If his country was at last at peace, he was not at peace himself. He could have called his new opera 'War and Peace,' for 'guerra' and 'pace' are words that define its long horizontal: he deliberately set the characters who fail to find peace in religious faith against a background of war. As for any answers to the questions of human existence – answers which for others religion might provide – Verdi still felt as he did when he wrote the earlier *Il Trovatore*, another work misunderstood by those with no feeling for the concerns that preoccupied Verdi.

Both *Trovatore* and *Forza* are derived from angry Spanish plays. Each develops from an incident which signifies that no one controls his own destiny: in *Trovatore*, a gypsy woman, in an irrational contradiction of every human instinct, mistakenly throws her own child into the flames where her mother is being burned at the stake; in *Forza*, the hero's pistol accidentally misfires and kills the heroine's father. We are not, these works would have it, in control of our own destinies.

And Verdi, in the swift and terrible scene at the end of each work, finds no meaning in human existence. At the end of *Trovatore*, brother brutally executes brother without either knowing who the other is. In the original ending of *Forza*, brother kills sister, and the hero, an Incan prince who became a Byronic soldier and then a humble priest, is so overwhelmed by the force of destiny that he leaps off a cliff into what he sees as the jaws of hell, despairing and calling on heaven to annihilate the whole human race.

Verdi changed that ending six years after the Russian première to the ending that most opera houses use today, inspired possibly by an encounter with an old man of vibrant faith, the poet and novelist Alessandro Manzoni. In the second and now standard ending, Verdi's Alvaro does not leap to his death but is persuaded by an old man of vibrant faith to find meaning in Christian forgiveness. The music in this second ending grows thematically out of what has preceded it. But the drama does not, and Verdi knew it. He was far from satisfied with the second ending. It was that shocking first ending that the opera had all along been leading to – a sudden explosion of terrible ironies: the hero out of compassion violates the sanctuary of the very woman he has been searching for, and brings down upon himself the curse, the *maledizione*, so massively intoned years before by the monks of the monastery where he has found refuge. He has been destroyed by the very religion he has served. His Leonora is killed by her vengeful brother, not only because the brother has sworn to save the family honour, but because the brother presumes that his sister and his enemy have been living in sin under the cover of religion.

The opera is very much about religion as Verdi saw it. He wrote for old Padre Guardiano religious music of great eloquence. (He once played the organ at a cloister called 'degli Angeli' where, I'm told, there is today a confessional that bears the nameplate 'Padre Guardiano.') On the other hand, he had little use for most of religion's practitioners: while he strove to keep his Fra Melitone a charming character in the *opera buffa* mould, his anti-clerical feelings kept getting in the way of his intentions. But above all else, religion as Verdi saw it was utterly helpless in the face of life's cruelties. Verdi became increasingly conscious of something cruel and irrational at the heart of nature. It just might be that Fate, not God, ruled the world, and that all man's believing, striving, searching, and suffering were for nothing. In fact, his good deeds could turn on him in terrible ironies. In *La Forza del Destino* there is no meaning in honourable love, in military glory, in religious faith and self-sacrifice. A blind *destino* forcibly and cruelly arranges what appear to be coincidences and uses them, across vast stretches of time and space, to destroy its innocent victims.

At the time Verdi wrote *Forza*, much of the civil and ecclesiastical censorship he had previously to deal with was no longer in force. He was freer to express his ideas, and he was further on his way to Iago's blasphemous credo and its terrible conclusion, 'After death there is nothing.' For most of his life, Verdi thought that way. His wife, the devout Giuseppina, wrote in sorrow that Verdi was happy in his agnosticism, that he called her mad when she spoke of God. I think he faced the concerns of *Forza* again, years later, in the *Requiem*, in *Otello*, and, years after that, in his *Te Deum*. And there, at the age of eighty-two, he seemed to find a measure of peace. The second ending given *La Forza del Destino* is not altogether inappropriate, for it is strangely prophetic: like Alvaro the soldier/priest in the second ending, Verdi would, in his final, quasi-liturgical pieces, express the hope that it might be a providential power, not an inscrutable fate, that directs the courses of human lives.

La Forza del Destino, with its two opposed and irreconcilable endings, remains a stark reminder that we have two choices in the matter of how we can view our lives. We can see life as inexorably fated, utterly beyond our control. Or we can see our lives as directed, however violent and senseless they seem, by a provident God. It is a choice as old as Greek tragedy, as old as the questions raised by Sophocles, whose tragedies are swept on by Fate, and by Aeschylus, who found an explanation for tragedy in the providential plan of a father god.

The operatic dramatist most influenced by the Greeks, Richard Wagner, never wrote anything like *Forza*. He always pulled the centrifugal elements of his massive dramas together at the close, so that we are left with a consistent, and ultimately consoling, view of the world. Such conclusions were not for Verdi, and certainly not for the Verdi who, in his maturity, wrote operas of ideas. For him the meaning of any human life was not to be sought, as in Wagner, in some archetypal myth, but in the confused conflicts of day-to-day existence. He was, in *Forza*, an existential-ist eighty years before Jean-Paul Sartre. And to dramatize his ideas he dared, after a long career in the theatre, to try his hand at a new kind of opera, one that juxtaposed and interrupted and contrasted, one that saw 'the whole checkered play of life' as he saw it – episodic, a series of loose ends, full of ironies and largely unintelligible.

What, finally, is the central idea that unifies all the details in Verdi's canvas? The idea that the great question of human existence is whether there is any meaning to human existence. It was a question to which Verdi, who took nothing on faith but thought seriously about life, found no answer. He was the kind of man for whom asking the question was more important than finding the answer.

11

Melt Egypt into Nile
Aida

Verdi's last two operas, *Otello* and *Falstaff,* are based on Shakespeare, are immensely respected by critics, and, especially in recent years, have won a wide public as well. The opera that precedes them is the un-Shakespearian *Aida,* his greatest popular success but so very successful that there is an occasional critical reaction against it. One reads that its characters are two-dimensional, its local colour laid on too thickly, its ballet interludes substandard, its 'circus atmosphere,' at least in most productions, too pronounced.

Over the years I had come to concur with those criticisms. In my salad days *Aida* was easily my favourite opera, but after close to forty years' listening, parts of it – the ballabili, for example, and the cabaletta 'Si, fuggiam' – might have been expected to wither and stale, and they had. Then I listened to the Toscanini recording of *Aida* at the same time I was rereading some of Shakespeare, the poet and dramatist Verdi loved above all others, the one he always kept within easy reach and might have had in mind even as he wrote *Aida.* Hearing the Italian's music with the Englishman's most appropriate play, *Antony and Cleopatra,* also in my head, I've revised my judgment on *Aida.* There is 'no winter in 't.' It is an autumn that grows 'the more by reaping.'

The two works are, of course, quite dissimilar. Shakespeare whisks us back and forth across the Mediterranean with more than forty quick scene changes, as we follow the careers of his Roman 'world sharers' Antony, Caesar, and Lepidus. Verdi, dealing with an Egypt centuries older, confines himself to seven scenes along the river that rises in Aida's land and ends in Radames's. Beneath their tunics and headpieces, Verdi's characters are clearly Italians and Shakespeare's Elizabethans. Neither dramatist had ever been to Egypt. Yet each has conjured up that land and conveyed the feel of it. And there is where the two works impinge, each on the other.

Shakespeare's conjuring device is, as it had to be for a stage without scenery, verbal imagery. The Nile, for instance, is never far out of his characters' vision. They speak of its ebb and swell, its ooze and slime, its caves and pyramids, its serpents, fishes, insects, birds, and crocodiles. And these images are used not for their pictorial value alone but to explain the personages who speak them.

Verdi, for his operatic Egypt, uses a sort of musical imagery. This is not to say that he resorts, as he is sometimes charged with doing, to indiscriminate picture-painting. He knew well enough that elaborate, realistic sets were being prepared for the Cairo première, and that his music need not reproduce the stage canvases. Instead, in what I choose to call *Aida*'s musical imagery, he alters his melodic line. There is a coiling, convoluted quality in many vocal and instrumental melodies in *Aida* that is quite unique in Verdi. Some of this is by way of local colour. The sinuous middle section of the dance in the temple is an obvious example:

No listener fails to note such 'exotic' effects. But the same serpentine quality invades the less exotic music associated with and sung by the characters, and it begins to define and delineate them for us. Aida's theme is usually noted for its exquisite tenderness. It also coils:

There is a persuasive chromatic quality about the theme that sets Aida apart from other Verdi heroines. Egyptian Radames might well have seen her beauty thus, as 'the pretty worm of Nilus,' and Aida, as he learns all too well, can use her sweetness to persuade, even to deceive.

Even more serpentine are the sensuous themes associated with Amneris. As she reclines amid her slaves and longs for the return of Radames ...

Ah! vie - ni, vie- ni, a - mor mio, rav - vi - va-mi

... one can hear Cleopatra's 'Give me to drink mandragora ... / That I might sleep out this great gap of time. / My Antony is away.' Much of Amneris's frenzied music could serve as a setting for Cleopatra's outbursts. Compare these twisted themes ...

Voi___ la   ter - ra ed i Nu - mi

... with Cleopatra's words as she hears that Antony has remarried: 'Thou shouldst come like a fury crowned with snakes ... / Melt Egypt into Nile, and kindly creatures / Turn all to serpents ... So half my Egypt were submerged and made / A cistern for scaled snakes.'

Radames is limned in music of a different cast. This commander of armies with eyes only for his black Aida is uncannily there in Shakespeare's opening lines – a 'plated Mars' whose eyes 'now bend, now turn / The office and devotion of their view / Upon a tawny front.' And in Verdi's opening 'Celeste Aida' we hear Shakespeare's 'scuffles of great fights' and 'the buckles on his breast' in the aria's brassy introduction, and then his 'dotage' and 'devotion' in its dreamy, rapturous release. 'Celeste Aida' has one brief undulating phrase ...

Il tuo bel   cie - lo vor- rei ri - dar - ti,

... at the point where Radames imagines Aida's native land. But most of the aria is, like the commander himself, straightforward. It moves in big melodic arcs. Radames's music is invariably robust and uncomplicated. When his very straightforwardness traps him, his 'Io son disonorato!' has a simple warrior's ring to it. It is Antony's 'I have offended reputation, / A most unnatural swerving.' I thought of Radames surrendering his weapon at the end of Verdi's Nile Scene when I read Antony's words, 'My sword, made weak by my affection, would / Obey it on all cause.' And when he said, very directly, 'She has robbed me of my sword.'

But Shakespeare's hero is not always so direct. He is largely defined in terms of verbal imagery. We see Antony's disintegration as dissolution, as a surrender to the liquid atmosphere of Egypt, and especially to the seeping Nile that endows Egypt with such life as no Roman can understand until he surrenders: 'Authority melts from me.' 'Let Rome in Tiber melt.' 'The crown o' th' earth doth melt.' In a superbly written scene in Cleopatra's palace, Antony observes that clouds and vapours can resemble now a lion, again 'a towered citadel, a pendant rock, / A forked mountain,' and 'that which is now a horse, even with a thought / The rack dislimns, and makes it indistinct / As water is in water.' Then he quietly tells his overawed servant, 'Now thy captain is / Even such a body.' This shifting, dissolving Antony is, to Roman eyes, an 'ebbed man,' like a swaying tropical plant that 'upon the stream, / Goes to, and back, lackeying the varying tide / To rot itself with motion.'

Can Verdi match this? He likely responded more to the exaltation and despair in such passages than to their wonderful fusion of imagery and character. But in *Aida*'s Nile Scene he does set his characters in a rich musical landscape, and that landscape works constantly on their emotions and, I think, begins to define them. First, it is as if we are sailing down the Nile with Amneris and Ramfis, on oars 'which to the tune of flutes kept stroke':

Into this fluttering stillness Aida enters, suspended like 'the swan's down feather, / That stands upon the swell at full of tide, / And neither way inclines.' If Radames is coming to say goodbye forever, she will throw herself into the great river. For a brief, vivid moment the Nile rises and coils frighteningly in the orchestra:

As the dank influence of the night and the river begin to cast their spell – or, as Shakespeare puts it, 'the poisonous damp of night disponge' – Amonasro evokes the green landscape of Ethiopia to tempt Aida, and she in turn uses it to tempt Radames. Each lover yields to the imagery's persuasiveness, and the luxuriant quality of Verdi's music is almost tangible:

This Nile Scene is a virtual textbook of scoring for wind instruments. Oboe, flute, clarinet, and bassoon wave and undulate in intricate patterns, conjuring up the steamy, shimmering night, the river and swaying trees. And while the instruments provide a kind of psychological canvas, the vocal line illustrates character, coiling in on itself at moments of introspection or suggestiveness or deviousness ...

Ri - ve - drai le fo - res - te im-bal-sa - ma - te,

... and opening out in more typically Verdian style at moments of extro-
verted passion:

Pen - sa che un po - po - lo vin to, stra - zia- to

In short, there is a kind of musical imagery at work, and like Shakespeare's verbal imagery it describes both landscape and character.

More than any other, the final scene of Aida, the Tomb Scene, can be
written in Shakespearian lines: 'Seal then, and all is done' ... 'Kingdoms
are clay' ... 'The bright day is done, / And we are for the dark.' Radames's
lovely 'Morir! Si pura e bella,' which lifts so gently over its rocking accompaniment of strings and soft clarinets, might be Antony's 'Where souls do
couch on flowers, we'll hand in hand.' And Aida's overarching 'O terra
addio,' a farewell to 'the little O, the earth,' is a strain, if ever there was
one, with 'immortal longings' in it:

O   ter - ra ad- di- o:ad- di - o   val - le   di pian- ti.

Verdi was concerned about the effect of both vocal and instrumental
parts at this point, a new effect he described as 'vaporous': the divided,
muted strings execute an unearthly succession of harmonics, the woodwinds whisper delicately, and the two lovers, singing separately at first,
finally blend their voices in soaring unison, while the whole orchestra
seems to quiver in one vast, cosmic tremolo. In no other music is there
anything to equal this 'vaporoso' effect of leaving earth for sky, of quietly
walking through space. Perhaps Shakespeare's lovers approximate it in
imagery as they forsake the 'dungy earth' and 'Nilus' slime' for the purer
elements. Antony, who saw himself as so much shifting vapour, wishes his
enemies would 'fight i' the fire or i' the air. We'd fight there too.' Cleo-

patra, about to die, says, 'I am fire and air; my other elements / I give to baser life.'

'Baser life' ... 'Nilus' slime' – the phrases remind me that I may have done an injustice to Verdi when I dubbed the serpentine middle section of his dance of the priestesses 'obvious.' In Act I it may seem an ordinary bit of colouring. But Verdi may only have been preparing us there for its subtle recurrence in Act IV: the same coiling, earthbound melody returns as the priests chant and the priestesses dance, but now the lovers' voices lift above it to sing, 'Everything is over for us on earth' and 'the sky is opening.' In terms of musical imagery, the sinuous melodic line of the dance means one thing – what 'the aspic leaves upon the caves of Nile' perhaps, while the spreading arc of 'O terra addio' means something else: leaving Nilus' slime for 'fire and air' or, as Verdi's lovers sing, 'flying into a ray of everlasting light.'

Finally, listening to *Aida* with ears freshened by Shakespeare, I was after many years alive again to its dramatic ironies. The fact that Aida has concealed her royal identity during her enslavement in Egypt affects every character and situation in the opera, from beginning to end. In the opening scene Radames thinks he can hope to marry a slave only if he wins unparalleled glory in battle – knowing it is Aida's country, but not knowing it is her father, he must fight. In the closing scene, Amneris, kneeling on the stone that has sealed the fate of the man she loves, does not and will never know that her rival was by birth not a slave but a princess like herself. Neither does she know that that rival has died with her beloved in the darkness below and is even now entering the realm of light with him. To know that, Amneris would have to look not to Egypt with its cruel, chanting priests and its impassive god Ptah; for that she must 'find out new heaven, new earth.' These may be small dramatic points compared to Shakespeare's, but as Verdi's vaporous 'O terra, addio' ebbs away, there is little question that the Bard's imagery has found its match in the composer's imaginative music.

12

A Figure as Old as Comedy
Falstaff

If you are one of the millions of young opera-lovers who have come to favour Verdi above all other composers, you may, on encountering his *Falstaff* for the first time, have felt some disappointment, even something of a shock. This is not *La Traviata*. It does not, when we first hear it, seem to have anything in common at all with *La Traviata*, or *Il Trovatore*, or *Aida*, or – name your favourite Verdi opera.

Yet for some people who have loved Verdi all their lives, *Falstaff* is their favourite of the master's works. And I don't mean just the famous conductors from Toscanini to Karajan to Solti to Bernstein who have recorded the work. I mean blue-collar opera-goers. I once saw *Falstaff* in Ravenna, crowded into a tiny upper box with three factory workers from Torino. They were old married men taking their vacations together, batching it while they made the rounds of the opera houses in northern Italy. They had the bluntness of skilled and honest tradesmen. And they told me honestly and bluntly that this was the best thing Verdi ever wrote. I thought that, after fifty years of listening, I knew *Falstaff* fairly well. But did my knowledge compare with theirs? Those three beefy fellows knew every bar of the score. They sang along with the music as it wafted upwards to our vantage point, and they clearly loved it. They knew that *Falstaff* was not a falling away from Verdi's earlier work, but a distillation, a crystallization of all that had gone before.

Every opera-lover comes, sooner or later, to value *Falstaff* specially, for its special qualities – a melodic line that is endlessly experimental, vocal ensembles of the finest craftsmanship, orchestral detail so intricate that this century's master of orchestration, Richard Strauss, wrote to old Verdi to say, 'I can find no words to describe the impression made on me by the extraordinary beauty of the score of *Falstaff*. It is the reawakening of your genius.'

This is not a different Verdi, but it *is* something of a reawakened one – a wise old man on the threshold of eighty, paradoxically filled with youth, with all his musical powers on the qui vive, returning to write one final opera, as he said, 'just for my own pleasure.'

Falstaff belongs in that special class of artistic masterpieces produced by artists in their old age, when the style that earlier made them famous is transcended, transfigured – often by touches of ironic comedy. I think of Sophocles' *Oedipus at Colonus*, Beethoven's last string quartets, the late films of Akira Kurosawa. These are unsettling and unquestionably great works, neither tragic nor comic but final statements by artists who, with the wisdom of age, can see at last *beyond* the tragic and the comic. As art historian Kenneth Clark once said, many 'old, even very old, artists have added something of immense value to the sum of human experience.' Critic John Russell agrees: 'Work done in old age' is often 'unprecedented, problematic, innovative, and above all fearless.' Such artists need no longer fear that their work will fail. So they release the inner demons that they have lived with all their lives.

With Verdi, the master of tragic song, the inner demons were comic demons, sprites he'd kept under lock and key for half a century. As he approached his eightieth year, he was finally ready to let them loose. In *Falstaff* he offers us what Clark calls 'a glimpse of some irrational and absolute truth that [can] be revealed only by a great artist in his old age.' No wonder those of us who have lived with opera for long lives value *Falstaff*. Verdi's vision can help us to advance to the end of our lives fearlessly, with wit and wisdom and, perhaps most important of all, humility – a realistic sense of our worth as human beings.

One of the moments in *Falstaff* that keeps *me* humble – as a Catholic priest and an honourary doctor of letters from the University of Windsor, Ontario – comes in the last scene, in Windsor Forest. Sir John Falstaff, whose belly is his god, is on his knees. Windsorites old and young, disguised as sprites, are pinching his paunch, singing 'pizzica, stuzzica' to make him repent of his sins. Meanwhile, the merry wives of Windsor, sounding like the nuns' chorus in *Il Trovatore*, sing in mock piety, 'Domine fallo casto,' to which Falstaff humbly adds, 'Savagli l'addomine.' This is a sly pun on 'Domine' (church Latin for 'Lord') and 'addomine' (ordinary Italian for 'abdomen'): the ladies pray, 'Lord, make him chaste,' and the fat knight adds to that prayer, 'But save his abdomen.'

The ladies who see to the merriment of that scene are only four of the ten memorably sketched characters in Verdi's final opera. Tito Gobbi once compared *Falstaff* to a Flemish painting crowded with figures: each figure 'has its own life but remains a vital part of the whole.' But it is also true to say that this opera is a character study of a single figure, larger than life – Sir John Falstaff himself. The fat knight and would-be lover is a lot older than the Shakespeare who named him Falstaff. His career on the stage goes back at least twenty-two centuries to the theatres of ancient Rome – to that comic type, the *miles gloriosus*, the ridiculous, deluded, braggart soldier who never gets the girl. We can see the old Roman *miles gloriosus* in many later operatic guises – as Dr Bartolo in Rossini, as Sergeant Belcore in Donizetti, and, yes, as Sixtus Beckmesser in Wagner.

But Verdi's Falstaff transcends all of those figures. For one thing – as we've said – he's fatter. This is not a politically correct opera. Sir John himself likes to remember the time when he was 'lovely and light, and so slim he could slip through a ring,' but the other characters see him as, and I quote, 'immense ... enormous ... a tub ... a whale ... a pile of lard ... a king of bellies ... a plump full moon ... round as an apple ... big as a ship ... a chair breaker ... a bed smasher.'

This presents a special challenge to the interpreter of the role, and I don't mean just the pillow stuck in the stomach of the costume. The baritone who plays the role must show us the difference between how Falstaff is perceived and what he really is. Is he a mischievous, lovable rascal, or a pathetically baited buffoon, or a shrewd old satyr who really knows more about life than all the other characters put together?

The last of these, I think, is the case. I believe Falstaff when he says, at the end of the opera, that he is not just witty himself, but the one who creates wit in others. Of course he has his faults, but, as John Mason Brown said of Shakespeare's figure, 'We *love* him for his faults.' Orson Welles, who played Falstaff on the screen, said, 'His faults are trivial. His goodness is like bread, like wine.'

Verdi saw to it that his librettist Boito fashioned a Falstaff who was not just the duped clown of Shakespeare's *The Merry Wives of Windsor*, but also the many-sided figure from the two *Henry IV* plays. Verdi's fat Falstaff is all of the things the old braggart soldier was two millennia back, and more. In the fugue that crowns the opera – and imagine Verdi ending his operatic career with a fugue! – Falstaff becomes a spokesman for Verdi himself. In that final fugue, the composer who in his other operas made us weep for our sufferings says wisely, through his wise old man, that we had better end our lives with our sense of humour intact, for 'Ride ben chi ride la risata final' – 'He who laughs last laughs best.' It pleased Verdi to lay his operatic pen down for the last time when he had set Falstaff and all the others singing 'Tutto nel mondo è burla' – 'Everything in the world is a jest.'

Verdi loved his fat knight, and on the completed score he quietly wrote him a touching farewell, in words discovered by Toscanini thirty years after Verdi died: 'Va, vecchio John' – 'On your way, old John.' Falstaff sings that line in the opera, and it develops into a little aria: 'On your way old John, on your way. This old body of yours can still squeeze out a little sweetness for you. All the women are crazy for you. Good old body of Sir John that I feed to the full, on your way – and thank you.' But at the end of the finished score, when Verdi wrote his farewell at the bottom of the page, he changed the words a little. He knew that his own career in opera was over, and he wrote, 'Va, vecchio John' –

On your way, old John,
You rascal,
You old comic type,
You master of mirth,
Eternally true in all your many guises.
On your way, on your way,
And fare you well.

It was Verdi's affectionate goodbye to his last operatic character, a figure as old as comedy, and one in whose human frailty and indomitability he was grateful to see something of himself.

Something of himself. Young people hearing *Falstaff* are, one may hope, too happy to need the message *Falstaff* has for us who have lived many years. But even they will hear themselves in the opera – in the utterly charming but utterly tiny duets of the young lovers. Verdi sprinkled that happy love all over the opera. Boito said he sprinkled it 'the way you sprinkle sugar on a cake.' The music of the young lovers and the music of all the characters, as it ripples on like a swift-flowing stream, tells us much about life. And one can only marvel at the shimmer, the gossamer glint, the sparkle of it as, in fine frenzy rolling, it crests for brief shining moments into little arias – the kind of arias we remember from *Il Trovatore* and *La Traviata*, but arias called to a halt before they can get too serious. And in another moment they are swept onward in the stream.

That is the way life appeared to the master of Italian opera when, after years in the theatre, he could see it steadily and see it whole. Life was too serious not to be taken lightly. And it was moving on quickly. He was eager to pay tribute to it, while it lasted in him.

That, if we are wise, is also the way life appears to us who are swiftly approaching Verdi's late years. And that is why we love his *Falstaff.*

13

The Exasperated Eagle
and the Stoic Saint
Les Troyens

Hector Berlioz sometimes wished he could have lived at the same time as Virgil, and known him intimately. 'I seem to see him,' he said, 'dreaming in his Sicilian villa: he must have been gentle, gracious, hospitable.' Other authors, especially Shakespeare and Goethe, may have had as much influence as Virgil on Berlioz's creative life, but it was Virgil who came to him first and never left him.

The characters of the *Aeneid* haunted his boyhood imagination. 'My mind was possessed by the glory,' he says of first reading about Mezentius and Lausus, Pallas and Evander, Amata and Latinus. 'I was like a sleep-walker.' Once he fell into a boy's daydream at vespers in his provincial parish church and, as he later recalls, 'I was with my Virgilian heroes again; I heard the clash of their arms, I saw Camilla the Amazon in all her beauty and swiftness, I watched the maiden Lavinia flushed with tears, and the ill-fated Turnus, his father Daunus, his sister Juturna, and heard the great palaces of Laurentium ring with lamentation – and was overwhelmed by an immense sadness. I left the church sobbing uncontrollably, and cried for the rest of the day, powerless to contain my epic grief.'

Those who know the massive opera Berlioz later wrote out of the *Aeneid*, his *Les Troyens*, will remark with some astonishment that the subject of these childhood transports are eleven Virgilian characters who never made their way into the composer's great work. They are all characters from the *Aeneid*'s last six books. *Les Troyens* is concerned with the first four of Virgil's twelve – and at that touches only briefly on the third.

Clearly, those early books moved Berlioz most of all. Another childhood incident: young Hector's father, a prudent and sensitive man who took responsibility for most of the boy's schooling, pretended not to notice how his son's lips trembled and voice faltered as together they

construed in Latin the *Aeneid*'s fourth book – the love story of Dido
and Aeneas. But when the son, himself named for the noblest Trojan of
them all, shuddered and 'stopped dead' at Dido's death, the father had
to notice. He prudently closed the text and ended the lesson. Virgil had
spoken too eloquently of epic passion.

There may be something of self-glorification in Berlioz's recording of
these incidents (Saint Augustine had confessed to the same Virgilian
grief famously some fifteen centuries before), but there is no insincerity
in Berlioz's confessions, and perhaps no exaggeration. Similar Virgilian
experiences continue on into his young manhood. When he had finally
won the Prix de Rome, after previous humiliating failures, he found life
in the Eternal City often unbearable, and would escape to the mountains
near Tivoli, with a gun or a guitar in hand, to hear the bells of Saint
Peter's from a distance and to watch from a precipice the plunge of a
stream that Virgil loved. Then 'some passage from the *Aeneid*, dormant in
my memory since childhood, would come back to me ... I would work
myself up into an incredible state of excitement ... [which] always ended
in floods of tears ... I longed for those poetic days when the heroes, sons
of the gods, walked the earth in glittering armour ... I wept for my own
private disappointments, my uncertain future, my interrupted career.'

Berlioz's Virgilian vision was Romantic and rose-coloured, but not idle,
and certainly not unproductive. In that Byronesque landscape of wild
hills and ruined monasteries, Virgil stimulated Berlioz's creative gifts and
strengthened him: 'What madness, many will say. Yes, but what happiness. Sensible people have no idea what it is to have this intense consciousness simply of being alive. One's heart dilates, one's imagination
expands and soars, one exists with a kind of frenzy; under the influence
of extreme nervous stimulation, one's very body seems made of iron.'
There the nineteenth-century artist speaks. Wagner might have said the
same of himself and his Germanic heroes.

When Berlioz finally came, at age fifty-three, to compose *Les Troyens*, he
wrote that 'the musical rendering of the characters and the expression of
their feelings and passions ... [were] from the beginning the easist part. I
have passed my life with this race of demi-gods; I feel as though they must
have known me, so well do I know them.' When the work was finished he
dedicated it 'to the divine Virgil,' and said, 'My musical and Virgilian passion has been sated.' Indeed, he wrote only one major work – *Béatrice et
Bénédict* – thereafter. His Virgilian opera was the culmination of his life's
ambitions. So his humiliation and disappointment at being unable to get
the work in its entirety onto any stage all but broke him: his first Dido was

with him when he died, and on the last page of his *Memoirs* he wrote, about being born out of his time, 'I am reconciled to not having known Virgil, whom I should have loved.' He never quite found his way to that Sicilian villa. In the end he added, with a thought for Estelle, 'the girl from the little white house' who also lived in his Proustian memory, 'The truth is, I am not reconciled.'

I have spent my life teaching classics, and teaching Virgil perhaps more than any other classical author. Yet I am puzzled by *Les Troyens*, though I have heard it many times, and seen the famous productions in New York and London, as well as the première in Geneva (its first complete production in a French-speaking city, more than a hundred years after its composition). It isn't just that Berlioz often strikes me, as he still strikes many listeners, as quirky and eccentric – while unquestionably touched with genius. The eccentricities of Berlioz's style are wonderful in themselves, worth having for themselves and, as they manifest themselves in *Les Troyens*, not always un-Virgilian. No, it's rather that Berlioz's Virgil is not the Virgil known to me, or to most twentieth-century readers. Did Berlioz really see Virgil, in or out of an imaginary Sicilian villa? Would he really have loved Virgil had he known him? I wonder.

In one way the two men are comparable, even kindred, spirits. Each had a strangely tuned musical ear. Virgil's hexameters are famous, his wielding of 'the stateliest measure ever moulded by the lips of man' justly celebrated by Tennyson. In his hands the interplay of sounding words and metrical rhythms, developed earlier in prose by Cicero and in verse by Lucretius, achieved a new poetic expressiveness. Speech became music. 'What a grand composer was Virgil,' Berlioz wrote. 'What a master of melody and harmony!'

Berlioz might have said much the same of himself. His sensitivity to the suggestive powers of instruments is perhaps unequalled in the history of Western music, and his long-lined melodies remain, after a century, absolutely unique, deflected as they are into altogether unexpected directions. Both he and Virgil had their early critics, and the criticism of both tended to centre around the strangeness of their syntaxes. The Roman general Agrippa said of Virgil that Latin ought not to be written like that; the French academicians said of Berlioz that music ought not to be written like that. In both cases the language was thought a *nova cacozelia*, a newfangled and perverse affectation. But it was the unpredictability of both styles that gave the two artists their emotional force, and in time the strangeness proved itself right. Virgil's unusual Latin shaped the languages of Europe for centuries, and Berlioz's special sensitivity is something today's composers can still learn from. (There is still much to be got from a study of the scene with Hector's ghost.)

But there, with the strangeness of syntax, the similarities between poet and composer pretty well end. Virgil and Berlioz are in many ways mutually opposed figures. Consider their personalities. Berlioz dominated any room he entered. He was as witty and elegant in his person as in his art. His conversation sparkled – though his bursts of laughter could be followed by brooding silences. His conducting, even of works that required forces of a hundred or more, was always, like himself, admirably precise and refined. Virgil, by contrast, had all his days something of the rustic about him. We are told that he spoke haltingly and almost like an uneducated man. Only when he recited his own verses did his voice, naturally weak, expand like a true Roman's. And he seldom recited, even in private. He was a recluse, rarely leaving his rural retreats. When he came to Rome he was known to step off the street into doorways to avoid company and conversation.

Théophile Gautier records that Berlioz had 'a splendid head, like an exasperated eagle.' Ernest Legouvé, the author of *Adrienne Lecouvreur*, described the head's great shock of reddish-blond hair as 'an immense umbrella or movable canopy overhanging the beak of a bird of prey.' To the German Heinrich Heine it was rather 'a great primeval forest towering above a rocky precipice.' In any case, it, the white skin that went with it, and the middling frame it topped were as different from Virgil's close-cropped head, dark complexion, and imposing farmer's stature as were the spirits that moved within the two.

Different, too, were their private lives. Berlioz fell in and out of love several times and married a famous Irish actress who aged gracelessly, became possessive, and gave him an unlikely son who made a small career in the French merchant navy. Virgil was childless, known all his life as a celibate, a kind of Stoic saint – though variously there are reports of passions for boys, and the second half of the *Aeneid* is overcast with a kind of homoerotic haze.

Berlioz went his own way artistically and produced highly original works, paying the cruel price of seeing them go unappreciated and even unperformed. His letter appealing to Napoleon III for a hearing at the Opéra makes pathetic reading. He was even persuaded not to send it, so that the emperor ultimately rejected him in other ways. Virgil, conversely, was supported by his emperor, Caesar Augustus, and reached a wide public immediately. What difficulties Virgil had with his epic were almost the reverse of Berlioz's: the emperor and the world eagerly awaited the *Aeneid*, while Virgil himself asked, in his mortal illness, that it be burned.

No one less than Augustus would have dared execute that request, and Augustus was not about to; he knew that the *Aeneid* was splendid in its ambiguities. Like the *Eclogues* and the *Georgics* before it, the *Aeneid* was dense with meanings and said a good deal more than its surfaces implied. Virgil wanted it destroyed, not, I think, because it never received his finishing touches, but because he was profoundly unhappy with the philosophic conclusions it drew from him. He intended to spend three years revising it and then to devote the rest of his life to philosophy.

There, surely, is the great difference between the Romantic composer and the classic poet. Berlioz's *Troyens* is a thing of surfaces, contrasts, and diffusions. It is spacious, noble, and deeply felt, and it keeps the main outlines of Virgil's incidents, but without Virgil's compression and levels of meaning. Berlioz provides a series of *tableaux vivants*, very much in the tradition of French *tragédie lyrique*, and ends with an unambiguous apotheosis of Augustan Rome. This is not Virgil.

The poet of the *Aeneid* – to consider him, at last, in himself – began his career specializing in small and medium-range genre writing. He proved his skill at both the stylized and the realistic evocation of Italy's countryside (in the pastoral *Eclogues* and the descriptive and didactic *Georgics*). And so he attracted the attention of Augustus when that not-yet-emperor was locked in world conflict with Antony and Cleopatra. When Augustus defeated Antony at the naval battle of Actium, in 31 BC, he brought an end to a century of civil war and began the massive labour of converting Rome from a ruined republic to a forward-looking empire. He needed effective propaganda to further his work (the effects of which are still felt in Europe and Asia today), and he was astute enough to realize that the best propaganda – the kind that sums up the past, changes the present, and speaks to the future – is great art written by great artists. His cultural attaché, Maecenas, surrounded him with promising literary talents. There was Livy to rewrite the history and Horace to rewrite the lyric poetry of the past for the long Roman future. But above all Augustus wanted an epic, an *Iliad* if he could have it, about his victory at Actium. He wanted a poem to justify his past, of which he was not altogether proud, and to help him forge a future.

That was an epic no one wanted to write – Virgil least of all. But Augustus had ways of applying pressure. Other poets who crossed the great man suffered: Ovid was banished to the Black Sea and never recalled, and Gallus, Virgil's friend and, reportedly, his equal in poetic skill, was publicly disgraced and his works destroyed. Gallus took his own life.

So Virgil undertook to do what Augustus wanted. But he was not ready to devote a large part of his life to mere propaganda. Instead of a versified chronicle about Augustus's career, he reached back beyond history, back even further than Rome's legendary foundation, to Homer's Trojan War, to the mythic story that a cousin of Hector's, Aeneas, had escaped from the captured city, taken shelter in Carthage, come to Italy, fought to establish himself there, and fathered the Trojan-Italian race that would some day found Rome.

As Virgil wrote, with studied slowness, Augustus, busy subduing north-west Spain and then warring in the Near East, kept asking to hear 'something from the *Aeneid*.' He may, when he finally saw his epic, have been surprised, even dismayed, to discover that he had to read hundreds of lines before he came to even an indirect reference to Actium. But if he was a sensitive man (and I think he was), he sensed soon enough that the new epic *was* what he had asked for. Aeneas was an emblem of himself, leading his people from a fallen republic to a rising empire. Dido was, on one level, Cleopatra, and Turnus was Antony. The poem was a *symbolic* portrayal of his recent wars. And more than that, it spoke symbolically of *all* the cruel wars of Rome's past. For Dido was also defeated Carthage, and Turnus was the vanquished tribes of Italy. The whole poem was a massive metaphor. It said, between the lines, that there was goodness and guilt on both sides in the civil wars just ended and in all of Rome's wars before that. It said many things, too, about the nature of God, the exist-ence of evil, the tragic choices involved in doing one's duty. (Its thematic words are fate, fury, and piety.) It was, finally, concerned with absolving national and personal guilt (read today: Vietnam and the Gulf War) and with building a better world. And it was mostly pessimistic about the possibilities.

The nineteenth century did not see Virgil this way, and Berlioz ought not to be faulted if he did not try to make his Virgilian opera an ambiva-lent comment on the Revolution and the Napoleonic Wars that had rav-aged his France, killed off its best men, and changed its vision. We ought not to be critical if he thought the *Aeneid* a justification of empire rather than, as many see it now, a searching meditation on it. Berlioz responded to and conveyed the surface levels and the big passions in Virgil's brave and beautiful poem. For the rest, he was scornful of theology, indifferent to philosophy, and impatient with the very idea of expressing moral values in his work. He was not a Virgilian Virgil would have recognized. I do not think that the two of them, had they met, would have had much to say to one another.

What Berlioz was – and it is not by any means inconsiderable – was a contemporary and in many ways an equal to his fellow sometime-Parisians

Balzac, Delacroix, Hugo, Chopin, and Liszt. He shared with them a Romantic desire to create a language utterly unique, a language instantly identifiable as his and his alone. If he forged something of his musical language from literature, it was from literature too great to be contained in any forms – from Shakespeare's free-flowing torrent of words and images and from Goethe's many-metred, recklessly idiosyncratic drama. Though Berlioz could not or would not articulate what he was doing, he was in fact proclaiming that Romantic impulse variously known as élan or life force or even the daemonic, something that could not be contained within the conventional forms of the stage pieces crafted out of Shakespeare and Goethe by the Gounods and Thomases of his day. His was a musical language all its own, and it drove him to shape his own musical forms with their own often incomprehensible plots (the *Symphonie Fantastique* and *Lélio*), to splinter *Hamlet, Romeo and Juliet*, and *Faust* into fragments in which expressiveness, not plot or character, was the chief consideration, in which the contrasts became the structures. It was a wonderful new language, but its syntax proved too personal to be altogether intelligible to Berlioz's contemporaries. (Today, when fragmentation in art is no longer a fault, we think we can read the language rightly.)

The main difficulty with *Les Troyens*, in its day and now, is that it is not Berlioz enough. Not Romantic enough. Approaching Virgil later than his other favourite authors, and hoping with a classical subject to write at last a stageworthy if not entirely conventional piece, Berlioz combined his new and brilliant style with the traditions of the French classical theatre. The result is an odd mélange of the picturesque, the piquant (in the justly famous excerpts and in orchestral details throughout), and the coldly classic (in the chiselled passion of the declamatory passages). *Les Troyens* may be the greatest of all French operas, but it is, almost paradoxically, not the best Berlioz, nor, in its dated classicism, does it encompass much of Virgil's still-modern vision.

It is easier to be impressed and charmed by *Les Troyens* than to be convinced by it. I am invariably impressed and charmed. Choose your favourite instrument – clarinet or flute or trombone – and follow it through the score, and marvel at the expressiveness of which, in Berlioz's hands, it is capable. Choose your favourite combination of vocal colours, and Berlioz will provide it – in duet, quintet, septet, octet. Always there is something to cause wonder. For his tragic subject, Berlioz finds room for an extraordinary number of characteristically witty touches. I think the music that accompanies the procession of Dido's construction workers, sailors, and farmers the most deliciously inappropriate music Berlioz ever wrote. Inappropriate, that is, by any conventional standards. No sailors on land or sea are suggested by the music provided. But the music *is* appropriate to setting the unique mood Berlioz had in mind – the exotic, not quite harmlessly barbaric, slightly unreal, delicately foreboding mood of Dido's African realm. Berlioz would regard the music as altogether functional. (Meanwhile, any director who must move those sailors across the stage will be completely at sea.)

There are many things about *Les Troyens* that appeal to the classicist in me, and as I have not seen them mentioned elsewhere they may be worth detailing here. They are expectedly subtle. No one seems to have noticed that Berlioz, wanting to give us a compleat Virgil, lovingly introduces the flavour and something of the language of Virgil's early *Eclogues* and *Georgics* into the song Iopas sings at Dido's court. (In the *Aeneid* Iopas not only evokes the *Eclogues* and *Georgics* but sings, with a subtlety that many critics have missed, of the labouring sun and abandoned moon – figures prophetic of Aeneas forsaking Dido.) I don't know where Berlioz got his uninteresting onstage Narbal, but he has created an interesting offstage character in the young sailor Hylas – swaying in the masthead, singing his own cradle song, and dropping off to sleep. Hylas's song has its gentle ironies (the oxymoronic 'heureuse misère' for one), and there are passing touches (the between-verses dialogue of two sentinels and an ominous orchestral surge) to indicate that the maternal, rocking sea will be the tomb of this young sailor. (Virgilians know he will die: in the *Eclogues* and *Georgics*, Hylas is the name of a mythic drowned youth; in the *Aeneid* the corresponding figure, Palinurus, also falls asleep on shipboard – and drops to his death in the waves.)

The frequent use of accented 6/8 time in Berlioz has always suggested Virgil's dactylic rhythms to me, and nowhere more than in the woodwind figure that introduces Dido's 'Adieu, fière cité' and in the ecstatic love duet 'Nuit d'ivresse.' And while it is often noted that that moonlit seascape of a duet uses Shakespeare ('On such a night as this ...'), it might be noted (again, I think, for the first time) that the Shakespearean phrases are shaped into amoebean verse – that series of sexual challenges and responses familiar to readers of the love poems of Catullus, the odes of Horace, and Virgil's own eclogues. In amoebean verse the challenger sets the metre, the rhyme scheme, and the image pattern; the responder changes them subtly to indicate sexual resistance or surrender. So, as Berlioz's Dido and Aeneas trade mythological references in 'Nuit d'ivresse,' her challenges acknowledge his beauty, his stature as a demigod, and his reluctance to yield to her advances; his responses acknowledge her vow of chastity, the madness of his love, and the dangers attendant on their union. As is the rule in amoebean verse, the loser is in indirect ways the winner: Berlioz's Dido loses in the poetic exchanges, but wins her Aeneas when she allows him to pardon her. Very classic and very deft.

Another such amoebean exchange, less rapturous, takes place between the two Trojan sentinels who comment on Hylas's song. The first sentinel's challenge ('I can already talk Phoenician with my Carthaginian girl here') prompts the other's response ('My girl here understands Trojan, and there's no talking back'). This is very like the comic exchanges given shepherds in Virgil's amoebean eclogues, and Berlioz intends it that way. But he introduces this exchange into a context of poignancy and ominousness. I don't think Virgil could have introduced the comic and the commonplace this ironically into his epic without losing control. In any case, he never tried to do so. The scene is definitely one up for Berlioz.

Most remarkable of all, Berlioz introduces into his 'Royal Hunt and Storm' a tree struck by lightning and falling in flaming pieces. This figure is not in Virgil's hunt, but it is absolutely right. Berlioz surely means it to remind us of Virgil's succession of famous trees at pivotal points in the *Aeneid.* In Book II, Troy falling is compared to a massive rowan crashing and trailing havoc in its wake; in Book IV, Aeneas himself is likened to an oak writhen by alpine winds but firmly rooted below in the underworld; in Book VI, at the entrance to Aeneas's own underworld, his unconscious, there stands a vast elm sheltering dreams that clutch beneath its leaves. So any Virgilian listening to the 'Royal Hunt' in *Les Troyens* knows that it is Trojan Aeneas himself who is symbolically brought low when that tree falls in the midst of Berlioz's swirling orchestral storm.

Add to these ingenious additions a few slips – which, as it is Berlioz slipping, just may be deliberate. He brings Panthus from Troy to Carthage, though Virgil explicitly, and with considerable point, has Panthus killed at Troy, a victim of Aeneas's misguided fury there. Add, too, those curious dramatic lapses that have always bedevilled Berlioz's early scenes at Troy. He never saw his first two acts staged, but anyone who has will sense that too much action is described rather than shown. This is misapplied classicism. It borders on the eccentric to eliminate so much sure-fire material in the fall-of-Troy sequences and to spend time on a love duet for two characters given scarcely a half-dozen lines in the original. And Berlioz's Trojan women stabbing themselves or leaping to their deaths correspond to nothing in the letter or spirit of Virgil, who ends his fall of Troy with a far more memorable scene – Aeneas taking his aged father on his shoulders and his little son by the hand and leading them out of the flaming city. This is an emblem of *pietas* that has caught the human imagination for twenty centuries. Any Virgilian will wish that Berlioz had set that scene instead of the unconvincing Masada-climax he has given us.

But then, we who dare to suggest such improvements aren't capable of writing a 'Nuit d'ivresse.' Nor has anyone of us ever written an opera quite like *Les Troyens*. An Italian composer would have provided more opportunities for vocal display; a German more philosophical depth. Berlioz is French, and the emphasis is rather on mood and contrast, gesture and inflection and stylized feeling. And to say that is not enough, for what other Frenchman could have written *Les Troyens?* It is, to use a Latin phrase, *sui generis.*

Could Latin Virgil have lived to see it, I think he would, like the rest of us, have puzzled over it. But he would have recognized it, sooner than we have, as a work of genius. He was no stranger to genius.

14

The Sins of Wagner's Youth
Rienzi

Nicola Laurenti, aka Cola di Rienzo, whom the young Richard Wagner put on the stage as Rienzi, is a historical figure. You can read about him at the end of Edward Gibbon's *Decline and Fall of the Roman Empire*. The fourteenth-century patriot in Gibbon's pages differs from Wagner's hero in several important respects, but Gibbon enables us to see what there was about him that would fire the imagination of the twenty-five-year-old composer: Rienzi was a visionary, a patriot with a flair for self-promotion, superbly confident in the rightness of his cause, and out to change the world. 'Never perhaps,' wrote Gibbon, 'has the energy and effect of a single mind been more remarkably felt.'

That sentence could have been written, with equal validity, about Richard Wagner. For a century now his controversial work has affected not just music and theatre, but painting, poetry, and politics. It also anticipated some of the findings of Freud and Jung, the novelistic techniques of Proust, Joyce, and Thomas Mann, and the structural analysis of myth associated with Claude Lévi-Strauss. While it is still commonplace to associate Wagner with the worst horrors of the Second World War, the late L.J. Rather, a man of science known for his cancer researches, contended, in a book called *The Dream of Self-Destruction*, that Wagner's *Ring* contains what we must know for survival in the nuclear age – if only we read it right. Looking back on Wagner at this point of time, we can say that he has been more successful in achieving his aims than Rienzi ever was. But then Wagner had more genius than Rienzi, and more luck.

Rienzi was a low-born Roman obsessed, in the declining Middle Ages, with the glories of the past. He declaimed Cicero and Sallust from memory as he looked down over his city's crumbling ruins – sometimes alone with his thoughts, more often surrounded by the downtrodden hoping for a leader. Like many Romans before and after him, he had a religious streak in his nature, so strong as to have prompted mystical experiences. And he dreamed great dreams.

Rienzi's mercurial career has been described for us in what is perhaps the best-known chapter in Luigi Barzini's book *The Italians*: Rome in the fourteenth century was a miserable place, deserted by the pope, who had moved to Avignon, and by the Holy Roman Emperor, who chose to live north of the Alps. Rome's noble families – the Colonnas and Orsinis – walled themselves up in impregnable castles inside the city, kept private armies to protect them, and fought one another. The commoners, largely ungoverned, had to brave streets alive with thieves, rapists, and murderers. Every night took its hellish toll. Every morning there were new corpses floating in the Tiber.

Rienzi got his first important position in Rome through the efforts of the poet Petrarch. He was made an apostolic notary. But he preferred to style himself, in line with the Rome of more than fourteen centuries before, as a tribune of the people, as their protector against oppression. The nobles were not very impressed with his fine words, his increasingly finer clothes, the all-night vigils during which he knelt through twenty masses in succession. The Colonnas, for their amusement, invited him to a banquet. At the table he pointed to each in turn and told them their forthcoming fates: one would be put in chains, one tortured, one hanged, one beheaded, one drawn and quartered. They laughed, but he kept his word.

With a small army, he took the Capitoline hill. And the commoners of Rome rallied round him. He organized a people's militia and ceremoniously proclaimed the restoration of the *res publica Romana* and a reign of liberty and justice. The nobles capitulated.

Rienzi, haranguing the crowds from his balcony, soon dreamed of uniting all of Italy under his Rome – not through war, but through ceremony and diplomacy. As his classically worded edicts went out to feudal lords far and wide, his banners grew brighter, his titles more imposing. He rode the streets in papal colours, on a great white horse, preceded by soldiers blowing silver trumpets and carrying the emblems of a Rome that once really did rule an empire. The most famous of his processionals took him to the Lateran (the Vatican of that day), where he bathed in the porphyry sarcophagus wherein Constantine was once miraculously cured of his leprosy, and slept on a great bed of state near the high altar. In the morning he flashed his sword to the four winds and commanded the

pope and the two claimants to the throne of the empire to return to
Rome and relinquish their powers, so that the people could choose one
man to head their restored republic, which would thereafter save and
rule the whole world.

He was thirty-three, and he compared himself to Jesus.

His excesses eventually brought him down. The commoners began to
long for the simpler times when the streets were filled with criminals, not
processionals. The warring noble families united to drive him out of the
city. He fled across the Alps. There the emperor caught him and sent him
in chains to the pope in Avignon. He pleaded eloquently for his pardon,
and got it. Restored to Rome, he rose again to power, and made the same
mistakes as before, and worse ones. He turned greedy, cruel, and vindictive. The people who once loved him now called for his death.

The end was not heroic. He fled his flaming palace in disguise, but he
forgot to remove his rings. He was recognized, captured, and pierced
through with the blunt weapons of the very commoners whose cause he
had championed. His corpse was dragged along the Corso, then hung by
its feet for two days, stoned and spat upon.

Luigi Barzini compares this astonishing career with Mussolini's. There
are many points of comparison. Sometimes history does repeat itself.
Mussolini was once warned by a friend, 'You'll die like Rienzi.' Mussolini
only spread his hands and said, 'But you see, I wear no rings. It will not
happen to me.' Yet it did, to the extent of his fleeing in disguise (with no
rings, perhaps, but with all his money), and being detected, murdered,
and strung up by his feet and reviled by his own people. There are features in Rienzi's make-up that suggest Napoleon as well. In fact, Napoleon had a book about Rienzi in his carriage as he made his ignominious
retreat from Moscow.

But above all, Hitler comes to mind. How could he not? *Rienzi*, only
eleventh best of Wagner's operas by almost any standard (and closer to
twelfth place than to tenth), was Hitler's avowed favourite in the Wagnerian canon. When he first saw it, in Linz at the age of seventeen, he con-
ceived his initial sense of what he thought his mission – to unite a divided
Germany, restore it to greatness, and conquer the world. 'In that hour it
began,' he later recalled, overlooking the fact that Wagner's Rienzi is in
the end deserted by his own people and consumed in flames. Hitler's fascination with *Rienzi* was strangely prophetic. He proudly kept the original
full-length score in his own possession, and it seems to have perished with
him in his flaming bunker. (We now have no surviving source for some of

the opera's orchestration. The Dresden theatre copy was lost in the horrendous fire-storm that destroyed that beautiful city when Allied bombs fell on it on Ash Wednesday, 1945.)

Napoleon, Mussolini, and Hitler may have been Rienzi figures. But it is the young Wagner himself we see most in the Rienzi he put on the stage – a visionary on the heroic upward curve of his fortunes, rising nobly to meet his inevitable death. Wagner's *Rienzi* came out of a popular three-volume novel he first read in the environs of Dresden – *Rienzi, the Last of the Roman Tribunes*, by Edward Bulwer-Lytton. Lord Lytton may have fallen from favour today (poetasters still make merry over one of his opening lines, 'It was a dark and stormy night'), but in Wagner's day and for many years after, Lytton's fiction, dramas, and translations of the classics had wide appeal and no little influence. When the young Wagner was in London, he tried to look up Lytton in the House of Lords. From the visitors' gallery he watched parliament in session, but he never met Lytton, who happened then to be out of town. One can only wonder whether an hour spent with the successful litterateur might have dampened some of the fledgling composer's visionary ardour.

The five-hour opera Wagner eventually created out of Lytton, begun in Riga and completed in Paris, was a frank bid for popularity in the French grand-opera format of Spontini, Auber, Halévy, and Meyerbeer. Wagner made sure that his *Rienzi* would be so vast that no provincial opera house could afford to mount it. He had his youthful eye on that great Babylon of the opera world, the Paris Opéra, which staged extravagant five-act historical pageants as a matter of policy, with Meyerbeer as the reigning musical dramatist.

But if Wagner's *Rienzi* was made for the Opéra, with the obligatory ballets and battles, prayers and processionals duly in place, if it was calculated, that is not to say that it was insincere. Wagner really believed in his hero. The changes he made in Lytton and in history he made out of a conviction that history's heroes, to be truly heroic, had to be what Hegel was then calling the human instruments of a higher power, a *Weltgeist*. Today we would call such a hero archetypal – cut to a pattern that would strike resonances in the hearts and minds of men and lead them to the end destined for them by history. That was Lytton's Rienzi. The English lord was proud that his novel contributed to the spirit of Italy's *risorgimento*. Verdi once thought of setting it, though, plagued as Verdi always was by political censors, he eventually gave up the thought. (Lytton's book was actually banned in some parts of Italy.)

So it fell to Wagner to put Rienzi on the stage. Everything that Wagner was in his mid-twenties went passionately into the writing of his new opera. The conductor Heinrich Dorn tells of the early stages of *Rienzi*'s composition, on a borrowed piano with clanking strings, with Wagner's wife Minna mopping his brow as he feverishly accompanied friends who divided the parts among them. 'The clatter of the broken strings,' Dorn says, 'blended with the rousing sound of liberty.'

Liberty. In the Germany of his day, which was no place for the down-trodden, Wagner wanted to be a Rienzi. When the opera finally took the stage – not in Paris, for the Opéra wasn't interested, but back in Dresden – it was his first success, initially far more successful than either of the works that followed it, *The Flying Dutchman* and *Tannhäuser*. And in Dresden Wagner soon *became* a kind of Rienzi – obsessed with the ideals of antiquity, sympathizing with the have-nots of society, writing on revolutionary subjects, even delivering an incendiary speech on the subject of republic versus monarch to the left-wing *Vaterlandsverein*. Performances of *Rienzi* had to be halted after that. The Saxon court could now see the opera plainly as the revolutionary tract it partly was.

There are glimpses of Wagner's Roman tribune in each of his later heroes. Rienzi is a forerunner of the Flying Dutchman, solitary and misunderstood; of Tannhäuser, defying civil and papal authority; of Lohengrin, coming to the defence of those in need and ready to lead an army against invaders; of Siegmund, with no woman in his life but his sister; of Siegfried, betrayed, killed, and consumed in flames; of Tristan, willing his own death; of Hans Sachs, pleading the cause of national unity; of Parsifal, pure in the midst of corruption and restoring vitality to the symbols of the past.

For about a century now, we have written off *Rienzi*. It has seemed buried under the weight of the deliberately faint praise given it by Hans von Bülow, who had a malicious way with a *bon mot*. How better to put down Verdi than to say that the *Requiem* was his best opera? How better to demote Wagner from the German musical trinity by coining the catch-phrase, still with us, 'Bach, Beethoven, and Brahms'? Von Bülow had his reasons for not liking Wagner, who had repaid him for years of dedicated service by stealing his wife. He had his small but real revenge when he dubbed Wagner's *Rienzi* 'the best opera Meyerbeer ever wrote.'

He was wrong. *Rienzi* is Meyerbeerian only in its externals. Wagner *had* to write on Meyerbeer's scale to establish himself. But Meyerbeer had none of the mythic sense, the passion, the identification with his hero, that went into the making of *Rienzi*. Meyerbeer was, at the time, a better craftsman than Wagner, and perhaps a better melodist. But he was devoted to giving the bourgeoisie what they wanted. Wagner wanted to stir them to revolt.

And so it was that the composer of *Rienzi* participated in the Dresden uprising of 1849, helping to plan strategy, secretly purchasing rifles and possibly even hand grenades, dodging bullets as he kept watch beneath the alarm bell of the Kreuzkirche. It was his fond hope that rebellion would establish a new order in Germany and indeed in all of Europe. He was putting the finishing touches on his *Lohengrin*, with its pan-German martial assemblies, and considering, as possible subjects for a new opera on revolution, Barbarossa, Achilles, and even Jesus. (He finally chose Siegfried.)

The Dresden revolution ended when Saxony called in Prussian troops. More than two hundred people were killed. Wagner's chief associates, the anarchist Mikhail Bakunin and the conductor August Röckel, were arrested and sentenced to long years in prison – the original sentence for each had been death. Wagner escaped, like Rienzi the first time, to flee into exile, a price on his head. It took him six years to start composing again. It was ten years before he heard his *Lohengrin*. It was twelve years before he could return to Germany.

By that time, he had evolved a new concept of theatre and a new manner of musical speech, and no longer felt any affinity with *Rienzi*. He looked back on the work as 'one of the sins of my youth.' 'I do not like the monster,' he said. When he built his theatre in Bayreuth he banned *Rienzi* by a provision in his will from production there. As recently as 1957, critics and audiences at the Festspielhaus indicated, when polled, that the Bayreuth ban on *Rienzi* ought to be continued. At one point in his life Wagner thought it a special irony that *Rienzi*, written for Paris, had not been performed in Paris, for Paris was a place where they might have liked it. But when the Paris première finally took place, more than a quarter-century after the first in Dresden, the opera was not the success everyone expected.

There is no question that *Rienzi* has its share of *gaucheries*, *bêtises*, and, especially, *longueurs*. The young Wagner tried dividing it, like Berlioz later with his *Troyens*, into two evenings, and found that the public wouldn't pay twice for one opera. Most performances were drastically cut. *Rienzi* readily yielded – and still, on the rare occasions when it is performed, yields – to cutting. It has been described as 'factitious, not organic,' as fashioned entirely of situations contrived to elicit emotional responses in music. That is one of the worst charges that can be levelled against an opera. It is true of much of Meyerbeer. And it is partly true of *Rienzi*.

What saves Wagner's massive French grand opera in German about a fourteenth-century Italian patriot, and what may keep it, at least intermittently, on the stages of the world in the coming century, is that in Cola di Rienzo the young Wagner found for the first time a figure he could believe in and identify with. It was out of the passionately committed, single-minded patriot Cola di Rienzo that the greater heroes of Wagner's subsequent operas inexorably came. And for that we are in *Rienzi*'s debt.

15

Long Day's Journey into Night
Tristan und Isolde

Some years ago a friend of mine went to see a performance of *Tristan und Isolde* at the old Metropolitan Opera House in New York, on 39th Street and Broadway. He sat alone in a box at what was by all reports a superlative performance and, as he put it himself, he suffered the torments of the damned. He thought Act I ear-splitting and intolerably long. Act II was occasionally quieter, but seemed even longer. And through both acts, he felt like that martyr in a medieval painting often mentioned in connection with *Tristan* – the unfortunate whose innards are slowly and painfully being extracted on a wheel. When the curtain rose on Act III, and my friend saw the tenor, who had already agonized through most of a long evening, sprawled on the stage delirious, while some melancholy pipe wailed interminably in the orchestra, he knew that he was in for at least another hour of the same tortures, and he fled the theatre.

Not without some feelings of guilt, mind you. He was a professor of French literature, and he knew all too well that *Tristan* is one of the most influential works of art of the past century. That's why I remarked, on his return from New York, that a new book had just come off the university presses, tracing some of the vast and continuing influence *Tristan* has had on art and thought through the century. The book was called *The First Hundred Years of Wagner's Tristan.*

'I knew it was long,' he said. 'But I didn't know it was *that* long!'

My friend's reaction was far from unique. Wagner himself despaired of the vastness of *Tristan*, even when he was composing it. Even before he experienced the immense practical difficulties of getting singers to sing it, he wrote in anguish to Mathilde Wesendonck, who, as her husband eventually discovered, had inspired much of the opera's love music: 'Child, this *Tristan* is turning into something terrifying. That last act! I'm afraid the opera will be forbidden, unless the whole thing is turned to parody by bad production. Only mediocre performances can save me. Good ones are bound to drive people mad.'

And when he had completed the work, Wagner wrote, 'Reading it through, I couldn't believe my eyes or ears. How terribly I shall have to pay for this work some day, *if* I ever succeed in getting it performed. I clearly foresee the most indescribable sufferings in store.'

However overstated all that seems, Wagner was, as usual, right in his forecasts. It wasn't just that his wife Minna discovered and denounced the affair with Frau Wesendonck, and that Wagner, already exiled from Germany for his participation in the Dresden uprising of 1849, now for private reasons had to leave Switzerland as well. It was that *Tristan und Isolde*, when at last it was completed, was accepted and then rejected by opera houses in a half-dozen countries across Europe. It was found unplayable and unsingable. Everywhere it languished unperformed. Several 'un-premières' came and went. In Vienna its scheduled première was finally cancelled after seventy-seven rehearsals. The Tristan of those rehearsals went mad.

It was a full six years before the opera finally reached the stage. That was in Munich, in 1865, after Wagner was permitted to live in Germany again. The strain of that production was again too much for the Tristan, who *died* of his exertions. He was Ludwig Schnorr von Carolsfeld, a giant of a man, still in his twenties, much admired both for his singing and his acting. But after the fourth and final performance of *Tristan*, he began to tear his hair and roar like a lion. It took three men to hold him down. 'I drove him to the abyss,' Wagner repented, while von Carolsfeld said from his deathbed, like a true Wagnerian, 'My Richard loved me. I die happy.' Nine years went by before *Tristan* got another production.

The opera has been particularly cruel to its Tristans. Wagnerites still talk about the Met performance in which the great Birgit Nilsson sang Isolde to three different Tristans, one in each act. But Isoldes too have suffered. The first, von Carolsfeld's wife, ruined her voice singing the role, retreated to spiritualism, and ended up quite mad. And then there was the first conductor, Hans von Bülow, who wrote: 'My intensive work on *Tristan*, that gigantic and devastating score, has literally finished me.' He records that his répétiteur was driven mad during rehearsals. He himself lost both his self-esteem and his wife: she left him for Richard Wagner. Then, almost to parallel the previous situation in Switzerland, all three of them – the composer, the husband, and the wife – were asked to leave Munich in the wake of the scandal.

One could say that these people were artists, and hypersensitive by nature. But the list of personal disasters that followed upon exposure to

Tristan is easily extended. Friedrich Nietzsche is only the most famous example. 'How is it possible,' he wrote, 'for a man who has listened to the very heartbeat of the world, and felt the unruly lust for life rush into the veins of the world – how is it possible for him to remain unshattered?'

Some will say that *Tristan*'s influence on great works of art has been equally pernicious. They are the people who don't like Richard Strauss and Arnold Schönberg, James Joyce and Marcel Proust and Thomas Mann, T.S. Eliot and Stéphane Mallarmé, Gabriele d'Annunzio and D.H. Lawrence – in short, the significant artists of the past hundred years.

Wagner interrupted his twenty-five-year efforts on the massive *Ring* cycle to write *Tristan*. He wanted *Tristan* to be something easy, something popular that he could get onto the stage right away, and so pay his debts and silence his critics. Meanwhile, the Emperor of Brazil asked for an opera for Rio de Janeiro. As operas there were done in Italian, Wagner began to think of the *Tristan* that was taking shape in his mind as a *Tristano ed Isotta*, a short, practical, easily staged work that would really sing, in the Italian style. But while Verdi, a decade later, was to succeed in accomplishing this sort of international success, writing *Aida* for the Khedive of Egypt, Wagner's correspondence with the Emperor of Brazil came to nothing. Only much later, when Wagner's festival at Bayreuth opened, did a rather sad traveller sign in at a local hotel simply as (name) Pedro (occupation) Emperor. By that time Wagner's projected Italian opera had become a German music drama of great length and complexity. And it is time, now, that we turn to it.

It begins with a famous orchestral prelude. The cellos, straining in their upper register, sing a four-note theme – a rising and then a dying fall. The last note of this theme overlaps with another four-note theme, sounded by the woodwinds, which pushes upwards by semitones, and will recur hundreds of times in the opera. Commentators have called this second theme 'yearning.'

When the two themes meet, they form a chord, the so-called *Tristan* chord, perhaps the most famous chord in the whole history of music:

There is no key signature at the start of this prelude. It may appear to be in the key of C, or perhaps A-minor. But the two amorphous themes give no hint of being in *any* key. A listener, then, would have to get his bearings from the underlying chords. But the first chord we hear, the *Tristan* chord formed when the two themes overlap, establishes no key relationships. A perfect fourth, the traditional basis of Western tonality, is combined with an augmented fourth (the 'diabolus in musica' regarded in the Middle Ages as an aberration). The resulting chord is, in technical language, unresolved. And the 'yearning theme' leads from it to a second chord which is also musically unfulfilled. We wait for a resolution. And all we get is a long moment of silence.

Then, reaching higher, the same music is repeated, and once more the two overlapping themes are prevented from finding any fulfilment. Reaching higher still, and expanding somewhat, the two themes fail again to reach the normal goal set for all Western music since the Middle Ages.

Finally, the second, yearning theme *seems* to strain upwards to a resolution: we hear the sweeping wave of an F-major chord – a moment of quite wonderful fulfilment. But musically this is not a resolution at all, for we have pushed through to a new tonality without ever settling ourselves in the one whence we came.

What *Tristan und Isolde* is really about (I'll anticipate my final remarks here) is 'a yearning for the infinite.' This young knight and his Irish princess must die, for nothing in life can fill the endless yearning that their love has brought them. And how does a composer express 'yearning for the infinite' in music? Wagner uses two themes that can find no resolution and a chord that strains at the very structure of music.

It has been said that the whole twelve-tone system in twentieth-century music has been derived from the *Tristan* chord – and for some people that means that *Tristan* is responsible for the disintegration of our traditional classical musical structures and for the dissonance of twentieth-century music. But in itself the chord is not new. It's in Liszt's song 'Ich möchte hin gehen.' It's in Mozart's E-minor string quartet. I'm told one can even find it *denied resolution* in such pre-Wagner composers as Chopin, Beethoven, and Pergolesi. I'm told that one can work his way through the encyclopaedic keyboard works of Bach and find whole structures that anticipate the chord relationships Wagner used in *Tristan*. The important difference is that none of those predecessors exploited the potential of the chord as relentlessly as Wagner does, or with the vast orchestral and vocal resources he marshals for their expression. We all feel, in the presence of the *Tristan* prelude, that we are in the presence of something new. And we are. A chord which we have been conditioned by other music to hear as transitional, to feel as tensed for the attainment of a goal, is over and over denied fulfilment. Tension, striving, yearning – these are built into the very structure of the music.

Wagner, explaining the *Tristan* prelude to Mathilde Wesendonck, compared the progression of the two themes to cloud formations, to 'the ebb and flow of the world's breath.' (He was reading Buddhist theories of the origin of the world at the time.) But what most of us hear, and sense, and all but see in the prelude as it moves onward wave on wave is that great *Tristan* image – the sea, viewed from the midst of its expanse, vast, fearful, inexorable, and beautiful.

When the curtain rises on Act I, we *are* at sea, on Tristan's ship, sailing from Ireland to Cornwall. Most of our view of the stern is obscured by sails. There is a kind of pavilion hung on shipboard to shelter Isolde and her servant girl Brangäne during the voyage. Over the side the sea is calm, and from the masthead there floats down the voice of a young English sailor, singing to the Irish girl he left on shore behind him:

Westward stray my eyes, eastward flies the ship.
Fresh blows the wind towards home.
My Irish child, where are you now?

Frisch weht der Wind der Heimat zu,
Mein Irisch Kind, wo weilest du?

Famous words, ruefully used by T.S. Eliot near the beginning of *The Waste Land*. Here, at the beginning of Act I, the words of the unseen sailor at the masthead are taken by Isolde on the deck as a personal insult. For *she* is an Irish girl abandoned by her lover. She starts up from the couch where she has been unable to sleep and breaks a silence of several days. 'Who dares to mock me? You, Brangäne, speak. Where are we?'

Her attendant Brangäne looks westward while the ship flies East and says, 'Blue streaks are rising in the West. Before evening we shall reach land.'

'Never,' cries Isolde, 'not today, not tomorrow.' And in a burst of frenzied song she rises to call on the winds to smash the ship and sink it in the waves. But the winds do not answer. Isolde cries out for air, and Brangäne lifts the curtain of the pavilion. The length of the ship can now be seen as far as the helm. And there, surrounded by his knights, with his faithful henchman Kurvenal, stands Tristan, arms folded, silently gazing on the sea. The sailor's voice floats down again from the mast, and the two unful-filled themes of the prelude recur. Isolde fixes her eyes coldly on Tristan as he stands outlined against the sky. 'His head,' she says, 'is destined for death. His heart is destined for death.'

No teller of this tale before Wagner ever suggested that Isolde intended to *kill* Tristan on the sea voyage from her Ireland to his England. Yet that is the implication here, and events soon bear it out: Isolde wants to destroy Tristan – perhaps even behead him – because they once fell in love over a glance, and now he is carrying her across the sea to marry her off to someone else – his uncle, Marke, the king of Cornwall.

'What do you think of that menial there?' Isolde asks her servant. 'The one who will not look at me. Go and command him to come to me at once.'

Brangäne makes her way along the deck, past the men busy at their work. Tristan is courteous but firm: they will reach land before the sun sets; till then, he cannot leave the helm. His servant Kurvenal is not so gentle: 'The head of your Irish hero Morold is hanging back in Ireland,' he sings. 'That is the way our English hero, Tristan, exacts tribute.' Soon the whole crew is hurling this insulting song at Brangäne, loud enough for Isolde to hear it.

Brangäne flees back in tears to Isolde, and the curtains and sails once again obscure the rest of the ship. Isolde *has* heard every insulting word, and, in a famous narrative, the whole bloody, vengeful tale of Tristan, Isolde, Morold, and King Marke comes spilling out. I'm going to tell it now, not in emotional outbursts, as Isolde does to her servant Brangäne and, later, to Tristan himself, but in an order reconstructed from Wag-ner's text and from the prose sketch he drafted from the old sagas. It's a complicated tale.

Long before Isolde boarded Tristan's ship, Ireland and England (more precisely, Ireland and Cornwall) were at war. Ireland claimed a tribute from England. When England wouldn't pay up, an Irish hero of splendid proportions, Morold, challenged the English to single combat on a soli-tary island. This Irish Morold was thought invincible in combat – his armour had been blessed by Isolde, to whom he was betrothed, and she was said to have magic powers. Of all the English knights, only Tristan, the young nephew of King Marke, dared accept Morold's challenge.

So Morold and Tristan – their visors closed – met in combat. Tristan was wounded, but he slew the dreaded Morold, hacking off his head. He buried the body on the island, but sent the head back to Ireland in place of the tribute demanded.

The distraught Isolde found in the head a splinter of the sword that had severed it, and she kept that splinter hidden, swearing vengeance on the hated Tristan, who had so brutally treated her betrothed.

Ireland and England then made a truce. But while all the others swore, Isolde kept silent. Her days thereafter were spent in utter silence.

Meanwhile, Tristan's wound would not heal. The English, thinking he would soon die, sorrowfully set him adrift in a little boat, without oars or sail. Fatefully the boat drifted to Ireland, and the dying man was carried, unrecognized, to the Irish court. So it was that Isolde, with her magical healing arts, cared for Tristan, bleeding his wound, not knowing who he was. She only learned the truth when she saw a notch in his sword – a notch into which the splinter left in Morold's head fit exactly: so the man she was tending was the very man she had vowed to kill! She took Tristan's gleaming sword and raised it over his head as he lay helpless before her. And then, to use her words,

> From his sickbed, he looked up –
> Not at the sword, not at my hand.
> He looked into my eyes.
> His suffering touched me.
> I let the sword fall.
> I healed the wound that Morold struck,
> And sent him home so that he would torment me no more with his eyes.

It is clear from Isolde's narration of these events, and even more from the music, reprising the two yearning themes of the prelude, that it was at this moment in the past, when Tristan's pleading eyes caught Isolde's and stayed her hand, that they fell in love.

She revealed his identity to no one. He pledged his love with 'a thousand oaths' and went back, healed, to England.

And there – returned, as it were, from the dead – he soon found himself feared, envied, and mistrusted. Some of the courtiers, especially a certain Melot, were not happy to see him returned. Tristan was next in line to the throne, for his uncle, King Marke, was childless and a widower. Tristan naturally explained to the court how he had survived: the beautiful Isolde had healed him in Ireland. The jealous courtiers suggested that this very Isolde might be a desirable match for the king: a wedding would end the blood feud between the two countries, and perhaps give Marke a true heir. King Marke agreed to this.

Tristan was caught between his promise to Isolde and his sworn loyalty to his king, and (though he bitterly repents of it later) he chose to serve his king and to preserve his honour. Despite his true feelings, Tristan supported the popular clamour that the old king marry Isolde and produce an heir. He even volunteered to go back to Ireland and claim Isolde for England's king.

So that is how the situation in Act I developed. Small wonder, then, that Tristan kept his eyes cast down on the return voyage. Small wonder that Isolde was confused, angry, and vindictive, and never spoke to anyone until that moment when, on Tristan's ship, the sailor's song from the mast drove her to speak, or rather sing, her fury – in piercing high B-flats and B-naturals.

That, in outline, is the substance of Isolde's narrative. Brangäne naively suggests that they make the best of the situation when they reach land and give the old king a love potion. Isolde sends for her magic drafts and reaches instead for the death potion – not for the king, but for Tristan and herself. At this pivotal moment, the crew sights land. The women are told to prepare for arrival. But Isolde says she must see Tristan first. There is a wrong that has to be righted. Then she tells the terrified Brangäne to prepare the death potion.

Tristan approaches, and the orchestra is heavy with foreboding: he *knows* why she is summoning him, and he is prepared to die. She spared him on his sickbed, but she will surely kill him now. They are alone together in the pavilion. Their exchange of words is terribly bitter – she all recrimination and half-suppressed fury, he quiet resignation, offering his sword again, urging her to strike this time.

'Put up your sword,' she says. 'Let us drink reconciliation.' The shouts of the crew taking in the sail break in on them, and Tristan starts up: 'Wo sind wir?' he asks. 'Where are we?'

'Hart am Ziel,' she answers. 'Close to the goal.' (The orchestra plays the motif that had accompanied her words, 'His head is destined for death,' and we know what goal she means.)

Tristan, thinking he is drinking poison, lifts the cup to his lips and drinks. She seizes the cup and drinks too, declaring, 'Traitor, I drink to you.'

The cup falls. There is a long silence. The orchestra reprises the prelude, as if the opera were only now beginning. In a sense it is. Tristan and Isolde have concealed and smothered their passion for one another for this hour that has passed on the stage. Now, on the brink of what they expect is death, there is no longer any need to conceal their passion. They stand transfixed, his pleading eyes looking into hers as they did once before when she came to kill him. They think they are dying but, strangely, they do not die. For Brangäne, or some power greater than Brangäne, has poured, not the death potion, but the love potion, into the cup. Now faithful Brangäne comes to tear Isolde from Tristan's arms, and faithful Kurvenal comes to separate Tristan from Isolde. Marke is approaching to the sound of trumpets ... Act I ends.

In Act II, we are in England, in the garden of King Marke's palace in Cornwall, as evening comes on. The king has gone hunting, and the sounds of the horns are still audible – though Isolde insists to Brangäne that the sounds are only the swaying of the leaves and the splashing of the fountains. It's a magical passage in the music. Isolde longs to extinguish the torch that blazes on the battlements. That will be a signal to Tristan to come to her, under night's cover. She dismisses Brangäne's fears about the courtier Melot. Is he not Tristan's closest friend? Why, it was Melot who planned this evening's tryst for them. Isolde seizes the torch and hurls it to the ground. The light goes out. Brangäne mounts a tower to keep watch. And in the darkness, Tristan appears, almost wild with passion.

Their forty-minute duet, often cut in performance to its melodic sections, now begins. It passes through a succession of phases. At the start, the lovers are breathless and almost inarticulate, and the orchestra swirls around them speaking the passion they cannot put in words. Then, in exchanges that begin to fall into intelligible sentences, they recall how they had been blinded up to now – he by his knight's code of honour that led him to break his promise to her, she by her desire to wreak vengeance on him. All of this they associate with the hated light of *day*. Then follows the quiet, familiar, and very beautiful hymn to *night*: 'O sink' hernieder, Nacht der Liebe' ('O night of love descend upon us'), the melody of which is derived from the famous *Tristan* chord. This is interrupted, in what many regard as the most enchanted moment in the opera, by the voice of Brangäne floating down from the tower and weaving its way through a luxuriant orchestral web:

I watch alone here through the night.
You, on whom love's dream smiles, hear my voice.
I foresee evil for the slumberers.
Take care, take care, the night will soon pass away.

Then, in a new phase of the duet, the lovers who almost drank death in Act I begin to think in a new way about dying. What if they were to die now, not hating, but loving each other? Would their love die with them? It could not if they were to become each the other, if they were to merge their identities. All death could do then would be to dissolve the physical limitations that enflesh them in separate identities. Death would come as a blessed power, to unite them. And, as Brangäne sends a second beautiful warning down from the tower, the lovers decide to die – Tristan singing now that he is Isolde, Isolde that she is Tristan. It's a Romantic idea, familiar from the strangely merged identities of Cathy and Heathcliff in *Wuthering Heights*. But as we shall see, it comes to mean something more than Romantic here. Tristan sings, to the most familiar melody in the opera:

> Then let us die so that, together, ever and always one,
> Without end, never waking, we may be united in love alone.

But before he can draw his sword again to slay – and so unite – them both, Brangäne shrieks from the tower, and Kurvenal rushes in to protect them. They have been discovered. King Marke, Melot, and the courtiers appear, and the day begins to dawn. 'Daylight,' says Tristan, and he adds significantly, 'for the last time.'

Melot, who set the trap, noisily claims that he has saved the king's honour. The king says, 'Have you really? Is that what you think?' At last we hear King Marke's side of the story: he has loved Tristan like a son, and chosen him for his heir. Now that Tristan has proved false, he doesn't know any more what honour is. We hear, too, that he has never touched Isolde, though she delighted his heart. And these two young people, whom he has loved so much, have paid him in pain. Who can tell why this was? It is a mournful Arthurian song, almost as if (with King Marke, Tristan, Isolde, and Melot) King Arthur, Lancelot, Guinevere, and Mordred were on stage. And, of course, the two medieval legends long ago blended here.

Tristan has no answer to the king's questions. The king is speaking of honour, oaths, and allegiances; he and Isolde are feeling their way through to an insight into the nature of love and death that reaches beyond kingship and allegiances. The orchestra reprises the prelude, as if the opera were only now beginning. In a sense, it is. Tristan turns to Isolde and asks, 'Will you follow Tristan to where he goes now? To that land he spoke of, where the sun does not shine?' It is an invitation for her to die with him, for the land is surely death.

Isolde answers, 'I followed Tristan once before, to a foreign land. Now he will journey into his heritage. How can I not follow him to that land that spans the whole world?'

He kisses her on the forehead, which is too much for Melot, who draws his sword. Tristan flings a challenge at his former friend and draws too. Often the audience doesn't understand what happens here, so quickly does it happen. Melot slashes Tristan with a single thrust – but then Tristan has never even raised his guard, for his intention is to *die* on Melot's sword, and then let Melot slay Isolde too. The drama might have ended there, with the lovers united in death. But King Marke intervenes to hold Melot back, and take Isolde away, and leave Tristan lying wounded. The opera cannot end there because, though Tristan and Isolde have reached an awareness of the mysterious connection between love and death, they (and we) haven't got to the heart of the matter yet. We have the third and greatest act still to experience.

Wagner composed the end of Act II and all of Act III, not in Zurich, which he had had to leave when his affair with Mathilde Wesendonck was discovered, but in a city he chose because it matched the mood of what he had still to write. He travelled south to Venice, where he rented rooms in a Gothic palazzo on the Grand Canal. The apartment was shabby but still proud, and from his balcony he could look out on la Serenissima, that most fascinating of cities, one which has always had a special, even fatal, appeal for Germans. Everything in Venice was a little unreal, and Wagner wanted to capture that. He wrote to Mathilde, 'Nothing here makes the immediate impact of real life, yet everything makes an effect, as in a work of art. I will stay here.'

There is something of death about Venice, as Thomas Mann told us in a famous short story. That deathly Venetian atmosphere went into the music of *Tristan*'s last act as surely as the passion of the Zurich love affair filled the first two acts.

In Venice Wagner would write *Tristan* music till mid-afternoon. Then he would fare by gondola to the square of San Marco for supper, and stroll the city or take a boat to the Lido to watch the sun sink into the sea, and return after dark to read alone in the stillness – mostly Schopen-hauer and a history of Buddhism. In the silences, ideas for *Parsifal*, still two decades and four mighty operas in the future, started crowding in on him. And he would often wake in the middle of the night and hear the silence broken by the distant cries of gondolieri calling to one another. They sounded indescribably mournful, like invitations to die.

Never before had he had conditions like this to work under. It was mag-ical. Wagner wrote to Mathilde how one night, returning home late along the darkened canals, his gondoliere, standing above him in the stern, broke out in a cry like the howl of an animal, swelling upwards and float-ing across the water to a dying fall. The cry haunted him, and very likely it gave him the inspiration for the 'alte Weise,' the 'ancient melody' that runs through Tristan's delirium in Act III.

Many Wagner-lovers regard Act III of *Tristan*, steeped as it is in fatal Venetian atmosphere but moving in massive waves of music towards ulti-mate transcendence, as the greatest act in any opera. It begins with a pre-lude that is both seascape and inscape: ascending thirds in the violins lead the eye across the sea to the horizon, all of it bleak and waste and empty. The curtain rises and we see what we have heard – an expanse of sea, calm and steaming in the sun, and, beneath the battlements of his castle in Brittany, Tristan lying motionless, dying of his wound, attended by his faithful Kurvenal. Then we hear one of the shepherds on Tristan's lands piping the 'alte Weise' Wagner seems to have derived from the gon-doliere's cry, full of longing and pain.

Eventually the shepherd appears, and asks Kurvenal if Tristan is still unconscious. Kurvenal says he fears his master will never regain con-sciousness unless Isolde comes by ship with healing arts to bleed him and tend his wound. If that happens, the shepherd is to signal Isolde's arrival by changing his mournful tune to a joyous one. But now, with no ship on the horizon, the shepherd can only speak another line T.S. Eliot remem-bered in *The Waste Land*: 'Öd und leer das Meer' – 'The sea is waste and desolate.' He puts his pipe to his lips and departs.

As the sailor's song in Act I awakened Isolde from her silence, the shep-herd's 'alte Weise' here awakens Tristan, gradually, from his coma. Kur-venal tells him how, after the duel with Melot, he brought him by ship here to his ancestral estates in Brittany, and has secretly sent for Isolde to come across the sea and heal him. But Tristan seems not to understand; he lies musing on the strange world he has seen in his unconsciousness. 'There was no sea,' he says, 'no land. Only a vast night. Only forgetful-ness.' It was a dark land of wonder – but Isolde was not there with him in the darkness, and his yearning for her has, he says, driven him upwards through his unconscious to the conscious land of light, to find her and bring her back with him. As his consciousness returns, Tristan works him-self up into a frenzy, and actually curses the sunlight and the conscious world. Then he sinks back delirious, the past and present blurring in his mind. 'The torch,' he sings, 'is still burning. Isolde is calling me to come out of the dark.' When Kurvenal assures him that Isolde has been sent for, Tristan imagines he sees her ship on the sea – only to hear the shep-herd's mournful tune insist that the sea is still 'waste and desolate.'

Joseph Kerman, in a penetrating analysis of this act in *Opera as Drama*, suggests that Tristan progresses spiritually through Act III along two large symmetrical cycles, each introduced by that 'alte Weise' piped by his shepherd. In the first cycle, just completed, Tristan affirms, some time before Freud and Jung, the reality of the human sub- (or un-) conscious. In fact, he affirms its reality *over* that of the conscious world. In the second cycle, which now begins, Tristan goes deeper. As from the sea wall the shepherd's 'alte Weise' comes sadly floating once again, Tristan *explores* his unconscious. He calls up his past, back to the day of his birth. Here is where, we now think, Proust got the idea for that vastest of twentieth-century novels, *À la recherche du temps perdu*, with memory on memory triggered by a sensory impression. And here is where, Sir Colin Davis once said, lowering his voice to a whisper, 'When you're conducting it, it's touch and go. You're just holding on. It's so overwhelming.'

Tristan remembers how the same shepherd's tune hung on the evening air when, as a boy, he first heard how his father died, and how it sounded again, in the early morning, when they told him that his mother had died giving him birth. The tune, he says, answers the question 'Why was I born?' with the response 'To yearn and then to die.' (Small wonder they named him Tristan – sadness.)

As the tune echoes through his memory, Tristan comes to see that his whole life has been nothing but unsatisfied yearning. That is the human condition, inherited from father and mother, nurtured by ambition, intensified by sexual passion, never fulfilled, driving him ever onward. Once again, he works himself up into a frenzy, and this time he curses – and this comes as a surprise to those who think this is a love story – he curses the love potion that he drank with Isolde. He had thought, when he drank, that he would die, and that that would end his yearning. Instead he drank an intensification of his yearning. He resolves now to renounce all desire, even his passion for Isolde.

The effect of this drains him of all his strength. Kurvenal thinks for a moment that Tristan has *died*. But no, the heart is still beating. And Tristan wakes to a sort of beatific vision: Isolde coming across the sea, walking on waves of flowers, smiling and bringing peace. He has suffered through to what Wagner thought, at least at that time of his life, was the ultimate human truth, buried deep in the unconscious – that only when a man renounces his insatiable desires can he come to the peace which is his true fulfilment.

The second cycle is complete: suddenly the shepherd is heard piping a joyous tune. Kurvenal sights Isolde's ship steering safely through the reefs, its flag flying. He hurries off to welcome it.

Tristan, left alone, tears off his bandages and lets the blood stream from his wound, for Isolde has come to heal him (he means, of course, to die with him). The massive symmetry of the whole drama now becomes increasingly clear. Isolde passed through two cycles in Act I, punctuated by the offstage sailor's song: in the first cycle she gave way to passion; in the second she resolved on death for Tristan and herself as the only way to end her passion. The two lovers together passed through two cycles in Act II, in the love duet punctuated by the offstage warning of Brangäne: in the first cycle they surrendered to their passion; in the second, they resolved to die together as the only true way to fulfil their love. Now, in the ongoing spiral that is *Tristan und Isolde*, Tristan has travelled along two massive cycles, punctuated by the offstage piping of the shepherd: in the first cycle he affirms the reality of a world beneath consciousness; in the second, he discovers that he can only find peace, and the meaning of life, when he has passed forever to that world, in death. He breathes his last word – Isolde – and dies just as she arrives to take him in her arms.

She doesn't understand at first. But then, as if from his dead lips, she hears a wisp of the familiar melody he sang to her in Act II: 'Let us die together.' She follows him, fainting, into unconsciousness. She doesn't react when the shepherd rushes in with the frantic news that a second ship, King Marke's, has come, and when Kurvenal rallies his little forces and slays the invading Melot, and is slain himself. She doesn't hear Brangäne calling to her, or King Marke, who has heard now about the love potion and is ready to forgive and unite the lovers. Why should Isolde hear any of this? Her dead Tristan is speaking to her of a wholly different reality. His eyes, she sings, are gazing upon her, his lips are smiling, his body is steeped in starlight. (She is now granted the beatific vision of him that he had of her.) The wisp of melody returns and expands. It is what Wagner called the 'Verklärung' (transfiguration); it will lead to the final transformation of the *Tristan* chord. But we have always called the melody, since Liszt first named it, the 'Liebestod' (the love death). 'Can't you hear,' Isolde asks of the others standing around her dead Tristan, 'can't you hear the music that he speaks?' Often in Wagner the orchestra says, with a musical motif, what the characters on stage cannot say. Here we have, I think, the greatest instance of this. Singing for the dead Tristan, the orchestra sounds and resounds the melody from in Act II, where he sang:

Let us die so that, together, ever and always one,
Without end, never waking, we may be united in love alone.

Those are the words Isolde hears in the Liebestod melody that surges around her on the opera's last page. Tristan is calling her to follow him into the world where they will never be separated from each other, and to find there infinite peace. And as Isolde surrenders to Tristan's orchestral pleading, and dies on his body, the restless yearning motif, unfulfilled on the first page and a hundred times thereafter, lifts at last to its resolution.

Tristan und Isolde is widely thought to be a glorification of physical or sexual or romantic love. I hope it can be seen from this synopsis that it hardly concerns itself at all with the sort of love felt by Mimi and Rodolfo, or Carmen and Don José, or by the many characters in *The Marriage of Figaro*. Most operas, Mozart's above all, affirm the joys and sorrows, the *human* dimensions of the love of man and woman. Wagner didn't concern himself with those sentiments – except briefly in *Die Meistersinger*, and even there Walther and Eva never get a love duet to sing or a musical theme to represent their love. The lovers in all of Wagner's operas point to something beyond themselves. In this opera, the lovers reject the sensuality and abandon of physical love for something we may quite rightly call meta-physical. The lovers learn and grow as they pass through the three acts. So, if we move with them, do we. Wagner certainly passed through phases as he wrote. One commonly hears it said that his affair with Mathilde Wesendonck was the 'inspiration' for *Tristan*. But the reverse is more likely: the vast effort of composing *Tristan* 'inspired' the affair with Frau Wesendonck. In any case, Wagner broke with her when it came time to compose the end of Act II and all of Act III. These no longer have anything to do with physical love. They are an attempt to reach a reality that lies beyond the physical. In fact, Act III ends with a death that has no physical cause at all. Isolde dies because the dead Tristan, singing to her in the orchestral music of the Liebestod, summons her. On any literal level, Wagner's revision of the old story is an absurdity, a betrayal of a rich medieval tradition and the *Tristan* poems of Malory, Chrétien, and Gottfried von Strassburg. But *this Tristan* demands to be experienced on levels other than the literal. I'd like to discuss it now on a level of metaphor, and after that to pass on to some levels of meaning.

First then, metaphor. There is much in Wagner's *Tristan*, words and music, that suggests the sea – that was the image it evoked most strongly for Baudelaire, Swinburne, Thomas Mann, and T.S. Eliot. Wagner, as we said, thought of the music of the prelude in terms of winds and cloud formations. But the image that most occurs in the text, beautifully realized in many 'painted-in-light' productions in the seventies, is oncoming darkness. *Tristan und Isolde* is a long day's journey into night. In the very first words of the opera we hear that Tristan's ship is sailing East, into the land of light, while Isolde's eyes are fixed West, into that dark Abendland where, already, 'blue streaks are rising.' *There* is where she is really travelling – back westwards into the land of night and 'death for us both' – 'Tod uns beiden.' Her dark plan is not, however, realized on the voyage. She and Tristan do not die when they drink the potion. He, without knowing the import of his words, predicts, 'Before the sun sinks, we shall reach land,' and the sun is still in the sky as King Marke and honour and duty come between them.

The association of light with all that is to be rejected and night with all that must be accepted then becomes the constant theme of the second act. The burning torch which keeps Tristan from Isolde is a 'sentinel' prolonging 'the hated day.' Isolde extinguishes it, and would do so 'even if it were the light of life.' Tristan wishes he could likewise 'put out the light of hateful day,' which brings only grief and pain. In that feverish passage of the love duet so often cut in performance, they renounce as so much false sunlight all their past notions of honour, his knightly service to Marke and her defiant fidelity to Morold. All this they now see as the high noon of their madness – like the sun, flickering, flaming, blinding the eyes and searing the brain. Tristan cries out in anguish, 'Oh, if only we could be consecrated to night,' and they begin their Liebesnacht, singing how, as the darkness surrounds them, they have the sun hidden inside them, the stars laughing in their breasts. As the lights of reason and memory fade away, and with them every illusory outline, even their own individual identities, the outside world disappears in the darkness and, they sing rapturously, they themselves are the world.

Then Brangäne's voice from the tower warns them that the night will inevitably pass, so they resolve to enter the darkness forever, to merge their identities forever. Only the intervention of those 'phantoms of light,' Marke and Melot, prevents them from ending their love duet on the point of Tristan's sword. This is a far different journey into night and death than the hate-filled journey of the first act. And it almost reaches its goal: Tristan secures Isolde's promise to follow him into that other land 'where the sun never shines,' and then drops his guard before Melot.

But Tristan is not killed in the duel – and the great third act is *his* long day's journey, as the first was *hers*: he wakes from his experience of 'the vast kingdom of the night of the world' and, while the sun overhead burns into his brain, he comes to see his passion for Isolde as the very essence of the whole hated world of light, and he renounces it. Dying, he cries, 'The torch is extinguished.' When she arrives to follow him, it is into a darkness so great that she cannot even see the 'creatures of light,' Marke and his attendants, standing round her.

Now suns, stars, and blessed nights have been part of the language of love for centuries. But in *Tristan* there is an obsessive, delirious quality about these images that is quite unlike, say, the sun and the stars in the love poems of Catullus, or Juliet as the sun and Romeo cut up in little stars. Moreover, Wagner deliberately inverts the traditional imagery: sunlight is rejected, darkness invoked. Then metaphor is turned to metaphysics: light is illusion, darkness reality. And, strangest of all, sexual love is, in Act II, welcomed as darkness and then, in Act III, cursed and rejected as light. What, we wonder, is Wagner saying in all of this?

The answer most ready to hand is that Wagner was investing his Western myth with Eastern, and specifically Buddhist, associations. (During his Tristan period he actually sketched another drama about two young lovers blessed by Buddha with a release from desire.) Wagner's reading in Buddhism would have acquainted him with that doctrine's first three truths. Those truths sound like an exegesis of *Tristan*'s third act – all human existence is pain; pain is caused by desire; the highest wisdom lies in overcoming desire. Only when this is accomplished may the soul experience the state of Nirvana. (Recall that only when Tristan has cursed desire, even his desire for Isolde, is he rewarded with his Nirvana-vision of her coming across the sea, smiling on waves of flowers.) Significantly, the word Nirvana means 'blowing out,' the extinguishing of the light of desire. (Recall Tristan's final, 'The torch is extinguished.') In that Buddhist darkness, to quote from Udana 9, 'shine no stars, nor is the sun to be seen there.' (Recall several passages in Acts II and III.) Chesterton once noted, contrasting the Buddhist afterlife with the Christian concept, 'The Christian heaven is a heaven where they love one another; the Buddhist heaven is a heaven where they *are* one another.' (Recall Tristan and Isolde resolving to die so they can merge their identities.) The word Buddha means 'awakened.' (Recall how in Act III both Tristan and Isolde must fall into a sleep of unconsciousness before they can waken to their Nirvana-visions of each other.)

Though the story of Tristan and Isolde is set in an era that was devoutly Christian – the early Middle Ages of the Holy Grail and King Arthur, of miracles, of devotion to the passion of Christ and the Virgin Mother – nowhere in Wagner's *Tristan* does anyone invoke or even mention anything Christian. The work is, as deliberately as some of Shakespeare's plays, divested of its medieval religious aspects (as *Tannhäuser* and *Lohengrin* were not) so that we can look to wider perspectives. One divinity *is* mentioned – by Isolde at the beginning of Act II – Frau Minne, the old German pagan love-goddess. But the imaginative world of Wagner's *Tristan* is closer to Buddhism than to any Western tradition, Christian *or* pagan. Joseph Kerman sees *Tristan* as a 'religious drama' that 'slowly and surely grips the audience,' in which we undergo 'a progress towards a state of illumination which transcends yearning and pain,' a sense of 'a compelling higher reality' beyond human understanding. 'If this,' he concludes, 'is not to be called a religious experience, it is hard to know what meaning to attach to the term.'

Buddhism certainly helps us get beneath the surface of *Tristan*, but still more details in the text seem to come from the metaphysics of Wagner's contemporary Arthur Schopenhauer, whose writings Wagner read over and over during his *Tristan* period. For Schopenhauer, our visible world (*Vorstellung*) is only one manifestation of the essential principle in the universe, *Wille* or will – a blind, undifferentiated power operating in nature as gravity and other physical forces, in animals as instinct, and in men and women (this, for the pessimistic Schopenhauer, was one of nature's cruellest impositions) as conscious passion. We humans are more pathetic than other creatures because we are relatively aware of the terrible gravitational pull of *Wille*, which hurtles us endlessly towards goals which, once achieved, prove unsatisfying and illusory. *Wille* is Schopenhauer's fundamental reality; the objects that meet our senses are mere phenomena illuminated by it. So in *Tristan* we may see *Wille* imaged in the sun – all purposeless yearning, lighting up illusory values. The lovers try to escape from it by dying, but this is no solution because (with Schopenhauer as with Buddhism) no one can find peace until he has overcome his own desires. The lovers must see *Wille* for what it is, and reject it. Extinguish it. This is what they accomplish, separately but each with a vision of the other, in Act III.

But it is easy to exaggerate the influence of these Eastern and Western ideas and ethical systems on Wagner. Denis de Rougement, whose book *Love in the Western World* is the classic study of the whole Tristan tradition, rightly insists that 'a composer of Wagner's calibre does not put "ideas" to music.' Many of the so-called Schopenhauer references in Wagner's text can actually be traced back to the thirteenth-century *Tristan* poem of Gottfried von Strassburg, while what look like Eastern elements can be traced to still older European tales of knighthood. De Rougement doesn't simplify our considerations, though. He complicates them. He demonstrates, from considerable evidence, that the Tristan myth first appeared in its complete form among the members of a heretical Christian cult, the

Cathars or Albigensians, a neo-Manichean sect that flourished in the eleventh century in the south of France. In the old Manichean world-view, a god of light was engaged in constant struggle with a god of darkness. For the eleventh-century Manichees, the Cathars, the physical world was evil. Humans should seek to escape from it. The sexual impulse in particular was wrong and was to be renounced. The sect, with its life-denying doctrines, its rejection of Church and Sacraments, was exterminated in a terrible persecution. But its myth survived. The troubadours of southern France had fashioned the tale of Tristan and Iseult to show that passion is destructive and had to be rejected before a man or a woman could find peace.

For de Rougement, Wagner is important because, after Europe had misunderstood and sentimentalized the myth (and made of it the beginnings of our modern love stories), Wagner rediscovered the original meaning in the old tale. Small wonder that Wagner began to realize, as he wrote, that *Tristan* was turning into something terrible, that ordinary people had better not see to the heart of what he was saying. He was eloquently preaching a centuries-old heresy, exposing Europe's chivalric tradition of honour and duty as illusory, and – most surprising of all – he was attacking at its heart the sentimental 'love story' that had become the substance of so much Western art – including, I might add, most operas.

De Rougement may well be right. But for me, it is not Buddhism, or Schopenhauer, or a medieval heresy I find most in *Tristan*. It is the spirit of Romantic Germany. As I listen, I think of Novalis and his languid *Hymns to Night*: 'I am light ... oh, if only I were night. Why am I not shadows and darkness?' I think of Hölderlin, contemplating the oncoming darkness in his *Hyperion*: 'Could this twilight be *our* element? Is shadow our soul's fatherland?' I think of that last product of German Romanticism, the marvellous succession of silent films produced in Germany in the twenties, with their expressionistic, almost neurotic use of darkness and light. I think especially of that philosopher of history Oswald Spengler, characterizing the German soul as enamoured of darkness, consumed with an urge to overcome the only reality it sees before it, a limitless expanse of space. For Spengler, the endless cadences of *Tristan* are precisely that – 'the artistic conquest of endless space' wherein 'everything merges in bodiless infinity.' The spirit of Wagner's *Tristan* broods mightily over Spengler's great book, even over its title page – though our English title, *The Decline of the West*, conveys little of the sunset and dark horizons of the German, *Der Untergang des Abendlands*. That title – literally 'the going under of the evening land' – is Isolde's foreboding, and

Brangäne's words from the deck ('Blue streaks are rising in the West') and the sailor's song from the masthead, those first words of the opera ('Westward stray the eyes, Eastward fares the ship'). The vision of our century's most famous poem in English, *The Waste Land* of T.S. Eliot, is of a Western civilization reduced to fragments of Sappho, St Augustine, and Shakespeare shored up against the oncoming darkness, with only the Eastern thunder of the Upanishads speaking peace.

Does *Tristan* preach Eastern Nirvana and Western denial of *Wille*? Is it a realization in art of the original love-myth of the Western World? Is it the ultimate expression of the German Romantic soul in love with darkness? Is it a forecast of the inevitable decline of Western civilization? Wagner's long day's journey into night is all of these things and, as Nietzsche remarked ruefully, 'The world is poor for anyone who has never been sick enough' to feel its power.

Sick enough? We are back where we began in these considerations. For the first hundred years of Wagner's *Tristan*, many people, not all of them unintelligent, have thought that the effect this music drama has on the submissive listener is unhealthy, dangerously introverted, life-denying. Elliott Zuckerman, the author of *The First Hundred Years of Wagner's Tristan*, used Wagner's opera to look back on a hundred years of destruction and decline. Jacques Maritain, whose neo-Thomist philosophy was an affirmation of a higher reality that *didn't* require a man to deny the reality of the world around him, whose teaching shaped two generations of Catholic intellectuals – not least at the college in Toronto where I have taught – maintained that he would have been a better man had he never submitted to *Tristan*.

W.H. Auden made these objections more precise, and more manageable. 'If we are to get the full benefit of Wagner's operas,' he said, 'we have simultaneously to *identify* ourselves with what we hear and see on stage – yes, all that is me – and to *distance* ourselves from it – but all that is precisely what in me I must overcome.' Auden didn't mean that he had to overcome his attachment to the music, but to the instinctual desires in himself that the music so powerfully expressed. And Wagner, one of our great intuitors, would have agreed with that. His *Tristan* affirms, most especially in its music, that deep in our unconscious we yearn for infinity, but that we can only find it when we have overcome our insatiable human desires. In affirming this, the opera gives expression to all manner of insatiable desires – primitive, frightening, vindictive, erotic – which we who have constructive roles in society have suppressed. We have relegated those desires beneath the level of consciousness, but none of us has ever really tamed them. Wagner's music reaches that subconscious level as no other music does. Wagner knew he was doing this. That is why he gave such prominence to the orchestra. 'In the orchestra,' he wrote, 'the primal urges of creation and nature are represented. What the orchestra expresses can never be clearly articulated, because it renders primal feeling itself.' (He may well have been thinking of Schopenhauer's *Wille.*) 'The vocal line,' he continues, 'is different from this. It represents ... human emotions that are intelligible and individuated.' No wonder, when we are first exposed to Wagner, that our attention goes to the orchestra – it seems to be saying so much more. For those who surrender to *Tristan*, the restless orchestra puts them in touch with the very depths of their unconscious feelings.

And in *Tristan* what we discover there may be frightening, but is ultimately, as with all great drama, life-affirming, even cleansing. We discover that, though in our human condition we feel hate and fear and lust and vengeance, our deepest desire is for an infinite reality apart from all of these, be it Nirvana, or release from *Wille*, or the vision that mystics like John of the Cross sensed in what he called the dark night of the soul. That is why we will need *Tristan* for the next hundred years. Our lives *are* poor if we never experience what mystical souls have called ecstasy: passing beyond the familiar realities of everyday experience, opening to the mystery that lies beyond our senses, below our consciousness, and beyond our deaths. Few works of art convey that mystery as *Tristan* does. And none, I think, so powerfully conveys our restlessness until we rest in it.

16

The Making of a Musical Legend

Palestrina

Hans Pfitzner called his twentieth-century opera *Palestrina* 'a musical legend' and thereby intentionally aligned it, not just with the sixteenth century in which it is set, but with still earlier Christian centuries, whose legends described in vivid detail the sufferings of God's chosen ones, the martyrs and miracle workers of his Church. Legends are based on history. They may not be literally true, but a good legend touches something archetypal and true in the consciousness of the one who writes and the one who reads. Everything about a legend, save the literal facts, is true.

Pfitzner's *Palestrina* is based on an apocryphal story and deals freely with historical facts. But it is fundamentally true. The story, a lovely one, tells how at the sixteenth-century Council of Trent the pope was determined to destroy all polyphonic music as worldly and corrupt, until angels dictated to the lowly Giovanni Pierluigi da Palestrina a polyphonic Mass (the *Missa Papae Marcelli*) so pious and pure that His Holiness changed his mind, and centuries of past music were thus saved from extinction. The truth of the legend is that God hides himself from the wise and powerful and speaks to and through his little ones.

Legends accumulate details as they are told and retold. Pfitzner, expanding his legend, represented the polyphonist Palestrina as disheartened by the success of the new monophonic music from Florence; as unable to write because of the death of his wife; as threatened by his friend Cardinal Borromeo if he does not produce a Mass to save polyphonic music; as driven to compose by a dream-vision of nine old master composers; as aided in the composition of the Mass by the apparition of his wife, who translates the angels' song for him; as imprisoned for his supposed failure to compose the Mass; as released from prison but destroyed physically by his sufferings; as thanked and blessed by the pope, and sought out for forgiveness by Borromeo, once the Mass is discovered and performed; as, finally, choosing solitude with his God over recognition from the world whose music he has saved.

Much of this is story-telling. The reform of Church music *was* an issue at the Council of Trent and for some time previous. The pope, Pius IV, was quite justifiably disturbed about the profane melodies and unintelligible words in most polyphonic settings of the Mass, whereas the Emperor Ferdinand was, as Pfitzner also indicates, eager to save polyphony despite its excesses. But decisions were left to a post-conciliar committee that included Borromeo. In 1565 several model Masses were composed and submitted. It cannot be established that Palestrina's *Missa Papae Marcelli* was among them. It had been written earlier, and the pope expressed his admiration for it later. Palestrina was never imprisoned. He had been pensioned off as papal choirmaster because he was married and technically ineligible for the post, but he was eventually reinstated for life. He was never particularly close to Borromeo, who approached not Palestrina but a certain Vincenzo Ruffo to compose a Mass as a model for reform. It was Ruffo who was personally thanked by the pope – a different pope, Gregory XIII, who singled him out from among a group of pilgrims and embraced and kissed him. Palestrina's wife died almost two decades after he composed the *Missa Papae Marcelli*. He remarried a year after her death, and lived on for more than a decade.

So it is mythic, not historical, truth that Pfitzner sought out and dramatized. Although he incorporated into his libretto actual quotations from the pope and the emperor, and worked into his score actual strains from Palestrina's Mass, his main purpose was to mine his facts and fictions for what they could say, on a deeper level, about an artist's duty to himself, his art, his fellow men, and his God. And what Pfitzner said, as his legend expanded into a musical triptych of vast proportions, is often touching, occasionally rueful, and ultimately, I like to think, profound.

As *Palestrina* is far from familiar outside of Germany, the expanded legend is worth rehearsing now in more detail. The centrepiece of Pfitzner's triptych – Act II, set at the Council of Trent – is a picture of the wide world, turbulent and cruel and unable to understand itself. The side panels, Acts I and III, are set in Rome, in the self-understanding of the artist's study, amid his manuscripts, his instruments, his visions. There, in the first act, Palestrina's best pupil decides to desert him for Florence and the new monophony (that is to say, for the Camerata and the experiments that will eventually give birth to opera). Palestrina's young son tells us that his father seems to feel the weight not only of such personal sorrows but also of the world's sorrows (that is to say, of the *lacrimae rerum* of which Virgil sang). Then Palestrina himself confides to Cardinal Borromeo that he sees the world as set on a course he cannot understand: artistic principles he thought eternal seem to be passing away forever. He also says (in the face of Borromeo's reminder that *his* work too will go up in flames if he will not compose an acceptable Mass) that his genius cannot work under constraint.

Left alone, Palestrina is close to despair. Then nine Renaissance masters appear to him from the past – not, as we might expect, to plead with him to save their works from extinction, but to tell him the astonishing truth that God needs him, that God commands him to write. He may think he cannot compose any longer, but (the masters seem to know Hans Sachs's 'Fliedermonolog') a poet sings because he must, and because he must, he can. A poet sings from a heaven-sent inner compulsion. God who fathered a Word on the brink of eternity is, they say, asking Palestrina now to follow his own creative example. God gives each of his creatures an earthly mission. Theirs has been to begin a musical tradition of unsurpassed excellence; Palestrina's is to become 'the last shining stone' that completes the succession.

The legend's angels surround Palestrina to inspire the Mass. But it is only when his departed wife appears at his side, only when he feels at one with humankind, that Palestrina is able to create. The joy of composing floods his soul, then leaves him asleep. In the morning his pupil and his son gather up the pages he has left. The bells of Rome's churches ring.

Act I is the beginning of a statement on the nature and purpose of art. Act II shows us how little the world understands. The ecclesiastics who have come to Trent from many lands to further the conflicting plans of the emperor and the pope know nothing about art, and so, Pfitzner intimates, they can know nothing about the revelations of God.

Among the Italians present, Novagerio first commands attention. He regards art as insignificant man-made stuff or, worse, the work of the devil. He thinks torture a blessing for insubordinate nonentities like Palestrina. He is a nasty piece of work – self-important, contemptuous, vicious when crossed – and yet on the surface he is genial and accommodating. On the other hand, Morone, anxious to save music, devout and inspiring in his great monologue, makes us believe for a moment that God really does speak through his Church in council. Pfitzner's use of leitmotifs reinforces the strength of Morone's words; indeed he gives the churchman a dramatic role and a musical ambience much like that Wagner gave to Hans Sachs. But unlike Sachs, Morone is single-minded in his attitude toward unbelievers, regards commoners as children, and is no match for the buffoonery of his Beckmesser, the Bishop of Budoja. That third Italian seems at first harmless enough, as he interrupts the council's prayers with his exclamations, indulges in a bathetic oration, and babbles on about his clerical expense account. But he soon proves himself small-minded and mean, encouraging the senile Patriarch of Assyria to speak and then laughing at him. (In an act full of ambivalences, the half-blind patriarch, looking like one of the Magi at the crib and speaking like Simeon in the temple, sees more clearly than any of the rest of them but, like most seers, is not listened to.)

The non-Italians are similarly ambivalent figures. The Cardinal of Lorraine, wise and conciliatory, turns testy and intransigent. The Archbishop of Prague, as his changing motif indicates, is now quietly devout, now savage and brusque. The Bishop of Cadiz, a clear thinker, is offset by his offensive lay associate, the Count Luna, a schemer who might have stepped onstage from between scenes of *Il Trovatore*.

And hovering over them all is the marvellously ambivalent Cardinal Madruscht, the 'German bear,' more warrior than churchman, who lives for duty and thinks order can and must be imposed. He seems a fair-minded host till, in a burst of desperate anger at the complete breakdown of discipline after the session, he orders his soldiers to open fire on the squabbling servants and commoners, who are only acting out on their own level the drama Their Eminences have acted out on theirs. As the wounded lie groaning on the floor, Madruscht asks of us the question we want to ask of him: 'Is this the meaning of the Holy Council?'

Large ironies pervade this long scene at Trent. There is nothing in the act more convincing than Morone's words, set to the beautiful motif of the council, 'Don't close your hearts to the Holy Spirit. He comes to us, yes, he comes to us, and gives us wisdom, peace, and unity.' Yet the Spaniards blasphemously laugh that Morone's 'Holy Spirit' is nothing more than numerical superiority: in any headcount the tonsured, oily Italian heads will win, for there are so many of them. And we who watch constantly think: the Mass that the council is furious with Palestrina for not writing has in fact been written, though the council knows it not. It has been dictated by a heaven that will not speak to its churchmen but will speak, even sing, to the lowly one the churchmen have thrown in prison.

Externally, Act II is spun on by the ambivalent and, in the end, ineffectual philistines we see; internally, through musical motifs, it is dominated by three unambivalent figures, all of them absent – the Emperor Ferdinand, Pope Pius IV, and Palestrina himself. The pope and the emperor, confronting one another, will decide the issue, not through their partisans' essentially meaningless machinations, but through an artist who works alone and apart. At the great ceremonial moment when the Holy Spirit is invoked to bless the council, it is the theme of the absent Palestrina that sounds; imprisoned though he is, it is through him that God speaks.

This message is made explicit in the brief final act when, the Mass finally discovered, the pope personally reinstates the composer, when Borromeo throws himself sobbing with remorse at Palestrina's feet, and when the lay composer, in a reversal of the roles of the ritual of ordination, places his hands on the cleric's head. The powerful Borromeo (later to be sainted by his Church) lifts his tear-stained face to say to the physically broken artist, in so many words, 'God speaks through you.' And the artist does not deny the truth of that statement. He only waits for death, bent over his keyboard, saying:

Now make from me, O God,
The final stone in one of your unnumbered successions.
And I shall be contented, and at peace.

The legend is complete: God's chosen one has heard his word, suffered to give it to us, and come through his martyrdom to union with his Creator.

What does Pfitzner's legend tell us? That art is a testament between God and man, a creature's share in his Creator's activity, providentially ordered in traditions that develop over centuries, achieved at great cost because the artist must suffer the world's persecutions, but worth every effort because without art the world would never hear the voice of the Artist who made it.

And yet, when all that is said, we have not really come to terms with Pfitzner's *Palestrina*, for Pfitzner made his musical legend into something less about Palestrina than about himself. It is, if not the last, at least one of the most precious stones in a succession of autobiographical German operas that are also personal artistic manifestos. Wagner's *Die Meistersinger* was the first of these, followed by *Palestrina*, Busoni's *Doktor Faust*, Hindemith's *Mathis der Maler*, and Schönberg's *Moses und Aron*. (One could even include Strauss's *Intermezzo* and *Capriccio* in this company, except that the worldly Strauss does not aim at the philosophical, not to say theological, perspectives of the others.)

In all of these works the composer wrote his own text, casting the creative artist as a solitary genius who sees more deeply into human events than do any of his contemporaries. In all of them the artist is appalled at what he sees and questions the worth of what he does. And arguably in all of them the artist receives a divine mandate to use his art to strengthen mankind. The five massive works represent five individual responses to the same profound question. Wagner's comedy, with its biblically named characters and its baptismal images, is the most objective and, I think, the wisest of them. The other works were written in the shadow of, or in the thick of, human events in Germany that would have driven any creative individual profoundly inward. Pfitzner wrote his during the First World War.

The autobiographical elements in Pfitzner's text are many and manifold. A lonely genius, he was regarded by his contemporaries, perhaps especially by Richard Strauss, as little more than a gifted crank. Stories that depict him as dogmatic and embittered are legion. They may not all be true, but it is certain that Pfitzner did alienate many, including those who, like Mahler, Walter, and Furtwängler, wanted to promote his music. Pfitzner was a narrow intellectual and a self-absorbed visionary. He had little use for democratic procedures or international cooperation. Subscribing to the notion of *Kultur* as the one great civilizing force, with Germany as its prime manifestation, he bitterly opposed anything he saw as undermining his nation's artistic heritage. As a consequence, his prose writings, as outspoken and occasionally as anti-Semitic as Wagner's, contributed to the climate that produced fascism. Though he came to despise and, at least once, confront the Nazis, he never renounced the single-mindedness of his ideas. He ended his life composing in near blindness, all his possessions lost in an air raid, suffering neglect and oblivion.

Pfitzner's gathering pessimism came largely from the realization that the great Central European tradition in music and thought was, in his lifetime, disintegrating. He thought of himself as the last in a succession that extended back through his beloved Schumann, also a polemicist, to Weber and Beethoven and Bach. When he looked about him, he saw only dodecaphonic modernists bent on the destruction of that tradition. His Germany, once a great civilizing force, with Luther and Kant and Schopenhauer and Eichendorff as its prophets, seemed to be crumbling about him. But he would keep his vision. He declared in a letter to Bruno Walter, 'I shall remain true to this land until my last breath.'

It is easy to see Pfitzner in the lonely Palestrina he put on the stage. But it does not require much effort, either, to see something of him – though

he hardly intended this – in each of the intractable nationalistic churchmen at the Council of Trent. He meant them, of course, to stand as figures for the ostensibly great of the world who accomplish nothing for all
their striving. But they are better characters than he intended them to be,
and they resist ready classification. Madruscht ordering his men to fire on
the commoners (Pfitzner's most daring fiction) has become a figure for
the good German gone tragically wrong, and the end of Act II can be
seen as a vision of Europe strewn – and, prophetically, to be strewn a second time – with corpses.

Wagner, to all appearances a terrible man, solved in his work the problems he could not solve in his life. In his soul-searching dramas, as he
divided himself into his Parsifals and Amfortases, his Kundrys and Kling-
sors, the self-destructive man came to understand himself and left us a
magnificent but profoundly ambivalent testament. I believe Pfitzner is
that same kind of artist. He is Palestrina and Borromeo at once, and when
the one blesses and forgives the other in the final scene of his opera he
seems to be attempting to reconcile his own ambivalences.

His opera has not won the public. This is partly because it is long,
demanding, and difficult to cast. But in addition, many have thought it
presumptuous, dangerously introverted, and politically suspect. Thomas
Mann, after an initial infatuation (he saw *Palestrina* five times in a single
year), found in it proto-fascist tendencies that disturbed him deeply.
Some years ago an international record jury decided against awarding its
'best of the year' prize to the Kubelik recording for the same reasons. As
with Wagner, so with Pfitzner – personal and political statements may be
read into the musical works with fatal ease. Both composers may have
laboured too mightily to put themselves into their music dramas.

But if we have come to terms with Wagner, may we not with Pfitzner?
By and large, our age has been reconciled ideologically with Wagner by
concentrating on elements in his texts he may not have consciously put
there; Carl Dahlhaus and Robert Donington and others have pointed out
what wonders the composer wrought intuitively. These are far more profound than the shallows of his conscious views. Wagner was, first and
always, an artist, and a very intuitive one. With Pfitzner we would be well
advised to regard his central affirmation that God speaks through his artists not as a self-righteous personal vindication, or as a dangerous denial
of the importance of liberal policies and democratic processes, but as a
kind of intuitive mythic truth, as something that, if properly understood,
is necessary to us, and nowhere else stated so beautifully.

It *is* dangerous, indeed it is the root of fascism, to take any human source as the voice of God. But must we deny then that God speaks to us in *any* way, or from *any* source? I have always believed that among his testaments are our great works of art, even though the interpretation of them is as problematic as is the interpretation of his scriptural testaments. Pfitzner, struggling to say something personal and political, affirms this higher truth, which is more than his personality and his politics, and he does it in music of often astonishing sincerity and persuasiveness. His ultimate affirmation comes from the legend, not the autobiography, in his text. That is why it is worth attending to. Legends are archetypally true.

God speaks to us through his artists. They are the instruments on which he plays. That is what Pfitzner's *Palestrina* affirms. If what it says is true, and I believe it is, then *Palestrina* deserves our attention and may in the end win our love.

17

The Moon Is Like the Moon
Salome

We are coming to a century's end, and the art and thought of one hundred years ago can not but have a special fascination for us. There is a term for the art of that time – *fin de siècle*, century's end. We associate it with the languid, overripe, neo-pagan yearnings of artists like Gustave Moreau and Aubrey Beardsley, and especially with an almost hallucinatory, delicately coloured play, inspired by Moreau's paintings and in turn inspiring Beardsley's illustrations, written in one mad night in elegant French by an impassioned Irishman: the *Salomé* of Oscar Wilde.

Nothing could be more *fin de siècle* than that *Salomé* – a languid, overripe, neo-pagan version the New Testament story of the beheading of John the Baptist, studded with images in the style of the Old Testament Canticle of Canticles, but written as if from the midst of some opium dream. No one was surprised when it failed in its first production in Paris, and was promptly banned by a shocked Lord Chamberlain in London. But Germany went crazy for it, especially when in the new century it appeared on the operatic stage there, in German, as *Salome* – rather severely cut, but shot through with strange music by another madman (or so he was thought at the time), Richard Strauss.

In the transition from French play to German opera, and from the end of one century to the start of another, the emphasis in *Salome* changed from languid elegance to something like brutal shock. Audiences knew they were in for a shocker when Strauss's curtain went up, not after an overture full of tunes, but on a neurotic growl from a solo clarinet, and when they saw on stage a lowering full moon, and in front of it a handsome young man in armour singing, like some sort of zombie, 'Wie schön ist die Prinzessin Salome heute nacht!' – 'How beautiful is the Princess Salome tonight!' When a little page-boy, obsessed with the young man obsessed with the Princess Salome, looked up at the moon and exclaimed, 'How strange the moon seems! She looks like a woman rising from a tomb.' And when the young man said in contradiction, 'The moon is like a little princess who has white doves for feet.'

Those are just the first two of a hundred-odd similes in this opera in which the Canticle of Canticles runs riot, and its delicate images are exploited and expanded to limn and hymn the thraldom of erotic attraction. We're not far into the opera before we realize that the moon that presides over the action reflects the mental state, not just of the young captain and the page-boy, but of each character in turn. So, when Salome herself appears, she says that the moon is 'like a silver flower, cool and chaste, beautiful as a virgin.' The besotted and effeminate Herod, when he takes the stage, says that the moon is 'like a drunken woman reeling through the clouds,' while his sober, no-nonsense queen Herodias only comments, bluntly, 'The moon is like the moon. That is all.'

But the similes of Oscar Wilde are nowhere near so bizarre as the music of Richard Strauss. He lets us know, with his own kind of bluntness, that it's not the *fin de siècle* any more. The twentieth century has begun, and the new style in art, especially in Germany, is expressionism. The idea now is to paint a world that will correspond outwardly to the twisted inner feelings of the men and women in it. So Strauss doesn't bother to give the all-important moon a musical theme, as a nineteenth-century composer would have done. Strauss knows that it is his expressionist's business to depict the distorted inner feelings of the characters who look up to the moon and see themselves and their obsessions there. And in depicting the characters he lays on the colours thicker than any operatic composer had ever done before.

John the Baptist (or Jochanaan, the Hebrew name he is given in Wilde's text) has two main themes. One, usually sounded on the French horns, we hear several times before we even see him. It depicts the Baptist as a holy man, young and fervent:

The other of the Baptist's themes appears when the moon darkens, like 'a dead woman who is trying to cover herself with a shroud,' and the holy man rises from his cistern prison. Now we see him differently – he is not young and fervent, but gaunt and terrible, a fanatic whose fatal attraction will cause Salome to uncover herself and meet her death:

Those two themes will undergo a myriad of changes in the opera's two-hour playing time. That first, fervent theme will take on an astonishingly sensuous character in the final scene, as Salome sings to the Baptist's severed head. The chilling second theme will eventually depict the great wings that Herod imagines are pursuing him through his palace. The very thought of the Baptist is, for Herod, an angel of death.

But I'd like to concentrate on three of the themes associated with Salome herself. At the opera's climax they will writhe their ways through the Dance of the Seven Veils. But long before that we hear them in the orchestra, each in what seems like a hundred different guises.

Our first Salome theme can sound at times like a Viennese waltz. And why not? If ever a young lady needed to pay a visit to number 19 Berggasse in Vienna it is the Princess Salome:

That theme will recur with shattering impact in the final scene, where an immense dissonance smashes it out of shape, and we know that Salome's mind has given way:

Salome's second theme appears when she first sees Jochanaan, and is both fascinated and repelled. 'He is terrible,' she says, 'truly terrible':

Later, that theme reappears – savagely percussive on the horns as the severed head is lifted from the cistern, truly terrible under a hair-raising trill as a cloud blacks out the moon and Salome kisses that head, and shockingly abrupt on the last page as the soldiers crush the princess to death with their shields.

Salome's third theme is as much vocal as orchestral. We never hear it without thinking of the words sung to it. We first hear it when the princess decides it is not the Baptist's flesh, or his hair, that is beautiful, but his mouth. 'I want to kiss your mouth, Jochanaan,' she sings:

When the Baptist rejects her and descends again into his prison, and she bends over the cistern peering into the darkness below, the brass instruments state that theme in this new, frightening form:

That is a musical statement waiting for words. And we get those words at the opera's most terrible moment, when Salome, asked what reward she wants for her dance, says 'Ich will den Kopf des Jochanaan!' – 'I want the head of Jochanaan!'

'Depraved' is an adjective sometimes given *Salome*. Depraved is what the first Salome thought it was when, in Dresden in 1905, she told Strauss, 'I won't do that. I'm a decent woman.' Depraved is what the Archbishop of Vienna – whose name, oddly enough, was Piffl – thought it was when he tried to have it banned. Depraved is what the Kaiser thought it was when he said of Strauss, 'This will be his ruin.' Depraved is what the Met board of directors thought it was when, in 1907, it was withdrawn after a single performance at the insistence of the outraged box-holder Strauss called 'a certain Mr Morgan.' Perhaps fittingly, the Met's current production is inspired partly by the Chrysler Building and partly by the slums of New York. But even in less provocative settings, even with the passage of a hundred years of performances, *Salome* still retains the power to shock, and commentators still feel called upon to defend it on moral grounds. Willam Mann made his case by arguing that the ultimate effect of *Salome* on its audience was an Aristotelian catharsis through pity and fear. He saw the princess as she herself sees the moon – a chaste virginal flower. She is, for Mann, a young girl tragically confused by the first stirrings of sexual desire, and haunted by the repressed memory of her father, who was imprisoned and killed in the same cistern where Jochanaan is kept. As we pity her and fear for her, Mann said, we feel not revulsion but a great wash of cleansing emotion.

Norman del Mar took a different tack. He saw *Salome* as part of the long battle waged by late Romanticists for a new kind of truth – the freedom to portray the ugliness as well as the beauty in human experience. If we do not face this ugliness, the implication is, we will never really know ourselves. (Wilde's own words in this regard were, 'People say that fiction is getting too morbid, but as far as psychology is concerned, it has never been morbid enough. We have merely touched the surface of the soul, that is all.')

I don't think that *Salome* is depraved. But I *would* say that it is, in the technical sense of the term, decadent. That is an epithet Wilde and the *fin de siècle* would have welcomed, and it seems an appropriate enough term to apply to many aspects of Strauss's score – the pathological excitement, the relentless striving for effect, the sometimes monstrous overweighting of orchestral resources, the sometimes outrageous demands made on the singers. Yet with the passing years we have come to terms with *Salome*. Audiences *have* left performances cleansed by some sort of catharsis, and found beauty in its portrayal of ugliness. Decadence in life we decry, but decadence in art has its positive aspects. By showing us the terrible depths of evil, art can give us moral vision – not the moral vision of the self-righteous man, complacent in the conviction of his own goodness, but the moral vision of the human being made suddenly conscious of the potential for evil as well as for good in his (or her) nature. Some decadent art has cast an almost theological light on the mysteries of suffering and sin. Huysmans moved from *À rebours* to *La Cathédrale*.

And *Salome*? *Salome* is like the moon, that poet's symbol of ambivalence. The light it casts is not bright and clear, but dim and mysterious. It tells us, as does so much of the art produced in this century of ours, not about our best qualities but about our obsessions, our ambiguities, our weaknesses, our fatal flaws. And those are a part of ourselves that, as we face a new millennium, we still need to know about.

18

Genius and *Morbidezza*: *Manon Lescaut*

The libretto of Puccini's first successful opera, *Manon Lescaut*, credits no author. Puccini used at least four librettists, accepted the additional suggestions of his publisher Ricordi, and – save for actual versification – may have been as responsible as any of them for the final result. Many hands were needed, for Massenet's seven-year-old opera on the same subject had already given all-too-memorable expression both to the brief period of happiness Manon Lescaut and her Chevalier Des Grieux had enjoyed on the Rue Vivienne and to his subsequent attempt to forget her at St Sulpice. And before Massenet, Auber had dramatized the crucial events in New Orleans that led to the hapless couple's fleeing that city to the wastes of an unknown continent. The new libretto would have to find new scenes.

Puccini wrote his own version of Massenet's essential opening scene, where the lovers meet in Amiens, but then, in striving not to duplicate the work of his predecessors, he had to make do for the rest of his opera with three more or less isolated episodes at locales slightly different from those the predecessors had used. He provided a kind of musical fill-in of the undramatized events by way of an intermezzo – but that comes when it is least needed, between Acts II and III. We have to turn to Massenet to fill us in during the first interval, and to Auber during the last.

All the same, most opera-goers feel that Puccini's music more than compensates for the libretto's inadequacies. For it is already the music of a genius. In four or, at the most, five of his later operas the melodies are more familiar and more beautifully crafted, but no opera by Puccini can boast so great a number of melodies as *Manon Lescaut* has in glorious profusion. They tumble and spill over one another like the jostling crowd in the square at Amiens, like the steady stream of admirers in Geronte di

Ravoir's elegant salon in Paris. I number close to fifty quotable tunes, some of then used recurrently, almost as leitmotifs, some of them (particularly those in the love duet in Act II) ringing out passionately and then never heard again.

Especially original is Puccini's way of picking a small connective strand out of an earlier context and making it a theme in its own right. This innocuous bit from the tenor's opening aria, at the words, 'Tell me my future':

Pa- le- sa - te- mi il de - sti - no

reappears at the start of Act II as a tingling, rapid, sinister figure on the flute, punctuated by shivery arpeggios from the other woodwinds: the future turns out to be glittery and decadent, quick with the feeling of danger.

Nothing previous in Puccini's work has prepared us for the torrent of melody and the thematic ingenuity to be found in *Manon Lescaut*. It is as if, after the promise of *Le Villi* and the comparative failure of *Edgar*, he were determined at all costs to force his way to recognition. He borrowed from his youthful *Mass* and from his minuets for strings for the madrigal and the dances in Act II, and from a string quartet for a doom-laden theme in Acts III and IV, but one wonders why he thought he had to. His melodic gift was, for the first time, in full flood, and today it still sweeps all other considerations before it. An all-stops-out performance of *Manon Lescaut* can be an overwhelming experience. Ask any long-memoried Metropolitan broadcast listener what his most memorable single afternoon was and he'll surely mention, along with broadcasts of the great Verdi and Wagner operas, the *Manon Lescaut* of 31 March 1956, with Dimitri Mitropoulos conducting, when Jussi Björling seemed actually to go mad at 'Pazzo io son' and Licia Albanese seemed to die before your very ears at 'L'amor mio non muor ...' But even in a routine performance, no listener fails to respond to the gravitational pull of Des Grieux's young-love-at-first-sight aria 'Donna non vidi mai,' to the so-called Destiny motif sounding triumphantly as the ship sets sail at the end of Act III, or to a score of other moments.

This was, in 1893, clearly a new voice in opera, with a potential beyond that sounded by Mascagni and Leoncavallo. Less than ten minutes into Act I of *Manon Lescaut*, Bernard Shaw exclaimed that Puccini looked to be Verdi's heir. The composer himself favoured Wagner: when he and Mascagni were starving students in Milan, they had pooled their resources to buy the score of *Parsifal* and searched it through together enthusiastically. Hence not only the proliferation of motifs but also the symphonic textures of *Manon Lescaut* – thicker in sound than anything in Puccini till the final *Turandot*. Wagnerian too, with the fervour of a disciple not yet launched on his own, are the harmonies. Every commentator hears *Tristan* in the unresolved love duet in Act II and again in the first theme in the Act III intermezzo:

That, however, is followed immediately by a melody unlike anything in Wagner. Puccini had found his own voice:

But it was a voice that, as Puccini came eventually to regret, sounded too exclusively in his work, and with too much of the composer's personal *morbidezza* – not morbidity, but a softness, a kind of despondent melancholy at the inevitability of suffering in human lives. This came to be something of a hallmark of Puccini's output. A quarter of a century ago, the composer Jan Meyerowitz found the pathos of a scene in *Manon Lescaut* (in which the women sentenced to deportation are marched in chains before the mob at Le Havre) disturbingly reminiscent of what he called the 'leering sweetness' he had seen in the faces of the SS guards at

Sachsenhausen. The deportation scene is not to be found in the Abbé Prévost's novel, which was Puccini's source, or in Auber, or in Massenet. It was introduced into *Manon Lescaut* at Puccini's own insistence. He already knew and would always know where his strengths lay.

He was not entirely happy about the knowledge. He strove mightily to vary his output after *La Bohème*, *Tosca*, and *Madama Butterfly* had conquered the world, and he certainly succeeded in the almost miraculous comedy *Gianni Schicchi*. But *Tosca*, for all its brutality, and *Madama Butterfly*, for all the intricacies and subtleties of its thematic development, had already determined what his course had to be, shot through as they were with the *morbidezza* that neither audiences nor composer could resist. In Puccini's last opera, when Liù's *morbidezza* was sacrificed to Turandot's cruelty, and Puccini had to carry on without it, he found himself faced with an artistic impasse. He was at the height of his powers, but when his suffering heroine was gone he struggled in vain to rise to the scene of transformation that was to crown his *Turandot*.

To the public at large, the fact that Puccini worked on a level less perceptive than Mozart, less heroic than Verdi, less mythic than Wagner has hardly mattered at all. And in this matter the public may, in the end, be wiser than the composer and his critics. Those critics lament that Massenet's *Manon* has in recent years been eclipsed by Puccini's, even though Massenet tells a coherent story with a three-dimensional heroine and Puccini gives us four virtually unconnected scenes and a largely unexplained heroine who suffers, with each successive appearance, ever further humiliation and degradation. What has made the difference with the public is of course a flood of passionate melody that is Puccini's and Puccini's alone – and perhaps too something that has been commented on less often but has always been there in Puccini's work, latent even beneath the youthful confidence of *Manon Lescaut*, something to set against Massenet's suave professionalism, something to advance as an answer to Meyerowitz and the other critics: a kind of vulnerability.

Puccini was, all his life, easily hurt. Once, when he was wealthy and successful but still artistically unfulfilled, he was crossing what amounted to his own private lake in his own motor boat, and a local fisherman shook his fist at him and shouted, 'It's yours now. Soon we will have our turn.' Puccini could scarcely control his wounded feelings till he got home: 'I have never intentionally caused anyone any harm. I have tried to make people happy. Why should that man hate me?'

Manon and the other Puccini heroines ask, in their several ways, the same question: 'Perchè me ne rimuneri così?' Puccini may have thought

– he certainly said – that his artistic impulse was rooted in his clinical observation of the sufferings of the women in his operas. But artists aren't always best at understanding themselves. (Most of them are notoriously unreliable at it.) Puccini seems in fact to have been as vulnerable as any of his heroines. If, as commentators relentlessly point out, he inflicted sufferings upon them, he too had felt such suffering.

That sensitivity is what those who love his operas instinctively understand, and what Björling and Albanese once unforgettably communicated to all of us, in *Manon Lescaut.*

19

Mists, Sails, Sounds, and Impressions

Pelléas et Mélisande

I've always thought that the final page of Claude Debussy's *Pélleas et Mélisande* – part lullaby, part requiem, with its slowly descending arpeggios, its distant bell tolling, its suggestion of the sea glimpsed through charmed magic casements and its muted trumpet sounding the flight of the soul from faery lands forlorn – is the most beautiful ending any opera was ever given. But then, I've been in love with the music of Debussy ever since, in my early teens, I first discovered the twenty-four piano Preludes performed on old 78s by Walter Gieseking, and first tried, with minimal success, to recreate those Debussy sound pictures under my fingers. What shimmering piano pieces they were! 'The Engulfed Cathedral,' 'The Girl with the Flaxen Hair,' 'Mists,' 'Sails,' and 'The Sounds and Fragrances Turn on the Night Air.'

I discovered the aural images of Debussy before I discovered the paintings of Monet and Manet, the poems of Mallarmé and Verlaine, the train of reminiscences that is Proust's quest for lost time, and the correspondences, in Baudelaire, between sounds, fragrances, and colours. It wasn't till my college days that I found how all of these artists interconnect, how they represent through different media that subtle, unearthly flowering of the arts that appeared, almost miraculously, to challenge academic traditions one hundred years ago in Paris – impressionist painting, symbolist poetry, stream-of-consciousness prose, and the music of Debussy.

The French artists of that innovative era were interested in representing, not the ordinary surfaces of human experience, but the impressions human experience conveyed, and the subliminal emotions it released. That meant, for painters, new approaches to light, tint, and outline. It meant, for prose writers, a new precision in expressing the vestiges left by experience on memory. It meant, for poets, a new perception of the images and symbols of dreams. And the forest, the castle, the moonlight, the girl with flaxen hair, the sea, the ship, the lighthouse, the peril, the fear of falling, the tenuousness of life, the elusiveness of whatever it might be that lies beyond the senses – all of these were the dreamlike concerns of the young musician who, at the turn of the century, had not yet written his 'Engulfed Cathedral,' or his tonal symphony *La Mer*, but who had already written the most romantic of his piano pieces, 'Clair de Lune,' and the first of his orchestral masterpieces, *The Afternoon of a Faun*.

Debussy's inspirations may make him sound like an idle dreamer, an aesthete, a mere sensualist. Actually he was, like the other French artists of his day, feverishly active, relentlessly precise, and wholly dedicated to capturing through his art what they captured through theirs – those aspects of experience that we cannot otherwise articulate. At sixteen Debussy shocked his conservatory teachers by challenging the established rules of harmony, theory, and counterpoint. He soon set about devising a new palette of sounds, blending Western medieval modes with Eastern pentatonic and whole-tone scales, juxtaposing chords that were, by academic standards, unrelated, and experimenting with what was thought at the time to be dissonance. He broke up the symmetrical patterns in which music, and song in particular, had been structured for at least two centuries. He was, in his quiet but determined way, a revolutionary, the first 'modern' composer of the nineteenth century.

And as the century turned, he wanted to write an opera. He would make some poet's words turn, as on the night air, into his new sounds. He had already set a few of the symbolist poems of Verlaine and Baudelaire to music. For his opera he hoped for a drama 'in which music begins at the point where speech is powerless ... Music,' he said, 'is made for the inexpressible. I want music to have an air of emerging from a shadow into which at times it should return.' In the opera house, he went on to say, 'they sing too much.'

He was thinking mainly of the works of that thundering Klingsor who dominated the operatic scene at the turn of the century, Richard Wagner. Wagner too had broken down musical barriers, and left the symbolist poets and impressionist painters in awe. But now Wagner was the new orthodoxy. He was done with his life, but his legacy, Wagnerism, was everywhere. And to a great degree the flowering of French art a hundred years ago was both a reaction against and a homage paid to the aesthetics of the powerful composer of *Tristan* and *Parsifal*.

Debussy had gone to Bayreuth to see those works. He loved the endlessly shifting harmonies of *Tristan*, and the medieval aura and stained-glass sound of *Parsifal.* But he did not love what he regarded as Wagnerian literalness and overemphasis, and especially not the prolonged and violent expressions of emotion in Wagner's texts. He wanted a text that achieved its ends through understatement and suggestion. How else was his music to convey on the stage the almost intangible impressions his friends were achieving in the other arts?

He longed to find a dramatist who, 'saying things by halves, would allow me to graft my dream onto his ... someone who would conceive characters not bound by time or place, someone who would leave me free to have more art than he, and to complete his work.'

In 1892, soon after Debussy expressed that hope, he found his playwright – a visionary Belgian, Maurice Maeterlinck, thirty years old like himself. Maeterlinck's new play, *Pelléas et Mélisande,* seemed to be exactly what Debussy wanted. It was a fluid succession of short scenes rather than, as with Wagner, three long acts requiring long spans of music. And there was nothing literal or unduly emphatic about this new play. It was a symbolist drama, all nuance and suggestion, set in a kingdom, Allemonde, that was nowhere and everywhere, and in an unspecified century, sometime in the Middle Ages, perhaps, but in effect outside of time, with characters who seemed suspended between willing and acting. And amazingly, the play was replete with the very images – the forest, the castle, the sea, the ship, the moonlight, the girl with the flaxen hair – that haunted the composer.

But there was – and this is not said often enough – a vast difference between the young composer and the young playwright. The fastidious Debussy, with his exquisite sense of irony, would have thought it unspeakably vulgar to explain what his dream images might mean. That would be, as Mallarmé had said, 'to suppress three-quarters of their aesthetic value.' They were not carriers of meaning, those images. They were carriers of feeling.

Maeterlinck, on the other hand, had been educated by Jesuits in the Christian mystics and the Greek classics, and did not hesitate to say, plainly, 'At the heart of my dramas lies the idea of a Christian God together with the ancient concept of Fate.' The old king in his *Pelléas et Mélisande* speaks of God and Fate as if they were interchangeable. At the time Maeterlinck wrote the play, he was deeply imbued with the conviction that human lives were determined by 'tremendous occult forces' which we cannot control – call them Fate or God or some undefined commingling of the two. We cannot understand them. We can only surrender to them. Hence the mysterious atmosphere in the play, and the ambivalent, passive, almost unintelligible statements made, especially, by the heroine.

Maeterlinck later moved from his fatalism to occultism, pantheism, and eventually to a final, fashionable agnosticism. And his literary reputation, after his Nobel Prize in 1911, steadily declined. His fame now rests largely on the play Debussy set to music – music which preserved almost all of the play and, to a great extent, redefined it. For Debussy said nothing about, and possibly cared little for, Maeterlinck's fatalism. He valued the play because its elusive, mysterious qualities presented him with an incomparable opportunity to apply his musical theories to drama.

It was not, he found, an easy task. It took him almost ten years to write *Pelléas*, and for several years after the première in 1902 he was still making changes in it. He wanted every bar to bear the imprint of his new, impressionistic style, to resonate with his own unique sound.

With the opening bars of *Pelléas* we know we are feeling our way into a new musical world. The opera begins in a dark forest, and Debussy sets his scene with a sombre theme built on a rising fifth. Could he have known that in the Middle Ages the rising fifth was the musical synonym for God, that it could serve as a synonym for Maeterlinck's Fate?:

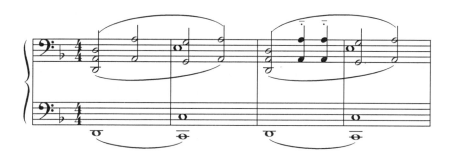

Debussy might object to our calling that theme 'Fate.' He had harsh words for Wagner's system of musical motifs associated with ideas and characters. All the same, he was not unwilling to adapt the contributions of others, including Wagner, when they suited his special purposes. Some the interludes between the scenes of *Pelléas* sound like the Wagner of

Parsifal. And throughout his opera, Debussy limns his characters with recurrent themes, though he does not employ the themes with Wagner's complexity and obsessiveness. Only four bars into the opera, we hear the theme associated with Golaud, a hunter lost in the forest, abandoned by his hounds, in pursuit of a bleeding, wounded beast which has escaped him. (The reminiscence of the opening of Dante's *Inferno* is surely intended.) Wagner would have given this hunter a brusque, violent motif. But Debussy's hunter is the only person in the drama who attempts to define his own destiny, to resist the Fate that envelops him. Debussy gives him a restless, tentative musical fragment that tries to free itself, but cannot, from its grounding in the Fate theme:

With a slight change in instrumentation and tonality, the two themes are repeated – a gentle, somber Fate and a man unable to escape from it. Then, suddenly, there is a gleam of light in the forest. Mélisande appears:

That is the theme, and light is the symbol, that will define Mélisande throughout the opera. Golaud is taken with her instantly. She is beautiful, like a child. She too is lost. She has been hurt. She will not say by whom.

She is weeping by a forest pool. Her crown lies submerged in its waters. She will not let Golaud touch her or retrieve her crown. She will throw herself into the water if he tries. She says he looks like a giant. He cannot stop looking into her eyes, which seem never to close. The innocence that shines out of them will eventually drive him close to madness.

The two introduce themselves: he is the grandson of Arkel, king of Allemonde (that is perhaps to say, of all the world). She is simply Mélisande. She will not answer his other questions. She will go with him if he promises not to touch her. He says he does not know where he is going. He is lost too. And the scene ends.

Debussy sets this scene in a subtle combination of speech and song that clearly owes a debt to Mussorgsky, the composer of *Boris Godunov*. But actually this kind of speech-song is as old in opera as the first operas themselves, those of the Florentine Camerata. And Debussy, with great care, makes his musical line match the inflections of the French language. But the most remarkable feature about the scene is how the images in the text combine with music whose style had been fashioned, a decade before, to depict those very images.

We can take, as another example of this, the scene in which Mélisande, now married to Golaud, has her first glimpse of the castle grounds in Allemonde. 'It's so dark here,' she exclaims. 'So many forests!' Geneviève, the mother of Golaud and his half-brother, Pelléas, quietly agrees: 'I was amazed, too, when I first came here. There are places where you never see the sun. But you get used to it. Look the other way – you'll see the light from the sea.' Yet, when Mélisande looks, the sea is misted over. Pelléas climbs up from the side of the sea and says, without realizing the full import of his words, 'Tonight you could sail out without knowing and never come back.' The three of them watch as, by the beacon from a single lighthouse shining through the mist, the ship that brought Mélisande to Allemonde sails away. We hear the almost ghostly chanting of the crew in the distance. A storm is coming on. Mélisande fears that the ship will be lost at sea. Finally, as Pelléas observes, the night falls quickly.

Pelléas offers to take Mélisande's hand and lead her back to the castle. But her arms are full of flowers. He says, 'Perhaps tomorrow I shall go away.' She says, 'Oh, why must you go?'

Her theme hovers in the air. The final chord is unresolved. It is the perfect expression in music of the ambivalences of the text. Must he go? Will he go? In the nowhere and everywhere that is Allemonde, there are no answers to such questions:

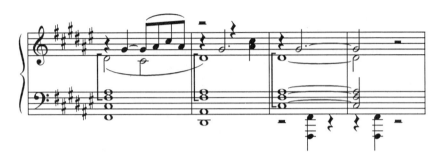

Or take the scene at a well near the castle. For once, the sun is shining, but Pelléas and Mélisande have come to the well for the shade of the trees. A well – if Debussy will permit me just this once to advance an archetypal explanation – suggests the depths of the unconscious. Mélisande exclaims at the translucence of the water. Pelléas tells her that it once had healing properties, and could restore sight to the blind. But now there are no more miracles at the Well of the Blind. The king himself cannot be cured. You can hear the water sleep. Is that to say that the characters in Allemonde have lost touch with their unconscious depths, that they have all to varying degrees surrendered, or must surrender, to the dark, quiet Fate that envelops and controls them?

Mélisande tries to see to the bottom of the well. Pelléas says it is as deep as the sea. She is sure that, if something bright were shining below, one *could* see to the bottom. He cautions her against leaning too far. She might fall. Her hands cannot reach the water's surface, but her long hair does, as she leans forward. In a moment, as he remembers that his brother found her beside a forest pool, she is tossing her wedding ring up to catch the sunlight, and it drops to the water's depths. Tossing the ring in the air over the well, when it might easily fall to the depths, seems, like all of Mélisande's actions, both deliberate and accidental. It might mean that she wants subliminally to abandon her husband for his brother. Or it might mean that she wants to illuminate for all of them the depths of the unconscious they have lost touch with. Or again, it might mean nothing at all. As Mallarmé had said, to explain it would be 'to suppress three-quarters of its aesthetic value.'

'What will we tell Golaud?' she asks.

'La verité,' he responds. 'The truth.' In fact, they will tell Golaud neither truth nor untruth. It is just striking twelve as the ring falls. Later they learn that at that very moment Golaud had been thrown from his horse.

Debussy matches this elusiveness with his inimitable music – all light and shadows, music that suggests but does not insist or assert, music that never rises above a forte. Richard Strauss, the composer of such splendidly noisy operas as *Salome* and *Elektra*, said, when he saw this opera, 'Yes, but I can't *hear* anything!' Henrik Ibsen, the author of such realistic social dramas as *Pillars of Society* and *An Enemy of the People*, said, when he read the text that inspired this opera, 'But what does it *mean?* I simply don't understand this sort of thing!' Both men were artists of the first rank; neither was an impressionist.

In the mid-twentieth century it used to be said that *Pelléas* was an eccentric work without a real place in the history of music, that it was 'freakish,' that it had no successors. Now, at the end of the century, we can see that Debussy's music, profoundly original even in the way it uses some of the techniques of other composers, has itself influenced much of opera right across the twentieth century – from Puccini's *Fanciulla del West* to Poulenc's *Dialogues of the Carmelites* to Messiaen's *St Francis*.

And it has long been clear that Maeterlinck's text, rife with symbols, unanswered questions, and elusive non-sequiturs, influenced the *Salomé* of Oscar Wilde that served as the text for Richard Strauss. It has also prompted orchestral music from such diverse composers as Schönberg, Sibelius, and Fauré. Other plays of Maeterlinck were soon set to music, by Paul Dukas and lesser composers, in the hope of creating another *Pelléas*. Now critics speak of the 'numerous progeny' of *Pélleas et Mélisande* – existentialist drama, the Theatre of the Absurd, and much of the music of the avant-garde.

But there is no question that the text has dated. It can no longer be performed without the music. Even in its day it was fatally easy for the irreverent to caricature, or for critics to expose as a conventional bourgeois situation deliberately, not to say perversely, couched in obscure language and laid over with symbols to give the suggestion of substance. But Debussy thought enough of the text to set it verbatim, cutting, for practical purposes, only four scenes and a few lines here and there. Maeterlinck, who knew nothing about music, had no objection to Debussy's setting till much later, when the opera was in production and he found that his mistress, Georgette Leblanc, was not going to play Mélisande. The director of the Opéra-Comique, Albert Carré, and André Messager, who was to conduct, wanted, and got, the marvellous Mary Garden for the part. (They may both have been romantically involved with her, but she was in any case the artist for the role.)

Maeterlinck, furious, made a scene at Debussy's house, threatening him with physical violence. He even consulted a clairvoyant to find out whether he should challenge Carré to a duel. (He was dissuaded.) He also lodged a formal complaint with the Société des Auteurs, wrote an open letter to *Le Figaro* disowning the opera and expressing his hope that it would be an 'immediate and utter failure,' and had distributed, at the first public dress rehearsal, a satirical attack on the production. All of this led, paradoxically, to an audience reaction against, not the performers, not the music, but the text.

When, eighteen years later, Maeterlinck actually heard the opera, he admitted he had been wrong. Debussy was dead by then. But Maeterlinck wrote to Mary Garden to say that her performance had enabled him at last to understand his own mysterious text and its elusive characters.

And can we, who have never seen Mary Garden's Mélisande, understand her and the other characters in Allemonde? If we limit ourselves to reading Maeterlinck's words, we will never understand them. The enigmatic Mélisande has been thought everything from a *damoiselle élue*, a pre-Raphaelite beauty, a story-book princess, to a *femme fatale*, a schemer, a deliberate destroyer of human happiness. Maeterlinck wrote a later play, *Ariane et Barbe-Bleu*, in which Mélisande is identified as one of Bluebeard's eight wives, escaped at last from his terrible castle. That might be why – Maggie Teyte, a famous Mélisande, insisted it *was* why – Mélisande is first seen weeping, hurt, a fugitive in the forest, unconcerned about the loss of the crown 'he' (that is to say, Bluebeard) gave her.

But that does not explain Mélisande's deviousness when she comes to Allemonde. C.J. Luten has observed that in the course of the opera Mélisande 'tells seventeen unarguable lies,' not counting her many half-truths and evasions. But the real point to be made about Mélisande is that she is not interested in logic and reason. There is no point in them. She knows intuitively that Maeterlinck's world, Allemonde, is ruled, not by logic and reason, but by Fate, that the course of her life there is fixed, no matter what she does. Pelléas feels he should leave it and never come back. Golaud is not sure he should return to it. Geneviève remembers her own adverse reaction when she first came to it. King Arkel has finally surrendered to spending the rest of his days in it.

Mélisande is wiser than any of them. Why are her answers so illogical, her actions so unmotivated? She knows that the world which is all-the-world-according-to-Maeterlinck is dominated by a dark, if quietly pitying, Fate.

The others only realize this in proportion to their ages. Old King Arkel knows it best. His surrender to Fate is all but complete. He cannot under-stand the human condition in which he finds himself, but he feels it deeply: 'Oh, the sadness of it,' he exclaims, 'the sadness of everything one sees.' This from a man who is all but blind.

Arkel's daughter Geneviève is a grandmother, but still young enough to think that Fate can be, if not avoided, at least ignored. 'Look the other way,' she says of the darkness. 'You'll see the light from the sea.' But the sea is shrouded, and a storm threatens the lone ship that ventures forth on it.

Golaud, the heir to the castle, the hunter, the husband, knows less of Fate, and actually tries to resist it. 'I am a man of blood and steel,' he says. He is pragmatic and resourceful. He concerns himself with social condi-tions, with his kingdoms's wars. He begets two children. He always makes the human effort to see the world around him with reason. 'Be reason-able, Mélisande,' he pleads at one touching moment. 'Be reasonable. You're crying because you can't see the sky? You're too old to cry about such a thing.' But the world in which Golaud lives is one where reason plays no role, where all is sense, and even sense is dimmed by mist and darkness. Fate rules. Mélisande unhappily accepts that. Golaud does not. That is why he alone of the characters does reprehensible things, and why he suffers the most. If we cannot feel with Golaud, the opera will be unintelligible to us, and we will not be moved by it. For in the world of Allemonde, Golaud, more than any of the others, is ourselves.

Pelléas, the grandson of King Arkel, is a youth awakening to sexuality, alive to sensual experience, and hardly aware of Fate. He is told often to try to escape from it. But, unaware as he is, he does not know what to do.

There is a fourth generation to this castled family. Yniold, the great-grandson of King Arkel, is a little boy far removed from any awareness of the power which foredestines all the lives in Allemonde. When, in Act IV, he is given his first glimpse of that power, he thinks, with childlike confi-dence, that by telling his elders about it he can forestall it.

And the last little family member, born in the opera's last scene, is the as yet unnamed baby daughter of Mélisande. She knows nothing yet of the power that sadly envelops them all, but the presentiment of sadness is already on her face. The future, we are told, will be no different than the past has been.

Call this view of the world beautiful, poetic, and true, or call it – as it can appear to be when divested of its poetic images – illogical, inane, and intolerable, it was in either case a view of the world that the world at large would long since have dismissed, had Allemonde not been waiting to be etched in Debussy's impressionistic colours, and subtly interpreted by Debussy's music.

Take the scene where Golaud enters with blood on his brow (he has passed through a hedge of thorns looking for the latest of his subjects dead of famine down by the sea). Helpless to stop the workings of Fate, and sure that his wife has been unfaithful to him with his brother, he draws his sword and brutally attacks Mélisande, in the presence of King Arkel. He is, as we said, the one character in the opera who attempts to carve out his own destiny. Where, in this shocking scene, should our sympathies go? Maeterlinck has the old king say, 'If I were God, I would have pity on the hearts of men,' and leaves it at that. But Debussy's orchestra develops, at length and with great poignancy, not Arkel's theme, not Mélisande's, but Golaud's. That savage man is the one God should pity.

In the last scene, after Golaud has killed Pelléas, and Mélisande lies dying after childbirth, his grief is terrible and he tries to convince himself of Mélisande's innocence: 'Isn't it enough to make the stones weep? They kissed like little children, like brother and sister.' Yet he is not sure of their innocence.

He tries, gently, to get the truth from Mélisande. He assures her that, even if she admits she has been unfaithful, he is ready to forgive her. But her answers are, as always, maddeningly elusive. In Allemonde, Maeterlinck's world in which all is foredestined, we never know the truth about ourselves. Golaud, in despair at ever finding out what has really happened, says to the old king, 'I shall never know. I shall die here in blindness.'

Then the sun sets on the sea and Mélisande quietly dies with her infant daughter placed next to her, after Golaud exclaims in a panic, 'Oh, I have to *tell* her something! Leave me alone with her. It wasn't my fault. It wasn't my fault.' A lesser composer would have underlined the pathos with a throbbing orchestra. Maeterlinck would have wanted it that way. (At the time of the première he was sorry he didn't give the rights to Puccini.) But Debussy lets us know that his opera is not so much about the elusiveness of truth as about the reality of impressions, about the wonder of the senses, which for him are the only true source of knowledge.

A distant bell tolls. Golaud's theme is quietly sounded for the last time, penitent and humbled. And then we get the ending that, as Maeterlinck eventually came to see, was the perfect ending for his drama: Maeterlinck's old king says, in the last and tenderest of his monologues, 'Don't stay here, Golaud. She needs silence now. It is terrible, but it is not your fault. She was a poor little creature, mysterious, like everyone in the world. She lies there as if she were the older sister of her child. Come, the child mustn't stay in this room. It must live now in her place. It is the turn of the poor little one.' And how does Debussy match this poignancy, as the twilight from the sea comes through the castle window? With a slowly descending melody, a gently tolling bell, and a muted trumpet depicting Mélisande's soul in flight. It is a final statement, not just of pity (with Maeterlinck) for the death of one who accepted her fate without question, but of wonder (with Debussy) at the sheer beauty of the world in which she lived her predestined life – the beauty of the world of images that impinge on our senses.

Not everyone, certainly not a professional Christian like myself, can respond to Maeterlinck's notion of Fate inexorably directing human lives and making all human action pitiable and futile. But everyone who has five senses can respond to Debussy's evocation of what it is to be alive to the wonder and the pathos of the world in which we all live.

The king submits, as always, to Maeterlinck's pessimism: death is the ending to a life of incomprehensible sadness, determined by a Fate we cannot control; the newborn baby will have to weep the same tears her mother wept. But in Debussy's ineffable music, half requiem, half lullaby – half for the mother, half for the child – there is more than merely sensuous beauty. There is a suggestion of transcendence of both pain and of purposelessness: there may be a realm beyond Allemonde of which the senses here give us only impressions.

There *may* be. That is the way with impressionist paintings, with symbolist poems, and with this opera. Beauty, if we can sense it, is all around us. But what truth is, what the meaning of life is – of that the wonderful music of Claude Debussy can only give impressions.

It Is Your Turn to Speak
Dialogues des Carmélites

My year in the novitiate was perhaps the happiest of my life. My novice master, who had seen Caruso sing and could detect the outlines of operatic arias in bird songs, seemed to me the oldest, gentlest, and wisest man in the world. I lived and prayed with twelve other novices who were close to me in age and shared my hopes and dreams. We read Shakespeare and studied Greek and Latin to keep our young minds busy, for we were going to be teachers one day. But it wasn't, primarily, a year of study. It was a life of close community. We learned to pray and to live with one another. We expanded the arable land behind the novitiate to twice its size, planted crops and tended them. We played a lot of baseball. We sang. We also observed long periods of silence, and when we spoke we often spoke about God.

It was a happy year because, though I was only seventeen, I knew what I was going to be doing with the rest of my life. I had consecrated that life. Every day had meaning. Though we didn't take any vows till the year was over, we were poor, chaste, and obedient. We were – or at least I was – almost unbelievably happy. I can remember saying, 'I think I might die for happiness,' and one of my fellow novices said, not just that he knew what I meant, but that he felt the same way. Another said, 'I don't know why everyone wouldn't want to live like this.'

Something of that innocence and joy, and much more, is communicated in Francis Poulenc's *Dialogues des Carmélites*, the story of another group of religious – sixteen Carmelite nuns whose purpose in life was to pray, who lived closely in community, and who bravely, not to say joyfully, went together to their deaths during the Reign of Terror during the last days of the French Revolution.

'No more living in community,' Poulenc's Carmelites are told when the

Revolution reaches the convent gates. But that blunt ordinance has no real power over the community life Poulenc's heroines lead, or over the dialogues that pass between them, even when they are separated from one another. The dialogues of Poulenc's Carmelites are exchanges of more than words, and they pass across time and space. They are – to use a term rarely if ever associated with the operatic stage but very familiar to Catholic intellectuals in Poulenc's day – exchanges of grace. Georges Bernanos, who wrote the text on which the opera is based, ended his most famous novel with the phrase, 'Everything is grace.'

Dialogues of the Carmelites, to give it its English title, dramatizes an idea that originated early in the history of Eastern Christianity and by the fifth century had worked its way into the creed of the universal church – the *koinonia ton hagion* or, in the West, the *communio sanctorum*. The Communion of Saints. As the idea developed in the West, especially in France, it came to mean that all members of the Church, living and dead, are bound together in a community, in a close-knit personal relationship with one another effected by grace – the share that each has in the life of God and, in specifically Christian terms, in the union of the Father with his Son in the Holy Spirit. Bernanos saw in this doctrine an answer to the greatest questions man has asked: What is God? Why is there evil in the world? Why do the innocent suffer? Have our lives any meaning?

The uncompromising Bernanos was super-patriot who married a girl named Jeanne d'Arc (a direct descendant of one of Joan of Arc's brothers) and had six children by her. He also believed with all his strength that the spiritual was no world apart, but a power that pervaded the natural world. And like the main character in his *Dialogues*, he was haunted all his life by a fear of death. He wrote his novels, plays, and essays out of passionate conviction and in fear.

But the story of the Carmelites of Compiègne goes back before Bernanos. When, on 17 July 1794, sixteen nuns from the Carmelite convent at Compiègne went to their deaths as 'enemies of the people,' one of their community, Mother Marie, was not with them. She had been called away to Paris when the new regime demanded some papers pertaining to her aristocratic family. She thus escaped arrest and, eventually, execution, for only a few days after the other sisters went to the guillotine, Robespierre himself was executed, on the ninth of Thermidor, and the Reign of Terror ended. The sisters were beatified twelve years later. Meanwhile, Mother Marie had kept a diary of the events that led up to their deaths, and this became the first of a series of works that preserved their memory.

Interest in 'the martyrs of Compiègne' revived in the early thirties of the twentieth century, when there were new terrors to face. A young German convert to Catholicism, Gertrud von le Fort, wrote a novella called *Die Letzte am Schafott* (*The Last Woman at the Scaffold*), which told the story of the Carmelites in a new and deeply personal way, grimly prescient of what was soon to happen to innocent people in Germany and across Europe. In the late forties an American, Emmet Lavery, fashioned a play from the German novella, and plans began in France to film the story with a wholly new script. A Dominican priest, Raymond Bruckberger, a popular celebrity in post-war Paris, outlined a scenario for the film, and asked Bernanos, the most prominent of French Catholic writers, to flesh it out with appropriate dialogue.

Bernanos, perhaps inevitably, overwrote. And he turned the proposed script into something of a personal manifesto. He was fifty-nine ('a good time to die,' he has the intuitive Sister Constance say in his text). He had, at the personal request of Charles de Gaulle, returned to France after self-imposed exile in Brazil during the war, and he did not like what he saw. His country's spiritual values, already undermined by the cowardice of those who had collaborated with the Nazis, seemed to be giving way under new waves of materialism and atheism. Bernanos projected his pessimistic view of post-war France, and his own very real fear of dying, onto the story of the Carmelites. His text is sometimes political, religious, and psychologically revealing at the same time.

Dialogue was all he had been asked to write, and *Dialogues of the Carmelites* was the unprepossessing title he gave his contribution to the forthcoming film. But his script was rejected by the film-makers. We don't know all of the ins and outs of the matter. The problem may have been Bernanos's insistent suggestion that his twentieth-century countrymen had, in a time of crisis, valued their lives more than their principles and disgraced the heroism of past generations of French men and women. Or it may have been the severe, not to say abstruse, theological discussions in which he has his Carmelites engage. There has always been criticism of his text. Conrad L. Osborne, an expert on operatic singing and a critic with a usually unerring sense of drama, said, on seeing John Dexter's now famous Met staging, that the arguments in the text were 'mere diddlings over abstractions of death and guilt, often quite sophistical and foolish ... pompous, querulous, and above all unclear.'

Perhaps that was Bruckberger's judgment as well. In any case, he proceeded with a much more straightforward script that was partly his own and partly that of his director, Philippe Agostini. For copyright reasons he had to change the title slightly. He added an article and changed plural to singular; the film was advertised as *Le Dialogue des Carmélites*. It had a brilliant cast – Jeanne Moreau, Alida Valli, Pierre Brasseur, and Jean-Louis Barrault – but it was attacked by the New Wave critics of *Cahiers du Cinéma* as being exactly the kind of empty historical chronicle their Nouvelle Vague was fighting against. (It didn't help that the new script was distinctly anti-republican.) The film sank pretty well without a trace. Today writers on opera will say, mistakenly, that it was never made.

Meanwhile, Bernanos's rejected script was mounted with considerable success as a straight play, and attracted the attention of Poulenc. Not a composer of great gifts, Poulenc had for decades written music best known for its wit and irreverence. He was thought by the smart set in Paris to be something of a clown – an oversized, clumsy man who looked like the leading French comedian of the day, Fernandel, and was something of a musical eclectic. His little piece about Babar the Elephant drew on the traditions of the music hall and the circus. His setting of Apollinaire's surreal, seriocomic *Les Mamelles de Tirésias* owed much to Chabrier and Ravel. Like the classical figure spoofed in that work, he was bisexual. He was subject to terrible depressions during his doomed love affairs. His final opera, the one-act, one-character *La Voix Humaine*, in which a desperate woman is unable to reach her lover by telephone because of crossed lines and wrong numbers, was, as Poulenc himself admitted, 'a musical confession.' No composer was more open. His friends said he was as spontaneous and simple as a child. But at heart he was anxious about many things, perhaps most especially about his faith. 'Blanche,' he once said of the heroine of his *Carmélites*, 'is me.'

Poulenc had abandoned Catholicism when he fell in with Paris's intellectual avant-garde – Eric Satie, Jean Cocteau, the surrealists, the Dadaists. Then, in 1936, a close friend was killed in an auto accident, and the composer went to the shrine of the black virgin of Rocamadour to pray, and to compose his *Litanie à la Vierge Noire*. That was the model for the Mass he eventually wrote in memory of his father, as well as for much other religious music, including the hymns that made their way into his *Carmélites*. By the middle of the century Poulenc needed the faith that the writing of his Carmelite opera gave him. His health was failing and, like Bernanos, he was afraid of death.

His music, too, had fallen from favour. He had no gift for the new atonality. He wrote most of his *Carmélites* in a graceful speech-song that preserved about a third of the Bernanos text, on musical staves without key signatures, as if he were applying the colours of his ever-changing keys to an absolutely clear canvas. He dedicated the finished score to Verdi and Monteverdi, Debussy and Mussorgsky, declaring them the major influences on him. Others have found in his opera further, rather predictable influences – Gregorian chant and the Stravinsky of *Symphony of Psalms* – and a few rather surprising ones – French boulevard tunes and George Gershwin harmonies. Above all, there was the omnipresent influence of Ravel.

The opera's music is stronger, not weaker, for being drawn from these varied sources. 'You must forgive my Carmelites,' Poulenc wrote. 'They can sing only tonal music.' In recent years, as atonality has become less and less the prevailing musical fashion, Poulenc's opera has taken its rightful place on the world's stages. It is in operatic form that the Carmelites of Compiègne have, in the end, spoken to us.

But what do their often mystifying conversations mean? Let us consider in turn each of the five women Poulenc and Bernanos portray in dialogue.

BLANCHE DE LA FORCE is, of the five, the invented character. She is the creation of the author of the German novella, who turned her German surname 'von le Fort' into the French 'de la Force' so as to project herself back into history and place herself among the Carmelites at Compiègne. The aristocratic name 'la Force' means 'strength.' But, ironically, the heroine who bears the name is congenitally weak, blanching so at every suggestion of the unknown that (had Bernanos heard the Second World War oratory of Franklin Roosevelt?) she comes to fear fear itself. Gertrud von le Fort described the heroine less epigrammatically: 'The great title of her family was like a placard she had no right to bear. No one who remembered her little face that paled so easily could call her anything but just Blanche.' Yet for all her fear Blanche has a presentiment, in the first scene of the opera, that her death, when it comes, will be like falling into the sea – fearful at first, and then easy. She sings this to a musical phrase of wide intervals that recurs at pivotal points throughout the score.

Blanche decides to enter the Carmelite convent because she thinks she will be protected there, find some measure of dignity and personal worth, and, when the Revolution comes, not disgrace her family. But the old Prioress who receives her sees instantly to the heart of the problem: 'Great trials await you, my child.'

Blanche answers, 'Why should I fear them, if God gives me the strength?' (In the French, this is, of course, 'If God gives me *la force*.') And the Prioress says, powerfully, 'What God wants to test in you is not your strength (*votre force*), but your weakness (*votre faiblesse*).' This is not 'chop-logic' or 'a reversible truism,' as some commentators have contended. It is part of the statement the opera eventually makes. Blanche will take, for her new name in religion, Sister Blanche of the Agony of Christ, a name that commemorates the moment in the Garden of Olives when Jesus himself went weak and felt fear. It is not as a de la Force, with pride and strength in blood and family title, that Blanche will be tested. While the other sisters will eventually go to their deaths summoned as *citoyennes* by their family names, Blanche, who has been hiding in fear, will go to her death anonymously. Her family name will not be called out. She will go alone, summoned in her weakness to the strength of community.

What gives her the strength to die with the others? We turn to four other Carmelites in dialogue, all of them historical figures.

Mme de Croissy, the OLD PRIORESS, was the grand-niece of Jean-Baptiste Colbert, who directed the mercantile policies of Louis XIV. Her intelligence and aristocratic breeding are immediately apparent in her opening words, where with subtlety and wit she apologizes for not rising from the chair in which she sits. The chair, though imposing, is no emblem of her position of authority in the convent, like the *tabouret* on which someone of her rank had the right to sit while in the presence of the Queen. It is only a necessity provided by her sisters because of her present infirmity. That is to say, its strength only emphasizes her weakness.

Even in her infirmity, the old Prioress strikes us as a strong, self-possessed, utterly committed and thoroughly seasoned *religieuse* – and so it comes as a great shock when, two scenes later, she dies in terror and despair, almost blaspheming, with a vision of Catholic France in disarray. It seems clear that Bernanos intended the old Prioress as a figure for himself. In the novella she is 'still young' when she dies. Bernanos makes her die at fifty-nine – his own age when, in his last year, he wrote his *Dialogues*, fearful for the future of his country.

SISTER CONSTANCE, our next Carmelite, is also high-born. But in the novitiate the aristocratic Constance de Saint-Denis has become only Sister Constance – a typical novice, irrepressibly cheerful, chattering on in the laundry to her fellow novice Blanche about the iron, the flannel, the blowing of noses, the countrified patois of one of the sisters, and how she, from the noble family of Saint-Denis, once danced with the peasants at her brother's wedding, and how they loved her for it. (The peasantry and the aristocracy are the two classes that, Bernanos thought, fearlessly preserved the true traditions of France during the time of Nazi occupation, and would ultimately save it. It was the middle class, the materialistic, god-less bourgeoisie who, he was sure, had betrayed France. While every social level had been represented among the historical sisters of Compiègne, Bernanos has no bourgeois women among his stage Carmelites.)

Constance gets all the best lines of dialogue, including the line the author wrote for himself: 'After all,' Constance says when the old Prioress is nearing death, 'she *is* fifty-nine. That's a good age to die.' Death holds no fear for Constance, just as she has never been afraid of life. 'If I could save the life of our dear Mother,' she says to Blanche, 'I would gladly offer my own life. Let us kneel together, and offer our poor little lives for the life of our Mother.'

'That's childish,' says Blanche.

'No. The thought came to me just now, and I don't think there is any-thing wrong with it. I have always hoped that I would die young.' Then to the wide-intervalled theme that Poulenc uses to underline the most important statements of the dialogues, Constance says, 'God is going to let you and me die together, on the same day. I don't know when. I only know that it is going to happen.'

Blanche refuses to make any such prayer, but Constance seems to know that Blanche will respond to it later. She has an intuitive understanding of the doctrine of the Communion of Saints, in fact an understanding wider and deeper than any theologian has ever suggested. For the child-like Constance, not only can one person, through prayer, touch another person's life. One person can exchange his (or, more to the point, her) death for another's.

Why is it that, though the serene old Prioress dies in terrible fear, the fearful Blanche goes to the guillotine serenely? Is it because, as an ordi-nary interpretation of the doctrine of the Communion of Saints would suggest, the others were praying for her? No, it is much more than that. It is because the old Prioress had already died Blanche's death for her. There was an exchange of deaths. Blanche received the peaceful, fearless death that the old Prioress might have died, because the old Prioress had already suffered through Blanche's frightening, terrible death for her. Blanche chose for her name in religion 'Sister Blanche of the Agony of Christ.' That religious name 'of the agony of Christ,' a commemoration of the time when Jesus himself asked that he not have to die, was the name that, years before, the old Prioress had chosen as well. Their deaths had always been linked.

Can one person heroically die another's death, to save that other from fear? Is such a thing possible? Is it good or even acceptable Christian theology? Bernanos wants us to believe that it is. He forces his Christian listeners to face the logical conclusions of their belief, saying in effect, 'If you really believe that all the people in the Church are in spiritual contact, in communion with one another, that grace passes from soul to soul, and that a prayer said for another really touches that other, then you must logically believe in the ultimate, all but unbelievable exchange of graces. You must believe that one of us can take on the suffering of another, take on his doubts and fears, and give in exchange his own faith and peace. You must believe that one can even die another's death for him. Or for her.'

If this truth has so far been hidden from the wise and the prudent, it has been revealed to little Constance. 'Think of the death of our poor Mother,' she says. 'Who would have thought that she would have so much trouble dying, that she would die so badly? It is as if, when He gave her her death, the good Lord made a mistake. It's like a cloakroom attendant's giving you someone else's coat. Yes, I think her death belonged to someone else. It was a death much too small for her. So small that the sleeves barely reached to her elbows.'

When Blanche reacts incredulously, 'Her death belonged to someone else ... what can that possibly mean?' the orchestra plays, and Constance sings, the broad-intervalled strain that marks the places in the text where Bernanos offers his new reading of one of the oldest teachings of the Church. Constance sings: 'It means that someone else, when the time comes to die, will be surprised to find it is so easy, that it fits so comfortably. We die not for ourselves alone, but for one another, or sometimes even in the place of another. Who knows?'

Who knows indeed if the beautiful doctrine of the Communion of Saints can be pushed so far? The old Prioress believes that it can, when she says to Blanche, 'To ward off danger from you, I would gladly have given my life. Now all I can give you is my death.' Poulenc too believes in these mysterious exchanges of grace, these dialogues that are more than words. In the last scene, when Constance sees Blanche cowering in the crowd, she smiles radiantly but says nothing. In the time-honoured way of opera, the music says what we must know. Poulenc repeats the luminous theme that accompanies all of the opera's intimations of the workings of grace.

Both text and music insist that these mysterious exchanges of grace are the real dialogues of the Carmelites. Consider the fates of the other two women in the story.

MOTHER MARIE OF THE INCARNATION was, historically, the most privileged of all the women in the convent. The natural daughter of the

Prince of Conti, she had royal blood in her veins, and had received an education worthy of her intelligence. Early in the opera, at the death of the old Prioress, she shows every promise of being strong enough to lead the sisters heroically to what she regards as their destined role in history – martyrdom. But she is not chosen to be the new prioress. And though she imposes her absolutist view on the community in the absence of the one chosen, arranging for the sisters to take a vow to die together, she herself is, by no choice of her own, away when the others are arrested. She is left alone at the end to preserve their history in her diary.

The fifth and final Carmelite is the NEW PRIORESS, Mme Lidoine, who, like her predecessor, is referred to by her family name. But unlike her predecessor, her name meant nothing at court. She is a humble peasant woman. (I'll never forget the effect Teresa Stratas made, a few years ago at the Metropolitan Opera, as this new Prioress. Radiating love and happiness, she went, in her opening scene, from sister to sister, clasping hands and speaking words of encouragement. Stratas had spent some time with Mother Teresa, and her characterization was, in body and spirit, a re-enactment of the simple goodness she had found.)

The new Prioress quietly answers the absolutism of Mother Marie: the Carmelites undertake their difficult lives not to be ostentatiously heroic but to pray, to make up for the evil done by others. With a peasant's instinct she sees more deeply than Mother Marie into the meaning of the Communion of Saints. Martyrdom is not something to be sought as a good in itself. It does, however, have its purpose. 'It restores the balance of grace in the world.' It can compensate for human weakness elsewhere.

When the time comes for the sisters to die, with Mother Marie absent, the new Prioress dies her death for her. Given in life a position she did not seek, she calmly accepts in the end a death she did not vow. Grace passes from soul to soul and fills up what is wanting. As Constance suggested, 'Perhaps what we call chance is actually the logic of God.'

The answers to the great questions of life are thus suggested in the dialogues throughout the opera – and they come crowding in overwhelmingly in the final scene. They are fearsome answers that hurtle at us as the guillotine blade drops with shuddering shock. But, like death itself, they are fearsome only at first, and then easy: There is evil in the world because, through our failure to do good, we allow its presence. The innocent suffer because we do not oppose evil. But their suffering lives have meaning because others in need can receive grace from them. And what is God? Grace, which moves freely among all good people and binds them together in community, is the closest understanding we have, in this life, of what God is. We have always defined grace as our share in God's life.

And grace is everything. Blanche says to her father in the opera's first scene, 'There is nothing so small that it does not bear the signature of God, just as all the immensity of Heaven lies in a drop of water.' If evil is only the absence of grace, and grace moves freely everywhere, and our sufferings can make up the balance of grace, why need we fear? The Carmelite saint of modern times, Thérèse of Lisieux, wrote simply, 'What does it matter? Everything is grace.' It was a statement Bernanos remembered.

The Carmelites die to compensate for the weaknesses of France, singing the hymn traditionally sung at the death of members of religious orders, the 'Salve Regina.' (The sisters of Compiègne composed, in a brave affront to their executioners, words of their own to the then-new revolutionary anthem, the Marseillaise, about their mounting joyfully to heaven, where as martyrs they would pray for France. But the anthem, now canonized itself by the Republic, would hardly have worked in the opera.)

As each sister is executed, the strain of the 'Salve Regina' thins out until only the voice of Constance, the last to mount the scaffold, is heard. Then there is utter silence as Constance stops singing, turns, catches sight of Blanche in the crowd, and gives her a radiant look. The orchestra plays one last time the wide-intervalled theme that sounded when Blanche sang, 'It takes your breath away for a moment, then it is easy,' and when Constance sang, 'Someone, when the time comes to die, will be surprised to find it is so easy. We die not for ourselves alone, but for each other, or sometimes even instead of each other.'

No words pass between the two young women, only that radiant musical theme. Constance turns back to the guillotine and resumes the 'Salve Regina.' Her life is cut off in the middle of the last word. Then Blanche, graced by the sacrificial deaths of the others, lifts her voice and moves calmly to her own death. She does not, as is commonly supposed, finish the 'Salve Regina.' She sings instead the last stanza of the great hymn 'Veni Creator':

Glory to God the Father,
and to his Son who rose from the dead,
and to the Spirit, for ages upon ages.

Blanche thereby affirms, not just that there life after death, but that the deaths of the nuns are exchanges of grace in the Communion of Saints wherein all believers, living and dead, are bound together in the life of God himself.

The opera, then, is about more than mere solidarity in the face of fear, though it is certainly about that. The first time I saw *Dialogues of the Carmelites* at the Metropolitan Opera, in mid-winter, I bought a ticket at the top of the highest balcony. I was reading my program, waiting for the opera to begin, when I suddenly noticed, looking down, that the main floor had been vacated. In a moment, an usher said calmly to us up top, row by row, 'Please do not panic. Take your coats and move quietly to the side exits and down to the street.' We did so, and when we emerged into the January cold, we gathered in front of the building and saw the glass-enclosed lobby of the Met – all five floors of it – filled with smoke. A militant group had thrown a tear-gas canister inside the main entrance. We were told to go home, that the smoke had penetrated the auditorium and the performance would have to be cancelled. But very few left. We waited in the bitter cold for almost an hour, and eventually we were re-admitted. The curtain finally rose on John Dexter's opening tableau – sixteen Carmelite nuns lying prostrate on a floor lit to form a cross – and we let out a communal cheer. In our small way, we, audience and performers, had demonstrated something of what Poulenc's music and Bernanos's words are all about. We had refused to panic in the face of threats, and achieved a minor but real triumph of solidarity and togetherness.

The opera is also more than a drama of catharsis, though it is certainly that. I've often taken a cross-town bus after performances of Mozart or Verdi at the Met, and the vehicle has been full to overflowing with opera-goers happily discussing the evening's singers and performance. But after the *Carmelites* – other people have told me the same has been true for them – there is absolute silence on that crowded bus as it makes its way from the Met across Central Park and to the Upper East Side. One time on that bus I was standing next to a girl who had seen the *Carmelites* and was carrying a biography of Lotte Lehmann. I broke the prevailing silence and asked her quietly, 'Do you like Lotte Lehmann?' She responded with a polite 'Yes,' and then said, 'Excuse me. I just can't talk now.'

The opera of Poulenc and Bernanos, more than an affirmation of solidarity, more than a moment of catharsis that stays with you after you leave the theatre, is an avowal that grace passes mysteriously from soul to soul. The truth of this has been demonstrated many times since 1794. Maximilian Kolbe affirmed it when, at Auschwitz, he volunteered to die for another. The other had a wife and family; Kolbe, a priest, had none. The other survived. The forces of evil, on that occasion and for as long as that occasion is remembered, were answered by a movement of grace. One good life touched another. The final work of Bernanos, the all-but-last opera of Poulenc, asks us to believe that such sacrifices are worth making. It asks us, if we cannot believe in a very heroic and demanding theology, at least to help one another, to see others' fears, sufferings, and needs, and to give of ourselves to alleviate them. In this world, one can only defeat evil by doing good.

Has *Dialogues of the Carmelites* any meaning for us as we face the future? Gertrud von le Fort ended her novella – and it is a subtly powerful book, well worth reading – with the narrator telling the reader, 'And now, my friend, it is your turn to speak! It is your turn.'

The dialogues continue.

21

An Opera Made of Songs
Porgy and Bess

I've often thought that the reason why George Gershwin's opera *Porgy and Bess* is still unappreciated in some critical circles is that some critical circles have too little appreciation of the golden age of American popular song.

The classic American popular song was born on 24 August 1914, when Julia Sanderson first sang Jerome Kern's 'They Didn't Believe Me,' to a lyric by Herbert Reynolds, on Broadway. By the time Julie Andrews sang Lerner and Loewe's charming 'What Do the Simple Folk Do?' with Richard Burton in *Camelot* in 1960, the popular song in America, apart from a few scattered numbers in increasingly few Broadway shows, was in irreversible decline. Its lifespan was about fifty years.

'They Didn't Believe Me' was written in the thirty-two-bar format that had marked American song for decades, and would for decades more. But it artfully changed the traditional AABA structure (A and B designating contrasting eight-bar musical sections) to something resembling ABAA', and it held its graceful melody to a span of no more than an octave. It thus broke, on the one hand, with earlier American traditions represented by the AABA songs of Stephen Foster and, on the other, with the operetta tradition, imported from Europe, that reached two octaves or more for high B-flats at emotional climaxes (and was still to yield more *New Moon*s and *Rose Marie*s on Broadway).

'They Didn't Believe Me' was written to be interpolated into the New York production of a London musical called, improbably enough, *The Girl from Utah*. It is difficult now to determine what the song did to advance the show's plot (about a girl who fled to London to escape marriage to a Mormon polygamist), or what it did to delineate the characters (though in the lyric the girl resolutely tells the boy she falls in love with in

London, 'I'm certainly going to tell them / That you're the man whose wife one day I'll be'). What the song *did* do was convey its very real emotion, not with the extravagance of operetta, but in a quiet conversational style in which, almost paradoxically, emotion is rendered more, not less, real. Its modest thirty-two-bar format allowed Julia Sanderson to make a statement and comment on it with the intimacy of a confession. Its little 'change from major to minor' (to quote from a subsequent Cole Porter lyric) in bars thirteen to sixteen was genuinely moving precisely because the scale was so small.

We are told that the night 'They Didn't Believe Me' was first sung on Broadway the charmed audience joined in at the final reprise. It was a song touched with real feeling, written with sophistication, and yet it was something anyone could sing. (Possibly that is why the critics chose at first to ignore it.) 'They Didn't Believe Me' was content with and confident about the potential for dramatic expressiveness in the small compass of the American popular song. It had no need for the larger scale of Victor Herbert, though that dean of Broadway operetta was perceptive enough to see what the new song was doing. 'This man will inherit my mantle,' he said of Kern. (Ten years later Kern met Oscar Hammerstein II, the man who would write the lyrics for his greatest score, at Victor Herbert's funeral service.)

In the more than eighty years that have passed since 1914, crooners and jazz improvisers have had their often too-free way with Kern's 'They Didn't Believe Me,' but they have not diminished its effectiveness. When it is rendered simply and directly by an expressive voice – say, the voice of Joan Morris – to an orchestration that preserves its original harmonies, it can still convey radiant feeling with startling immediacy.

Even simpler and more moving, if sung as its composer intended, is a deceptively modest 1924 song not written for a show (but often included in revues), Irving Berlin's 'What'll I Do.' Its lyric, poised half-way between resignation and despair, repeating the title at the end of every eight-bar section except the bridge, is simplicity itself. Its structure – AAA'A, with the almost mandatory thirty-two bars – is even less complicated than that of 'They Didn't Believe Me.' It rhymes 'do' with 'you' and 'blue.' Its pensive waltz tune might have been composed by a child, the only complication being its use of the first eight bars a fourth higher as the 'bridge' at the song's half-way point. But Berlin, for all his lack of pretentions, was no child. He knew how to express feeling in an eight-bar melody (this one so poignant that performers invariably hesitate over its cadences), how to heighten the tension by repeating the eight bars with slightly darker words, how to intensify the mood simply by lifting his melody that major fourth for the song's bridge, and how to find a kind of resolution at the end by returning the melody intact to its original key. The emotional effect conveyed in 'What'll I Do' is out of all proportion to the means used.

(It seems to me that I used those words earlier about Gluck's operatic reform, about his return to the simplest and truest musical expressivity for operatic purposes. Gluck, relatively uneducated musically, was able nonetheless to draw on a century of Italian and French classical styles to achieve his aims; Berlin, unable even to read music, had within his reach only the café music his struggling parents remembered from Central Europe and, closer to home, indigenous American musical styles, notably blues and jazz. Yet Berlin's distillation of past traditions in 'What'll I Do' is as artful in its small way as is Gluck's paring away of baroque ornament in his *Orfeo*.)

Surpassing both the Kern and the Berlin songs in compressed emotional power is Richard Rodgers's still relatively uncomplicated 'Spring Is Here,' written to a lyric by Lorenz Hart for *I Married an Angel* in 1938. Though the deft, perennially unhappy lyricist penned a number of frothy verses for the rest of the show, he expressed something of his own disillusionment, not to say bitterness, in the words of this one song.

As for Rodgers, his songs had a way of releasing the power latent in a lyric by setting the important lines to an upwardly moving scale. (The ascending melody at the end of 1937's 'Where or When,' rising one interval of the major scale with each successive bar, is a case in point: nowhere in music is the surprise attendant on an experience of déjà vu more memorably suggested.) Rodgers's music for 'Spring Is Here' is an ingenious ABAB' thirty-two-bar structure in which the emotional payoff comes when the two rising scales of the first B section (accompanying Hart's words 'No desire, no ambition leads me / Maybe it's because nobody needs me') are compressed at the end into a single rising scale to accompany the words 'Maybe it's because nobody loves me.' There the underlying harmony opens up the rising melody like dew opening a flower. The rueful effect, when the song is sensitively performed, is shattering. So is the unexpected ending, when the song turns in on itself (one feels it is the only thing the song can do) and the singer exclaims, 'Spring is here, I hear.'

Rodgers's songs were not necessarily better when he began to work with Oscar Hammerstein II, but they were unfailingly designed for the shows they wrote together, furthering plot and delineating character without losing the distinctive qualities that had made the Broadway song so quietly compelling. Rodgers's songs with Hammerstein observe the (usually AABA) thirty-two-bar format until some dramatic necessity requires that they burst its bonds. In 'If I Loved You,' one of the great songs from *Carousel* (1945), the repressed heroine, who insists that she does not love the bullying hero (she sees the danger in him that he cannot come to terms with), imagines what it would be like to be in love with him. As she sings, her imagination takes her past her inarticulateness, fear, and longing (Rodgers uses descending scales for those) to the point where 'in the mist of day' he would leave her, 'never, never to never know' ... what? At that point the thirty-two bars are up. But the words are not, and the melody has reached a harmonic impasse. The heroine is compelled to push beyond the framework of the song two more bars to a poignant high note in which, though the language is still mere supposition, she all but admits that she does love the man she claims not to. Then she realizes she has said too much. In two closing measures she quietly returns to her opening statement, to say, in effect, that the things she has just sung about would happen only 'if I loved you.' Nonetheless, she is thereafter utterly changed.

Such songs (we have spoken of one from each of the four decades from 1914 to 1945) can be written off as sentimental only by a listener unattuned to their strengths. Paul Griffiths has noted that Kurt Weill, in *Mahagonny*, 'used American popular music in a critical sense, as a degraded language.' But *Mahagonny* was one of Weill's earlier tantrums. He tried thereafter to write something worthy of Kern and the others, and succeeded, a few times and late in his career, with 'September Song,' 'Speak Low,' and 'My Ship.' (It might be observed that three songs do not a songwriter make, but then Weill had other talents.)

There is much more to be said about the underappreciated strengths of more complex American songs with wider vocal ranges – Kern's interestingly chromatic 'The Touch of Your Hand' and 'All the Things You Are' for Broadway, Porter's beguine-tortured 'In the Still of the Night' and 'I Concentrate on You' for the movies, and those creations of Harold Arlen, 'Blues in the Night' and 'Come Rain or Come Shine,' that simply transcend their original venues. Much too could be said about the theatrical effect of the Broadway songs that developed plot (Leonard Bernstein's for *West Side Story*), established character (Frederick Loewe's for *My Fair Lady*), supplied the required ambience (Frank Loesser's for *Guys and Dolls*), and did everything but paint the scenery (Richard Rodgers's for *Oklahoma!*). But where, to return to the concerns this book, does opera come in?

The American popular song reached its most expressive state in the decades when it was becoming increasingly clear that American opera was not going to develop from the European-style *Mona*s and *Merry Mount*s the Met expensively produced and nobody wanted to hear. Hopes began to run high that an indigenous operatic tradition would spring out of the new Rodgers and Hammerstein 'musical play' in which story, music, and dance conspired together. But when the team's stylized and ambitious *Allegro* failed, they settled for a decade into a less arduous mode (often venturesome in subject matter) that ended with *The Sound of Music*. Some of Rodgers's songs for this all-time money-maker were interesting, but on the whole his music seemed heading into a Ruritania that popular song had long since outgrown. The end was near. It was 1959.

Since then the repertories of German opera houses have never been without their American musicals – *Kiss Me, Kate, Annie Get Your Gun, Fiddler on the Roof* – but no American opera worthy of the name.

There are, however, two earlier Broadway scores that are worthy of the operatic stages of the world. There is, first, the Mississippi opera without which we might never have had the other pieces – the 1927 Kern-Hammerstein *Show Boat*, with a score of almost Wagnerian length, replete with at least two dozen accomplished songs (including six of the greatest ever written), and with a book that was the first Broadway attempt to tell with music a story of some depth and complexity. *Show Boat* ought to be in the repertory of every American opera house. But it has never had an official script or score, and until the recent recording by John McGlinn it has never been given the scholarly attention it has deserved and needed.

A small but telling vignette: I once saw *Show Boat* produced by one of Germany's middling opera companies. It was savaged, spoofed, and tricked up with orchestrations appropriate to a Broadway sixty years later than its period. When I asked a local doyen for an explanation, he replied, 'Well, we had to do something. It's not as good as *Hello Dolly!*'

What few impresarios seem to realize is that *Show Boat*, unlike its predecessors on Broadway and unlike most of the *Hello Dolly*s that followed it, is *about* something. It was the first musical built around an idea: individual lives come, in the end, to nothing; the forces of nature, silently omniscient, go on forever. *Show Boat* is also a compendium of American song styles from the 1880s to the 1920s, and of the performing traditions – melodrama, minstrel, negro spiritual, ballad singing, vaudeville, ragtime, jazz – in which the songs were written. The constant in all of this diversity is Kern's own pioneering style, grown from the days of 'They Didn't Believe Me' to an artful, kaleidoscopic blend of indigenous American elements with Viennese operetta and with his own patented conversational idiom.

Show Boat also dared to dramatize on the American stage something of the racial inequalities that had for more than a century been part of the fabric of American life. Its 'miscegenation scene' was, in 1927, more powerful than anyone could gather from any of the *Show Boat* films (Universal's in 1929 and 1936, and MGM's in 1951) or from subsequent stage revivals, where the scene's framing chorale 'Mis'ry's Comin' Aroun'' was either reduced to background status or completely deleted. Deleted too in subsequent versions was *Show Boat*'s very first word: the curtain originally went up to the deliberately shocking lines, 'Niggers all work on de Mississippi / Niggers all work while de white folks play.' That first word has not been sung on the stage since, despite its general acceptance today in the works of Mark Twain and Joseph Conrad. It still needs to be said that Oscar Hammerstein, who was later to write the lyric 'You've got to be taught to hate' in *South Pacific*, was not a bigot, and may in fact have been the first Broadway lyricist to use dialect to dignify, not to caricature, black people – in *Show Boat*.

The plight of American blacks, one of the great American stories, cried out for music, for more music even than Jerome Kern had given it in 'Ol' Man River.' And that brings us, at long last, to George Gershwin's *Porgy and Bess*. Long regarded as a misguided enterprise by an overambitious songwriter, it was in most respects a failure at its New York première on Broadway in 1935. And though it has since gone from strength to strength, it has still to find, not just the critical acceptance it deserves, but its proper place in the world's opera houses. The morning-after reviews of its première at Glyndebourne in 1986 told with some astonishment how the English festival's well-heeled, traditionally reserved patrons found themselves, by the end of the evening, standing and cheering, with tears streaming down their faces. *Porgy* had triumphed once more in what might have been thought the most unlikely of places. It was a repetition of what had happened many times across some thirty years, at La Scala and the Bolshoi and other houses, but somehow it is always news when *Porgy* succeeds.

The two most durable and pernicious charges levelled against *Porgy* are, first, that it deals in demeaning racial stereotypes (the very idea of a Jewish composer in Manhattan's wealthy Upper East Side writing an opera about underprivileged Carolina blacks has seemed to some pre-

sumptuous) and, second, that it is musically gauche, with ineffective recitatives, stop-and-go connective passages, and melodic peaks which are
little more than overextended popular songs.

It seems to me that Gershwin himself has provided the best answer to
these criticisms, not in the oft-quoted statement made in the *New York
Times* after the Broadway opening (*Porgy* had to be seen as a 'folk opera'),
but in a remark made to the *Herald Tribune* in the midst of composition:
'If I am successful [*Porgy*] will resemble a combination of the drama and
romance of *Carmen* and the beauty of *Meistersinger*, if you can imagine
that.'

Perhaps it is not quite a matter of *Porgy* having *Carmen*'s 'drama and
romance' – though I am a hundred times more touched by Porgy's loss of
Bess than I am by Don José's lament for his 'Carmen adorée.' The point
about *Porgy* vis-à-vis *Carmen* is that neither opera 'deals in demeaning
stereotypes.' A Jewish immigrant's son's depiction of black people gambling and brawling, working and praying need not be, and in the event
is not, any more condescending and offensive than is the middle-class
French composer's depiction of Spanish gypsies gambling and brawling,
working and – well, not quite praying.

When I first saw *Porgy* in what might be thought an unlikely place,
Essen, in a foreign language, German, with a quintet of American blacks
in the lead roles and a chorus of Ruhr Rhinelanders (Gosh, and we'd
fought a war against them!) performing with the Americans, and in black
face, I was more moved by it than at any time before or since. I saw – with
the perspective provided by new degrees of both detachment and involve-
ment – that Gershwin's opera no more dealt in stereotypes than did
Carmen or *Cavalleria Rusticana* or *Boris Godunov* or *Wozzeck*. More than
that, the composer's love for his characters was writ large all over his
opera, and that love was unfailingly communicated to me. What did it
matter that the characters were black and I was white, any more than that
they were fervent Protestants and I a professional Catholic, or that they
were miserably poor and I had money enough to be teaching in Europe?
Nothing mattered except that they were people with a depth of feeling I
felt privileged to be part of. That emotional communication is what opera
is all about, and Gershwin knew it.

Porgy, Gershwin promised, would also be like *Die Meistersinger*. Perhaps,
once again, it is not quite a matter of its having the 'beauty' of *Die Meistersinger* – though both operas express their sense of the community of
human lives in radiant choral outpourings. It is certainly not a matter of
Porgy, which can be improved by cutting, having anything like *Die Meister-*

singer's unsurpassed architectonic splendours. No, in the face of the persistent criticism of Gershwin's work, the point about *Porgy* vis-à-vis *Die Meistersinger* is that neither has 'ineffective recitatives, stop-and-go connective passages, and melodic peaks which are little more than overextended popular songs.' The recitatives in both are quickened by leitmotivic fragments (those in *Porgy* still not adequately perceived), and the transitions in both are skilfully managed (those in *Porgy* still ineptly handled in most stagings). Most important of all, both are replete with recurrent songs that carry the weight of the drama.

Walther's Prize Song, reprised many times in *Die Meistersinger*, gathers associations with every repetition, so that by the end it has come to mean almost everything the opera itself means. And it is much the same with the songs in *Porgy*. The most famous of them, 'Summertime,' a lullaby that always presages violence to come, is reprised three times, always ironically – during the crap game that ends in the death of Serena's husband ('there's a-nuttin' can harm you'); during the hurricane that ends with the deaths of the baby's father and mother ('with Daddy an' Mammy standin' by'); and by Bess to the orphaned baby immediately before Porgy kills Crown and she is lured away in despair to a place where 'the livin' is easy.' The song's lulling vision of a world at peace is contradicted at every turn by the events we witness in Catfish Row.

Lawrence Starr, in an indispensible article in the journal *American Music*, points out some of this and much more about 'Summertime,' and adds that it is high time we reconsider the givens of *Porgy* criticism.

It can be said – and I'd like to say it here – that the songs of *Porgy and Bess* do all of the things the best American popular songs do, and do them supremely well. Though almost all of them observe the familiar AABA structure, they consistently, for dramatic puposes, burst the bonds of the thirty-two-bar format. They are fine melodies in themselves, ingeniously harmonized and (this makes *Porgy* unique among the musicals I have spoken about) orchestrated with great skill by their composer. But the strength of the songs lies in their dramatic effectiveness, their sympathetic understanding of the characters for whom they are written, and their direct communication of emotion through the relatively small-scaled, intimate forms they share with 'They Didn't Believe Me' – the song that first turned the admiring sixteen-year-old Gershwin toward composing.

Is *Porgy* the best score ever composed for Broadway? It seems quite possible that it is, but ever since its composer made that statement to the press about it being a 'folk opera,' *Porgy* has been thought, in the

Broadway musical sweepstakes, to be *hors de combat*. Musical or opera, Gershwin's score is challenged, in this listener's opinion, only by Kern's for *Show Boat*, by Porter's for *Kiss Me, Kate* (with its witty quasi-Shakespearian pieces), perhaps by Loewe's for *Camelot* (but when I told them in 1960 that it might be the last substantial Broadway musical they didn't believe me), and certainly by Rodgers's for *Carousel*. But more than any of these, it is *Porgy* that makes human drama out of lovingly delineated three-dimensional characters, and it is *Porgy* in which wonderful songs conspire with everything else to make an opera.

Is there a future for indigenous American opera? Perhaps our new composers will be able to learn from the forerunner who took his inspiration from his country's songwriters as well as from the composers of *Carmen* and *Die Meistersinger*.

22

The Music Wrote Itself

Oklahoma!

When *Oklahoma!* first blossomed on Broadway in 1943, the adjective invariably applied to it was 'fresh.' It was many other things, too, but what most came at you from the stage of the St. James Theater, or almost minute-to-minute over the radio, or from the piano in virtually any living room that had one, was a freshness best described by librettist Oscar Hammerstein II himself, when he wrote that the wavin' wheat could sure smell sweet when the wind came right behind the rain.

We were in the thick of the Second World War then, and it was becoming increasingly clear that the fighting wasn't going to be over as soon as we'd thought. We were going to be Johnny Doughboy at the front and Rosie the Riveter on the home front for the foreseeable future. Everyone was caught up in the war effort – and that meant that when we at home looked for music and drama the plays would be *Watch on the Rhine*, the movies *Behind the Rising Sun*, and the popular songs, even the good ones like 'You'll Never Know' and 'As Time Goes By,' would, regardless of their creators' intentions, be weighted with wartime sentiments. That there would be no *Meistersinger* or *Madama Butterfly* at the Met and next to no Wagner at the Philharmonic. And that we shouldn't complain about it. 'What's the matter? Don't you know there's a war on?'

And then came *Oklahoma!* 'Fresh' was the word. Rain showers in virtually every song. A bright golden haze. The red sun setting, the blue moon shining, the stars breaking through, the starlight looking swell on us. Scurrying chicks and ducks, a little brown maverick winking her eye, a lark waking up in the meadow, a hawk making lazy circles in the sky. Shutters and eyes-in-glass windows and velveteen settees. June bugs zooming and honey bees cajoling. Instantly quotable lines like 'All the cattle are standin' like statues' and (perhaps the most famous line ever written for a

Broadway musical) 'The corn is as high as a elephant's eye.' And all of it set to instantly memorable Richard Rodgers music. It was frankly escapist (even the inescapable fact that corn doesn't and never has grown high in Oklahoma), but it probably did more for morale than all the less truthful propaganda pieces put together. Oscar Hammerstein, the librettist of *Show Boat*, had seen to it that *Oklahoma!* would also be built around an idea – the idea that people who really loved the land they lived close to could overcome their differences and build together a new world: 'Soon be livin' in a brand new state.'

The war was hardly over when the word for *Oklahoma!* was no longer 'fresh' but 'landmark.' It became the longest-running musical Broadway had ever seen, and the first to reach, along with Britain and Australia and South Africa and Japan, virtually all of the musical capitals of continental Europe. It was the first American musical to have four companies running simultaneously, the first to have an original cast album of virtually the entire score. Even though it had given free performances for soldiers at home and abroad, it had still piled up grosses big enough to pay off the national debt. And all of the stories that were told of its troubled birthing – that Rodgers had been devastated at the departure of his former partner Lorenz Hart; that Hammerstein, even with the help of Jerome Kern, hadn't had a hit in years; that both Hart and Kern had said that the new show wouldn't work; that the Theater Guild which produced it was on the brink of bankruptcy; that both composer and librettist had to make the rounds of the Park Avenue penthouses, hat in hand, singing the songs and pleading for money; that MGM, who owned the rights to the original play, refused to make a small investment in the musical in return for 50 per cent of the profits – all of those stories are true. Broadway scuttlebut predicted disaster.

But there was no stopping a show with a score that gave the Coldstream Guards a whole armload of tunes for Buckingham Palace parades, a show with a set of lyrics that gave Columbia University's Gilbert Highet a twentieth-century example of the pastoral tradition, a show with a ballet that conspired with the story and the songs so effectively it sent historians of drama back to the seventeenth century to find an equivalent, and a show that, to MGM's chagrin, paid back a 2500 per cent return to its investors.

More than that, in 1943 *Oklahoma!* was a celebration of the confident spirit that was to make the United States, somewhat to its own surprise, a post-war superpower. Its message (and I use the word advisedly) was that the best things in life were ready to hand for those who were confident, generous, and hard-working enough to reach out for them. It was the first chapter in the Rodgers and Hammerstein gospel of the common man, developed further in *Carousel, South Pacific, The King and I,* and *The Sound of Music.*

But times have changed. What is *Oklahoma!* today? Most of its innovations have long since been assimilated into diverse Broadway styles, while other effective elements – the integration of book and music, the psychologizing ballet, the calculated suspension on the penultimate syllable of a song – have, for better or worse, been discarded by modern practitioners of the musical. As Rodgers and Hammerstein went on to write their later works, as *Oklahoma!* itself pointed up the pioneering features in such earlier pieces as Kern's *Show Boat*, Gershwin's *Porgy and Bess*, and Rodgers's own *Pal Joey*, one heard the word 'landmark' less and less. And when the cozy optimism of the post-war years was blasted away by the war in Vietnam, when the Rodgers and Hammerstein formula was attacked head-on by top-forty rock music and unsentimental Sondheimian music theatre, when the public began to favour high-tech megabuck Andrew Lloyd Webber enterprises, *Oklahoma!* came to seem as much a period piece as *Pinafore* or *The Merry Widow,* and in some respects less vital than they. Has it any right to a place on the operatic stage today?

The answer of course is yes, not least because American opera has something to learn from *Oklahoma!,* something that it might have learned in the forties, except that tuneless Sprechgesang was then the norm for new operas. But now that the twelve-tone and other twentieth-century systems have pretty well spun themselves out, now that our operatic fare reaches from Cavalli to Cage, from Gagliano to Glass (and people in the theatre are able to adjust their sights accordingly), it is not too much to hope that the staging by opera companies of pieces like *Oklahoma!* might teach fledgling American composers to make singing once again the primary means of dramatic expression, to write once again for the voice without abusing or exploiting it, to use melody to depict a character and advance a plot.

It would be easy to point out the abiding strengths of *Oklahoma!,* but any audience with its sights properly adjusted can spot them quickly enough. I'd like simply to point out some of the charming subtleties in the fifty-five-year-old musical's still popular songs – points I haven't seen made before.

'Kansas City'   In his previous collaboration with Lorenz Hart, Rodgers's ace card had been the straightforward but powerful use of the rising scale

– 'Where or When' and 'Spring Is Here' are superb examples: a complex emotional effect is achieved at the climaxes of those songs by recourse to the most elementary of musical means, an upward-moving major scale. The musical climax of the comic 'Kansas City' expects us to remember this. Rodgers, as if to mark the change in musical style he wisely adopted when he shifted from the mordantly urbane Hart to the earthier Hammerstein, parodied his best effect of the past: he had the least sophisticated member of the cast use a rising scale to exclaim, with growing excitement, that in Kansas City 'you can walk to privvies in the rain and never wet your feet.' Humility (the composer's) has seldom been so endearing.

'Pore Jud Is Daid'   When the hero invites the unsavoury, self-pitying villain to consider how, if he were dead, people might like him at last, and the villain gets a verse of his own and sings in parallel thirds with the hero (shades of 'Mira, O Norma'!), the ironic little song sets the tone for all the best subsequent 'wondering numbers' on Broadway – Eliza and the sweeps thinking how loverly it would be to be swells, King Arthur and Queen Guenevere wondering what simple folk do and hopefully dancing the hornpipe, Petruchio remembering the bachelor life that late he led, *und so weiter.*

'Oklahoma!'   When the Staatsoper in what was then East Berlin did an operatic version of *Lysistrata*, the chorus members knelt on one knee along the footlights, arms extended, and belted out an up-tempo version of one of the surviving fragments of ancient Greek music, with weird rising phrases from the sopranos. Somebody behind the Iron Curtain had clearly remembered the show-stopping title song of *Oklahoma!*, with its line-'em-up-at-the-footlights chorus, its imitation choo-choo-train reprise for the men, and its remarkable mounting chromatic phrases for the women. Just the thing for updating Aristophanes.

'People Will Say We're in Love'   The hit song in the show is actually thirty-two bars of piquant banter between amiably malicious lovers. Hammerstein seems to have remembered the amoebean verses of Horace's odes and the 'proviso scene' in Congreve's *The Way of the World.* Rodgers, not to be outdone, remembered a phrase from the song's introductory verse, 'Why do the neighbors gossip all day?' and decked each of the first three lines of Hammerstein's quatrains with that 'gossiping neighbors' motif. Seldom has a composer so deliciously undercut the expansiveness of his own melody. Seldom has romantic love been so conscious of itself. And the public at large had never heard anything like it before. As the songs from *Oklahoma!* took over the pop charts from the early summer of 1943 clear through to the spring of 1944, the ever-fresh 'People Will Say We're in Love' stayed on the radio Hit Parade for a full thirty weeks – a record never surpassed. It was a triumphant vindication of popular taste.

'Many a New Day' The verse to this song is the unsung glory of the score. It is recitative poised on the brink of song. Rodgers once said, apropos of the even more accomplished 'Twin Soliloquies' in *South Pacific,* 'Don't tell Kurt Weill, but when the script calls for recitative I write melody.' (I often wish, when listening to Weill, that someone *had* told him.)

'All er Nothin'' and 'I Caint Say No' Although Hammerstein was indebted to Lynn Riggs's original play for some of the best things in his lyrics, the whole of *Oklahoma!*'s subplot is his own invention, and these delightfully not-so-dumb songs do exactly what subplot material should do – cast the main subject in relief. (Set 'All er Nothin'' next to 'People Will Say' and 'I Caint Say No' next to 'Many a New Day' and the personalities of all four characters in song light up.) The lyrics to the two subplot-songs tapped a whole new vein in the citified Rodgers – he was in the barnyard for the first time, and just as enthusiastic and uncondescending about his cowboy and farm girl as another composer was about his Papageno and Papagena.

'The Surrey with the Fringe on Top' A single clip-clopping rhythm forms the basis for every line of this song, and continues for three sets of thirty-two-bar lyrics, a bridge, and a little coda, without ever wearing out its welcome. And, in the patented Rodgers and Hammerstein tradition, when the music stops the two lovers are not quite the same people they were when it started. That happens in Mozart too. And if Rodgers was more modest in his means and, like others in his profession, chose not to do his own orchestrations, he had nonetheless a Mozartian sense of how to craft a song and make it work dramatically. Musical-comedy music is not, as some tend to think, made with less art than serious music. 'It's worth keeping this in mind,' wrote David Hamilton apropos of a Viennese waltz, 'not so that we will treat light music more solemnly, but so that we should widen our perceptions, and not miss any of its special distinctions.'

'Out of My Dreams' Speaking of Viennese waltzes, is it ridiculous for an

Indian-territory farm girl to sing one as she voices desires and fears she only half understands? Rodgers, America's best composer of waltzes, didn't think that it was – and central Europeans, hearing 'Out of My Dreams' every day as theme music on the post-war GI network, thought that what they were hearing actually *was* a Viennese waltz. What's more, Agnes De Mille, who choreographed the show, didn't think the Viennese element out of place either. She had the waltz song lead directly into a famous Freudian ballet. The heroine's half-understood desires came frighteningly out of her dreams and played themselves out on stage. Fearful fantasies do not surface only at number 19 Berggasse.

'Oh, What a Beautiful Morning'   Isn't the bluesy note that accompanies the syllable 'morn' all wrong for the show, and especially wrong for the first line in the first refrain of the first song in the show? No, not wrong. Deliciously daring. That bluesy wrong note, more even than Hammerstein's marvellously evocative words, really made the song sing. Two days after the opening, Rodgers heard kids trying it out on the sidewalks of New York. He always claimed that, given a good lyric, he could write a song almost in the time it took to play it. With 'Oh, What a Beautiful Morning,' he recalled, 'I just put the lyric on the piano and the music wrote itself.' (What wrote itself was a waltz, of course.)

And is it right for a curly-headed cowpuncher to contemplate the bright golden haze on the meadow in a Rodgers waltz? You bet your sombrero and chaps it is!

23

HURRY UP PLEASE ITS TIME

Our century is hurrying to its end, and anyone who has lived through even a small part of it is likely now to wonder what it has meant, where we are headed, and what will speak for us after we are gone. He might also wonder, if he has any interest in such matters, what twentieth-century opera has had to say about the ten turbulent decades that have produced it, and what hope it holds for the future.

These are daunting questions. I wouldn't be addressing them had I not been invited to, and I apologize in advance for what will surely appear as insularity, partisan feeling, naiveté, or just plain ignorance in the views that follow. Few of us have the gift of prophecy, and no one completely understands the art of his own age. Even the artist, if he is wise, will not attempt to explain what he has made. A man is fortunate if he understands something of the past, and of himself.

I teach classics. When I first came to university as a student in the forties, the talk of my college campus was 'The Terrors of the Year Two Thousand,' a lecture given by the eminent medievalist (and crypto-Wagnerian) Etienne Gilson. It was his believer's answer to the existentialism of his fellow Parisian Jean-Paul Sartre. The bomb had just been dropped on Hiroshima. Gilson observed, in awe, 'Formerly, it was by obeying her that one mastered nature, now it is by destroying her.' Human destiny, he said, was henceforth utterly changed. What Nietzsche's Zarathustra signalled when, sorrowing, he pronounced the death of God was now imminent – the arrival, triumphant, of Dionysus.

So, I was told, my century – which began with Nietzsche torn to pieces like, perhaps even by, the fierce Dionysus he vowed to serve – would end with H.G. Wells's cautionary tale *The Island of Dr. Moreau* inverted: we would be transforming, not beasts into men, but men into beasts! What was I to make of it all? The myths and the metaphors had their fascination, but, after all, the year two thousand was then impossibly far away. No one in his teens thinks much about centuries, let alone millennia.

I went my own way, read classics, and came to Virgil, the Father of the West. Suddenly it *was* a matter of considering things millennially. And because Virgil lived so long ago, what he said about the future was, with history's hindsight, clearer than the forecasts of more contemporary prophets. At the end of the long centuries BC, Virgil was awaiting the year one, though of course he couldn't have known that's what later ages were going to call it. He had the sense of being poised on the edge of a new era. After a century of wars – civil wars that had become world wars – he wondered whether his world could possibly hope to renew itself. The prophecy in his fourth *Eclogue* of an impending Golden Age, marked by the birth of a divine child, had turned in his sixth *Eclogue* to a vision of a Dark Age in irreversible decline. He sued to the one source that could always renew itself, nature, and sought answers there, and wrote his *Georgics*, using the myth of Orpheus failing to resurrect Eurydice as a vehicle for his pessimism. Finally, he brought the literature of the thousand years past to bear on the hopes and fears of the present, and wrote a majestically sad epic for the future, the *Aeneid.*

For all his pessimism, Virgil saw before he died a world made peaceful, a transformation, a rebirth and renewal. An Augustan Age. The Roman he wrote for was still in power when the baby was born in Bethlehem who was to dominate the new millennium – in fact the next two millennia. Virgil was, for a long time, thought to have predicted that birth.

As we head towards the year two thousand, the bimillennium (which Stanley Kubrick, odysseying towards another baby's birth, insists should begin in the year 2001), who is our Virgil? If art exists to comment on the past, express the present, and, to some extent, predict the future, who in our century's art – in its opera – can tell us who and where we are? Is there any work of art to speak to and for us – or must we go under with Nietzsche?

The twentieth has been a century marked by an astonishing advance in the natural sciences and technology as well as by increasing ecological problems, economic depressions, oppressive totalitarian regimes, and an almost unbroken series of wars, two of them on an unprecedented scale, the last marked by the systematic slaughter of millions, also unprecedented. (It really has no precedent: Genghis Khan was a brute, whereas Nazi Germany was an industrialized nation that had inherited a great tradition in music, philosophy, and science.) Many hoped, when the terrors of the two wars were fully revealed, that a further war would be fore-stalled: if trench warfare was inhuman, and the Holocaust incomprehensible, atomic war was surely 'unthinkable.' Meanwhile, new nations were emerging violently, and they made the art-producing, empire-building nationalism of the past seem utterly passé. The twentieth saw more change than any century in the memory of man, and until a decade before its end about a third of the earth's population had come to live, often perforce, under a new religion – Marxism.

In art and thought, the years before and after the First World War witnessed the emergence of a number of isms, all of them ostensibly more sophisticated and less self-dramatizing than last century's Romanticism, but none of them destined to provide artists with an alternative to it. Georg Lukács thought that the major ism, Marxism, would be the Romanticism of the twentieth century. He was wrong. Since the Second World War we have seen an ugly bureaucratization of culture in the Marxist East and, in the West, a wholly unMarxist emergence of the irrational in art and in society.

We've also seen the challenge to and near collapse of the premises on which Western culture has been based. Those beleaguered premises are, I should say, the belief in a providential God; a concept of man as a creature of intrinsic individual worth, flawed but capable of growth in virtue; faith in human reason and the progress that can come from its exercise; and respect for and willingness to learn from the accumulated wisdom of the past, especially the wisdom found in classic Greek and subsequent European traditions. As the decades of our century succeeded each other, we've seen an increasing disillusionment with these givens, and both delight and despair as belief in them waned. Some observers have seen a corresponding decline in the quality of our art, music, literature, and philosophy. Others see only change. For a few, and they are not unintelligent, it is all for the best. There are, after all, other traditions.

At the half-way mark in our century, the most quoted poem in the English language – the poem of my generation in college – was *The Waste Land*. Western civilization was reduced to butt-ends, to fragments of Sappho, St Augustine, and Shakespeare shored against the ruins; only the Eastern thunder of the Upanishads spoke peace. Soon it would all be over. HURRY UP PLEASE ITS TIME

Today Eliot's has yielded to the still bleaker vision of Yeats. Our end-of-century poem is the oft-quoted *Second Coming*:

Things fall apart: the centre cannot hold;
Mere anarchy is loosed upon the world ...
The darkness drops again; but now I know
That twenty centuries of stony sleep
Were vexed to nightmare by a rocking cradle,
And what rough beast, its hour come round at last,
Slouches towards Bethlehem to be born?

Perhaps Yeats is our Virgil. He knew decades ago that there would be more fear than hope in our ninth-decade expectations. Who sings now of the dawning of an Age of Aquarius? The post-Christian future is imminent, and it is frightening precisely because the past, which man has always relied on, has come apart. 'The past,' says Robert Nisbet in his *History of the Idea of Progress*, 'is sacred ground for any genuine, creative, and free civilization.' Without it, 'human beings are condemned to a form of isolation in time that easily becomes self-destructive.' That is where our artists, including our best composers of opera, seem to be.

It was not always so in the West. Throughout the four centuries in which opera developed, Nisbet observes, 'the ascendancy of the West over the rest of the world was not just a matter of ethnocentric belief but a military and political reality [that] ... could be made to seem foreordained, inevitable, and irreversible.' Opera, as much as any other art form born in Europe, reflected this. 'But within an astonishingly short time, what had required more than two thousand years to create as condition and as belief has come to an end.' HURRY UP PLEASE ITS TIME

Today's artists are separated from their public as never before. They think themselves fortunate if those in power pay them even token respect. In the first century, Caesar Augustus *listened* to the Virgil he asked to write. In the twentieth, our best rulers have never had to act on what they heard from their laureates, while our totalitarians have had bourgeois and old-fashioned tastes. Stalin liked, not Shostakovich, but *The Queen of Spades*. Hitler in his bunker listened, not to Wagner as is popularly believed, but to *The Merry Widow*.

All the same, proper understanding of the first decades of our century, from a musical and from several other points of view, begins with Wagner. He whom Nietzsche canonized, for a while at least, has had, according to Bryan Magee, 'greater influence than any other single artist on the culture of our age.' Sceptics who thought that influence played out by the end of the nineteenth century have seen it take new forms in the twentieth, and continue unabated. Opponents who thought that influence unremittingly harmful have had to reckon with its unexpected flowering in the best of our literature, art, music, and even social sciences. We have seen the East-West dislocation experienced by the sailor watching the wind at the beginning of *Tristan*, and the despair of the shepherd looking out over the waste sea before the end of that same work, become images for Eliot's *Waste Land* and Spengler's *Decline of the West*. We have seen the last-act monologues of Tristan, his descent through memory to levels of conscious and unconscious experience, prompt and pervade the greatest twentieth-century novels – those streams of consciousness produced by Proust, Joyce, and Mann.

There are Wagnerian patterns also in Conrad, Lawrence, Forster, Woolf, and Cather. In the theatre Shaw embraced Wagner's concept of persuading the audience to entertain ideas by 'emotionalizing the intellect,' and Diaghilev applied the principles of the *Gesamtkunstwerk* to Russian traditions in the dance. Symbolist poets (including the Russians) found sustenance in Wagner's art-for-art's-sake theories, while impressionist painters tried to capture his sound textures in colour. In music, Mahler, Schönberg, and Strauss are only the foremost of Wagner's descendants. Other important figures – Debussy and Stravinsky, Cocteau and Brecht – defined themselves by opposition to Wagnerism, as it came to be called. Lévi-Strauss developed his structural analysis of myth out of Wagner's use of leitmotifs. Some of the most remarkable insights of Freud and Jung were anticipated by Wagner's use of archetypal myths on the stage. The staging itself influenced modern theatre through Adolphe Appia and Wieland Wagner. The old Klingsor of Bayreuth, who introduced the idea of a festival long before our Stratfords and Salzburgs came into being, also taught subsequent generations how music – not only his own – was to be conducted, and how audiences were to listen to it.

Wagner also has his chiliastic significances. In *Tristan* and the *Ring* and *Parsifal*, as well as in the prose works that surrounded their appearance, Wagner said what few others in his seemingly progressive century were saying – that the West was actually in decline, owing partly to its technology and its dehumanizing industrialization, partly to its loss of spiritual values. At the end of the *Ring* he seemed to predict that some suprarational force might, to use his word, redeem the world – but, after changing his mind five times about the wording of this, he left it to his music to define what still has not found practical definition. In *Die Meistersinger* he expressed his hope that art (was it too immodest of him to suggest his own art?), would provide understanding and help build a better future. Instead (was he too vainglorious to have seen this possibility?), his art was used as propaganda for evil purposes, and evil on a scale never known before.

(Virgil, no less intuitive and influential and by all odds a better prophet, asked at his death that his *Aeneid* be burned. His reason, the stream-of-consciousness novelist Hermann Broch has suggested, was that he saw that his epic meditation on empire might be used in the future to justify oppression and evil.)

Almost paradoxically, Wagner's direct influence on operatic composition has been small. But the Wagnerian and anti-Wagnerian movements of the first part of the century – naturalism, symbolism, impressionism, expressionism, Dadaism, surrealism, neoclassicism – all left their imprint on opera. Witness the work of, respectively, Puccini, Strauss, Debussy, Bartók, Virgil Thomson, the younger Poulenc, and the older Stravinsky.

No event of the new century had a greater effect on art than the Great War. Most of the conditions that had, for three centuries, produced opera in Europe – a sense of national destiny, the aristocratic notion of *noblesse oblige*, class systems, conservative traditions in politics, religion, and education – the First World War in effect ended. A telling comment on this was provided by the century's new art form, film, and specifically by the film I regard as the finest ever made, Jean Renoir's *La Grande Illusion*. When its patrician officers de Boeldieu and von Rauffenstein go to their respective soldier's fates, they represent a centuries-old Europe dying. The climate that favoured the creation of *Figaro* and *Lohengrin* and *Otello* (or, from a bourgeois point of view, of Gounod's *Faust*, the most popular opera of the time, quoted by the film's common soldiers) no longer obtained.

After the First World War there were no more successful operas along the lines of those early-twentieth-century pieces *Don Quichotte*, *Rusalka*, *Le Coq d'Or*, *Tiefland*, and *L'Amore dei Tre Re*. In a short time, even that sturdiest of growths, Italian *verismo*, was dead – though, the taste for opera being still very much alive, the best of the past continued to be performed and, with the democratization of taste, Puccini's readily accessible, phonogenic, almost cinematic pieces came to be performed more than ever before, more often in recent years than even the perennials of Verdi.

The vital creative impulse between the wars was still from Wagner, though I suspect that not even he would have foreseen the forms it was to take. The significant work, anticipating new developments in both the music and the drama of opera, was once again *Tristan*. Its relentless chromaticism, and in particular the atonality of its opening chord, pointed the way to the first of the new century's major developments, musically speaking – the twelve-tone system, illustrated operatically in Schönberg's

Moses und Aron and Berg's *Lulu*, and to some extent in his earlier *Wozzeck*. It is now clear that these are three of the important operas of our time, their characters emblematic of twentieth-century man – rootless, doubt-ridden, materialistic, obsessed with sex. But Berg and Schönberg's cerebral, astringent, ear-wearying twelve-tone system, it is by now equally clear, was no substitute for the less intellectualized musical traditions of the past. Nor were the other musical styles, stubbornly academic, that followed. Popular response – ask Verdi and Wagner how important that is! – was and remains at most fitfully enthusiastic about them all. As twentieth-century opera houses became, increasingly, classic repertory theatres, the public seemed not to mind. There was much still to be learned from the great works of the past. There was the whole of the Baroque and half of Mozart and Verdi to be rediscovered. There was, suddenly, Italian bel canto to speak in unexpectedly modern terms. The new operas, by comparison, seemed barren of melody. And that – it is no longer thought naive to state the truth bluntly – was the main problem with them. Drama cannot sing without song.

It was no different with the other fine arts. They all, in their several ways, learned to express the uncertainties of a world that industrialized war, a world where science had outdistanced art, in styles far removed from the styles of the past. In his study of existentialism, William Barrett, speaking of 'the age that has discovered and harnessed atomic energy, that has made airplanes that fly faster than the sun,' remarks that 'if an observer from Mars were to turn his attention from these external appurtenances of power to the shape of man as revealed in our novels, plays, painting, and sculpture, he would find there a creature full of holes and gaps, faceless, riddled with doubts and negations, starkly finite.'

While we cannot, then, blame the opening chord of *Tristan* for everything that has happened since in music, it was none the less *Tristan* – and especially its third act, where the orchestra helps the hero feel his leitmotivic way out of his sufferings – that was the harbinger of a second distinctly twentieth-century operatic trend, something that we may hope will ensure opera's survival as a creative art form in the century to come. George Martin has put this well: 'It was opera's peculiar quality that the orchestra could contradict a singer's expressed thoughts or indicate his subconscious fears and hopes. Opera, more than most art forms, therefore, was in a position to absorb easily the discoveries of the century's most startling new science, psychoanalysis.'

So out of Freud's Vienna came Hofmannsthal's symbol-laden, increasingly psychoanalytic libretti for Richard Strauss. (As Martin put it, 'Menelaus is cured of his war neuroses, including a desire to murder Helen for her guilt in causing the war, by acting out his inner feelings.') The psychologizing trend is soon detectible elsewhere. As the wife unlocks each door in Bartók's *Bluebeard's Castle*, she unlocks a new aspect of her husband's psyche. When the husband in Korngold's *Die Tote Stadt* sinks into a dream, he finds release from the subliminal hold his dead wife has had on him. Two monodramas of Schönberg depict the nightmare aspect of eroticism in the male (*Die Glückliche Hand*) and the female (*Erwartung*). Zimmermann's *Die Soldaten* is a study of sexual neurosis, Prokofiev's *Fiery Angel* of schizophrenia, Poulenc's *Dialogues des Carmélites*, at least partly, of the fear of fear. Britten's Peter Grimes, Claggart, Governess of Bly, Owen Wingrave, and Aschenbach are psychological sketches of a sort seldom if ever found in opera before. In most of his work Britten (like Wagner in effect if not in method) seems to be trying to understand his tormented inner self. His compatriot Michael Tippett made *The Midsummer Marriage* and other operas out of Jungian archetypes (and, as they were mainly his own archetypes, failed to win the audience he deserved). Busoni in *Doktor Faust*, Hindemith in *Mathis der Maler*, even the very traditional Pfitzner in *Palestrina*, explored the psychology of the artist in elaborate works that are to some extent autobiographical.

Perhaps Puccini, always astute in marking the newest trends and assimilating them, is the readiest index of this development. At the century's start it was enough for him to show Tosca and Butterfly suffering; two decades later he felt he had to provide, via the orchestra, some psychological rationale for his Turandot's cruelty and capitulation (and, being a nineteenth-century Italian at heart, he found he couldn't complete the task).

It is possible, too, to mark a third trend. In choice of subject, twentieth-century opera composers have become increasingly attuned to the intellectual and especially the literary currents of the day. A list of notable writers and notable operas of the century will almost automatically result in matching columns:

Apollinaire	*Les Mamelles de Tirésias* (Poulenc)
Auden	*The Rake's Progress* (Stravinsky)
Bernanos	*Dialogues des Carmélites* (Poulenc)
Brecht	*Mahagonny* (Weill)
Čapek	*The Makropoulos Case* (Janáček)
Claudel	*Jeanne d'Arc au Bûcher* (Honegger)
Cocteau	*Oedipus Rex* (Stravinsky)
Colette	*L'Enfant et les Sortilèges* (Ravel)

Hofmannsthal	*Elektra, Der Rosenkavalier* (Strauss)
Maeterlinck	*Pelléas et Mélisande* (Debussy)
Synge	*Riders to the Sea* (Vaughan Williams)
Wedekind	*Lulu* (Berg)
Wilde	*Salome* (Strauss)

In each of these instances the libretto is either original work from the literary figure or a more-or-less verbatim reproduction of his/her original play. A similar list could be made of libretti drawn from twentieth-century fiction, with the adaptation remarkably close to the original, as in Britten's operas based on Henry James's *The Turn of the Screw* and Thomas Mann's *Death in Venice*. Estimable if less durable operas have been crafted from such other twentieth-century authors as Chekhov, Conrad, D'Annunzio, Dürrenmatt, Eliot, García Lorca, Greene, Hauptmann, Kafka, Pirandello, Strindberg, and Yeats. This represents a use of the best contemporary literature far more extensive than in any of the previous centuries of opera's history. Even when contemporary opera chooses subjects from the past, it depicts the past, not as picturesque à la nineteenth-century opera, but as prophetic. Our composers have used such harbingers of modern alienation as Euripides, the Shakespeare of *Lear*, Gozzi, the Goethe of the second part of *Faust*, Dostoevsky, Büchner, and Poe.

On the strength of these observations I should guess that, in addition to the works already mentioned, the next century will still be performing, as representative of our day, operas by Shostakovich, Szymanowski, Penderecki, and Martinů; by de Falla and Dallapiccola; by Orff, von Einem, Henze, and Reimann. And perhaps by Stockhausen and Birtwistle. I have that expectation even though in the seventies Henze felt that opera was finished and Pierre Boulez issued the call to blow up the opera houses. Both were, after all, striving towards new forms of what they didn't want to think of as opera. But it may be that the three trends we have spoken of have in fact spent themselves. Even the interest in psychology. The century that began, operatically speaking, with Debussy's elusively symbolic *Pelléas* steadfastly refusing to analyse its characters now promises similarly to end with Philip Glass unanalytically limning the surfaces of his characters in bright, easy-listening orchestral solmizations.

In the United States the hope that an indigenous operatic tradition would develop from jazz and ASCAP styles has gone largely unfulfilled. We've been granted one masterpiece, Gershwin's *Porgy and Bess*, and a score of enduring Broadway musicals graced with superbly crafted songs by Kern, Berlin, Rodgers, Porter, Arlen, Loesser, and Loewe. But American folk idioms have blessed us only twice – when filtered through the creative irreverence of Virgil Thomson and Gertrude Stein, in *Four Saints in Three Acts* and *The Mother of Us All*. Adaptations of O'Neill, Steinbeck, Arthur Miller, and Tennessee Williams have come and, it seems, gone. Menotti, Moore, Barber, Bernstein, Floyd, and Argento are names surely to be remembered, yet each has, after promising beginnings, disappointed to some degree. And in the United States as elsewhere, electronically produced music, the subject of much hopeful experimentation, has shown itself almost wholly incapable of delineating character or developing a dramatic situation. (The biggest fiasco has been rock opera – a sociological phenomenon of some consequence, perhaps, but as art hardly more than a misnomer, a contradiction in terms.)

Can anyone say that what has been accomplished by the composers of the major political power of the century has told Americans what they must know about themselves? Can we make such a claim when the estimable Stephen Sondheim examines a hundred years of Japanese-American relations in *Pacific Overtures* without even touching on the bombing of Hiroshima and Nagasaki? When no composer (save, perhaps, Puccini – but hardly, so far, John Adams) has forced us to face the 'innocent American' Europeans and the rest of the world regard as dangerously unaware? When no successful American opera has dealt with either of the great wars? It was left to the Russian Prokofiev, in the little-known *Semyon Kotko* and *The Story of a Real Man*, to do that, in works of some merit. But as both were opposed in his homeland, we have had small opportunity to hear them over here.

It may of course be wrong-headed to expect opera to deal with contemporary issues realistically. By nature 'an exotic and irrational entertainment' (the phrase is Dr Johnson's), it has generally dealt with important matters through myth and metaphor. This is no slight to its seriousness. Philosophy too – from Plato to Nietzsche and Sartre, and even to Gilson, answering them – has resorted to myth and metaphor when faced with the insoluble or the unknown. And that brings me to my final remarks.

As we hurry towards the year two thousand, I'm sometimes asked to name what I think 'the opera of the century' might be. If I were up against the wall, or sent to that proverbial desert island with the grim prospect of taking with me only one opera of my own times, I wouldn't, from personal preference, choose either of the top two in popularity, *Tosca* and *Madama Butterfly*, which in any case are in every respect but their dates nineteenth-century pieces. I could easily be persuaded to choose *Der Rosenkavalier*, which has moments to challenge any opera ever written at any time. *Salome, Elektra,* and *Die Frau ohne Schatten* would do any century proud, and Strauss's *Capriccio* is some sort of last-farewell miracle. A convincing case could be made for *Pelléas et Mélisande,* or for *Moses und Aron,* or for *Wozzeck* as speaking more eloquently than any other opera about who we were in this century of ours. It no longer seems special pleading to rank *Jenůfa* and perhaps other works of Janáček, and *Peter Grimes* and perhaps other works of Britten, among the foremost accomplishments of our times.

That said, I'd like to end these considerations by rehearsing, at some length, why I would cite Strauss's *Ariadne auf Naxos* as the most significant and in many ways the best opera of the century.

Ariadne was first performed in 1912 as the play-within-a-play in a German production of Molière's *Le Bourgeois Gentilhomme.* It was not too successful then, grafted as it was on to the end of a mammoth Max Reinhardt production of a spoken drama. But it was eventually rescued from oblivion by its composer and librettist, detached from the Molière play, equipped with a forty-five-minute prologue, and launched on its own as a full-length opera – in Vienna during the First World War. That production, in 1916, with Lotte Lehmann, Maria Jeritza, and Selma Kurz, was the stuff theatrical dreams are made of.

All the same, the war prevented *Ariadne* from reaching a wide audience. In fact, it wasn't until after the Second World War that it made its way around the world. And only in recent decades – as we've passed beyond our twelve-tone expectations and learned not to condescend to Strauss's once unfashionable post-Wagnerian style, as we've come to look for meanings, especially symbolic and psychological meanings, in that maligned literary form, the libretto – only since then has *Ariadne* advanced to a commanding position as one of the century's great works of art.

Ariadne is about, in one word, *Verwandlung* – transformation. By 1912 Strauss had already written the famous orchestral piece he called *Death and Transfiguration,* and the *Zarathustra* that was to become our age's anticipation of the year 2001. Later, as the bombs fell on Munich and Dresden, he would write for solo strings his moving *Metamorphosen* – transformations. So it was right that, in mid-career, the splendid poet Hugo von Hofmannsthal should give him, in *Ariadne,* a libretto that touches gently on those Straussian concerns – death, transfiguration, Zarathustra, metamorphosis, transformation.

I teach the myths of Greece and Rome – Homer's epic of the return of the hero across magic seas, Aeschylus's drama of man discovering fire, Virgil's song of nature renewing itself, and Ovid's *Metamorphoses*, those fifteen books of stories about transformations of men into beasts and women into stars. Myths are made for every century. If there is a single theme in Ovid's maze of myths, it is transformation: humankind, like the many species of nature's fauna and flora, must adapt to change. As the world around us changes, we must change as well. Nature's irrevocable law is 'transform yourself or die.' There are two figures in Greek myth most associated with transformations: Hermes, the mercurial god who, with his magic wand, unseals our eyes after death to escort us to our places in the next life, and Circe, the seductive island witch who, with songs, potions, and a magic wand, transforms amorous men into beasts. Hermes and Circe do not actually appear in *Ariadne*, but they're hovering just out of sight.

Also hovering just out of sight in the prologue to *Ariadne* is the richest man in Vienna. We never see him. He only announces, through his Major-Domo, that the opera he has commissioned for his private theatre that evening will have to be followed by a low comic piece. That leaves the young composer of the commissioned work utterly stunned. He has written a serious opera – a desert-island opera in fact – about nothing less than 'the secret of life.' And now his new masterpiece about the love of Bacchus and Ariadne will have to share the evening with a vulgar commedia dell'arte farce about the love of Harlequin and Columbine. What an insensitive nouveau-riche sort this richest man in Vienna must be! Well at least, the young composer is assured by his teacher, his work will be first on the program. Intelligent people will remember it and forget the rest.

Then a sudden announcement leaves *all* the theatre folk stunned. The Major-Domo reappears to say that the richest man in Vienna can't afford to miss his fireworks later that evening, so he has decided that, to provide the needed time, the two theatrical offerings must be run together. The tragic opera and the comic masquerade will be performed *gleichzeitig* – simultaneously. And the performance must end at exactly nine o'clock.

The young composer panics – until his eyes fall, amid the confusion, on Zerbinetta, the comic lead in the rival Italian company. He should, as a serious German artist, despise her, but instead he feels strange new emotions rise within him. He senses that, even at this last minute, changes not only can but must be made in his *opera seria*. There is a fresh melody buzzing in his head, and it doesn't fit his tragedy at all. It's not for heroic characters. It's for Cupid. It's about youth and pleasure and everything opposed to death and transfiguration. The comedienne, perhaps anxious to get as much playing time as possible that evening, or perhaps only interested in making a conquest, sizes the composer up quickly and works on his sympathies. She tells him she plays coquette roles against her will. Most of the time she is lonely and sad. She longs for one man to be faithful to till death.

It's a most unusual little duet the composer and the comedienne sing – like comedy longing for tragedy and tragedy longing for comedy. For the first time, the composer sees comedy as 'sweet, incomprehensible, unearthly.' It is a new vision, and it transforms him. Neither the tragic nor the comic is all. The depths of human experience are infinite. And music can sound those depths. Perhaps *his* music can encompass both tragic and comic at once. 'Music,' he sings exultantly, 'is a holy art.'

Then the comedienne escapes his embrace and runs away. His own leading lady, the tragedienne, agrees to play Ariadne only when assured that the audience will see between her and the comedians an infinite gulf. Doubts and regrets crowd in on our young composer. He almost despairs as all the players scramble to meet their curtain. But scramble they must. The richest man in Vienna is waiting to see the strangely mixed command performance. HURRY UP PLEASE ITS TIME

The last time I saw *Ariadne* I heard at this point a tired business man, coming up the aisle, say, 'I don't understand it.'

Well, what *is* going on here?

In one word, transformation. 'Transformation,' Hofmannsthal said in a letter to Strauss, 'is the life of life itself.' It keeps life alive. Nothing in the world can survive unless it adapts itself to nature's ever-changing conditions. If we are not, at a moment of crisis, to go under, to die, we must change. Transform ourselves. Renew ourselves.

There was a time when *opera* was in danger of dying. *Opera seria*, based on heroic mythological figures sung by vain and vapid creatures, seemed in the mid-eighteenth century hopelessly dated, moribund, bound for the boneyard. Only *opera buffa*, a distinctly minor genre grown out of pantomime comedy and concerned with ordinary folk – only that was capable of survival. Or so it seemed, until some unseen power providentially decreed, while there was still time, that the two be blended.

A young genius appeared in Vienna. He had written promising *opere serie* about Scipio and Mithridates and Idomeneus. And then, though Vienna hardly appreciated it at first, he began to produce works in which the *seria* and the *buffa*, the tragic and the comic, were wondrously combined. Though these works appeared to be mainly about cupids and coquettes, they sounded surprising depths, and for two centuries since many people have found in them, as much as in any works of art, 'the secret of life.' Many people have said that God sent that young genius to us. God certainly took him away sooner than anyone other than He thought wise. But before that, God – or whatever we want to call that unseen power hovering then over Vienna – decreed that His composer fuse the tragic and the comic on the stage. Before opera died. And before the nine o'clock of his own brief life had struck. There was so little time. The genius died, tragically young. Opera survived.

The young man's name, of course, was Mozart. If you will, Amadeus Mozart. I like to think that the first part of *Ariadne*, the prologue, is about him.

After intermission we see the improvised opera. We see the little stage in the house of the richest man in Vienna from the other side. Viewed now from the front, it represents the Greek island of Naxos, floating for our pleasure in a turquoise sea. Now it is as if each of us watching is the richest man in Vienna.

The island is presided over by the three spirits who represent water, trees, and winds. (They can also be thought to represent the springs, groves, and breezes by which the Muses inspire art.) They sing in close harmony, like the three ladies in Mozart's *Magic Flute*, or the three Rhinemaidens in Wagner's *Ring*. Deserted on the island is the beautiful Ariadne. It's hard to believe that the lovely princess who now appears onstage is the same mindless prima donna we saw backstage. But there she is, transformed now by the theatre's magic into a classic figure of suffering.

Ariadne has loved but one man, prince Theseus of Athens, and he has carried her off romantically on his ship, only to abandon her cruelly on this island. She sings her sorrow in an aria – and the first of the clowns, Harlequin, appears and tells her, in a little baritone solo, that, whatever her grief, she must will to live. But Ariadne, after her terrible desertion, now sees life as an illusion – imperfect and impermanent. She thinks instead of death and, in a second aria, voices her beautiful, mythic idea of what death is. He is a lover, but not a false lover like Theseus. He will come to her gently, and take her away to a land where all is pure, perfect, incorruptible. He should, because he is death, be frightening, but he is not. He is – she sees him clearly now – the god of transformations, Hermes, and he will come across the tides with a golden wand, to waft her soul onwards like a leaf on the wind.

The comic characters, unable to comprehend any of this, attempt a further diversion for the visionary abandoned princess: the four clowns cavort merrily and Zerbinetta sings a big coloratura aria, Italian style. There is much to laugh at in their antics. We are even made to laugh at ourselves. We opera-goers are so easily fooled. We explode into applause when Zerbinetta's show-stopping aria reaches its climactic high note, and it turns out this is not the end of the piece at all. Strauss induces us to clap too early and then, when we are caught interrupting the music, directs his Zerbinetta to end the aria, not on a stratospheric high D but, as she holds a finger to her lips, on an almost whispered 'Stumm, stumm!' – 'Quiet, quiet!' Directed at us.

The big coloratura aria, like each successive piece in the opera, is about *Verwandlung*. Ariadne may think that a woman should be faithful to one man only, and love him for his transforming love, as some kind of god, forever. But Zerbinetta will have none of that. She careers from lover to lover. *Every* lover comes to her like a god, kisses her, and, for the moment, transforms her. Then she leaves him.

They are opposites, Ariadne and Zerbinetta, the A and the Z of the transforming experience of falling in love. With the comic Zerbinetta, falling in love happens over and over, and has an immediate meaning. With the tragic Ariadne, it happens one transcendent time, and has ultimate meaning: it is something like dying, yet it is the entrance to new life.

In the final tableau of *Ariadne auf Naxos*, we see this happen. The spirits of water, leaf, and wind sing that a ship is approaching Naxos. In the distance, we hear a tenor voice. It is the young god Bacchus. Greek gods only gradually enter into their powers, and Bacchus on his ship is still passing through the adventures that will lead him to the fullness of his godhead. There are dangers still to be met. The three spirits sing how only now, on this sea, he has braved the island where the enchantress Circe with magic potions changes men into beasts. But Circe has had no power over him.

As the orchestra reiterates, appropriately enough, the evolutionary first chord of Wagner's *Tristan*, and the chromatic theme that attends it, a ship anchors at the island. Ariadne exclaims in fright as Bacchus – to savage, fearful sounds – steps ashore. Then the two come face to face. They are, of course, the foolish soprano and the foppish tenor we laughed at before the intermission, when we saw them backstage. But now Strauss's truly beautiful music works a metamorphosis. They are young, radiant, vulnerable, ready to reach outward to some new, transcendent experience. Ariadne, the deserted princess resolved to die, stands expectantly before Bacchus, the life-giving god not yet sure of his godhead.

At first each takes the other for someone else. She thinks he is Hermes, mythic emblem of change, angel of death. 'How will you make the trans-formation in me?' she asks. 'With your hands? With your wand? Or will you give me a potion to drink?'

He thinks she is another Circe, mythic emblem of change, evil enchant-ress. 'Are you the goddess of this island?' he asks. 'Do you sing magic songs at your loom? Do you take your guest within and pour out for him a magic drink?'

They kiss. She expects to die, for death is what Hermes brings to his votaries. But instead she is awakened to a new life. He expects to be turned into a beast, for that is what Circe does to her lovers. But instead he feels himself, at last, become a god.

The music, too, is utterly magical. Strauss has already transformed the echoing song of waters and leaves ('Wie der Wellen ... wie der Blätter') into Ariadne's prayer for metamorphosis ('Du wirst mich befreien'). Now he transforms Harlequin's little song about love, hate, hope, and fear ('Lieben, Hassen, Hoffen, Zagen') into a lullaby ('Töne, töne, süsse Stimme'). As the spirits of nature sing that sweetly rocking lullaby, Ari-adne sinks down to be reborn. The last breath of her old becomes the first breath of her new life. Her lover's mantle casts a shadow in which, like a child in the cradle, she sees her mother's eyes. When the darkness lifts, the cave where she thought she would die has become the bower where the love of a god awakens her to new life. The sail of his ship becomes a canopy to waft them together to the stars.

Clearly this is, on one level, about the dawning of sexual awareness. *Ariadne* was written for the same Vienna that taught Freud to interpret the symbolism of dreams. But on a deeper level it is about the possibility of renewal and rebirth. There is more of Virgil than of Ovid in this drama-tized myth. It is prophetic, but hopefully expectant in a way that Yeats, with his rocking cradle and rough beast slouching to be born, or Wells, with his island of hideously transformed brutes, could not be. It antici-pates, not some apocalyptic horror, but the awesome rebirth of the star child in Kubrick's *2001*, and the breathless vision of the theologian-scientist Teilhard de Chardin: 'The earth is far from having completed its sidereal evolution. We may envisage all kinds of mischance which might in theory put an end to our evolutionary progress: but the fact remains that for 300 million years Life has paradoxically flourished in the Improb-able. Does this not suggest that its advance may be sustained by *some sort of complicity on the part of the "blind" forces of the Universe?*'

How wonderful of Hofmannsthal to have converted Nietzsche's fright-ening Antichrist, Dionysus, into the transforming and transformed Bacchus! How insightful of Strauss to have resisted his librettist's insistence that Zerbinetta's last comment must be cynical, and to have left her, like us, overawed at what she witnesses! How appropriate that the opera of the century be composed by a German, a son of the most civilized and most barbarous nation the age has seen, to the words of a poet who was part Jewish, from the people that suffered most and also – in Marx, Einstein, and Freud – most profoundly changed our era's notions of itself! How fitting that it be set in Vienna, that dream city, that city George Steiner called the 'demonic cauldron on the brown Danube,' where this century saw the beginnings of atonality and psychoanalysis, the flowering of its most influential literature, and the devising of its most hateful solution; the city in which Hofmannsthal 'sensed the coming collapse, the emptiness ahead' and strove through his libretti to find, in the Virgilian Hermann Broch's words, 'a higher reality.' How astonishing that this psychologizing, eminently literary opera should reach its climax in the opening phrase of *Tristan* and end celebrating the possibility of rebirth!

The duet of Bacchus and Ariadne rises to positively Wagnerian heights of exaltation. Like Wagner's Tristan, Strauss's Bacchus sings that he is now something different from what he was: 'Ich bin ein anderer als ich war.' Like Wagner's Isolde, Strauss's Ariadne sings that she is more than the world itself. She ascends, as in Ovid's *Metamorphoses*, to become the constellation we call the Crown.

Bacchus and Ariadne mount upwards through the skies, defying earthly gravity, transfigured by love. She will be safe from harm in her new cosmos, for she has made him a god. He sings, 'The everlasting stars will die before ever you fall from my arms.' The comic actors watch in amazement, and then close the curtain.

Even from this rough-and-ready summary of *Ariadne*, we can see, first, something of how it evokes virtually the whole history of opera, from its beginnings in the late Renaissance, when some Florentine scholars decided to put Greek myths on the stage, through its French and Italian development as tragic *opera seria* and comic *opera buffa*, to Mozart's eighteenth-century Viennese fusion of the two, to nineteenth-century Italian coloratura arias, to – in the final scene – German Wagner, his atonal chord, his mythic anticipations of Freud, and his evolutionary vision. Through the centuries opera has survived by transforming itself.

And why use the myth of Ariadne and Bacchus to express all this? I think because, ever since Monteverdi, Ariadne has been something of a symbol for opera. And because those Florentines who invented opera didn't really start out to invent opera at all. They wanted to re-create

Greek tragedy, which began out of the worship of Dionysus – or, to give him the name Hofmannsthal prefers, Bacchus. Drama, when it was born, was meant to celebrate *his* myths, and he is its god.

And as drama was transformed into opera, so too, if we can see and believe in what *Ariadne* is saying, we can be transformed. Strauss, a businesslike but hardly disingenuous man, as much as said of the libretto, 'I don't understand it,' and the intuitive Hofmannsthal explained: *Ariadne* was about 'whether to hold fast to that which is lost, to cling to it even to death – or to live, to live on ... to transform oneself.'

This is a simple fact of nature, sung by every echo, wave, and leaf. It is what the young composer said his opera was about: the secret of life. It may be the only answer, in the end, for the unexplainable human suffering and loss our century has known.

Verwandlung, renewing oneself, bringing the past to bear on the present, trying to lead at least a decent life in a world where so little makes sense – all of these were concerns of German poets at the beginning of this century. As that century now hurries to its end, sometimes I'm asked, as a professor of Greek and Latin poetry that is two thousand years old, who I think 'the poet of this century' might be. Well, if I were up against the wall, or sent again to that proverbial desert island with only one volume of this century's poems to take with me, I'd bid a sad farewell to Yeats and Eliot, to Lorca and Valéry and, yes, Hugo von Hofmannsthal. And I'd take to my desert island the works of Rainer Maria Rilke.

In a museum in Munich there stands an archaic torso of Apollo, twenty-five centuries old. Rilke confronted that noble stone in a famous poem, noting how the statue's head was missing, and its limbs broken away, and yet somehow the work of art had survived. More than that, it still had the power to see. It was as if the lost eyes had somehow sunk within the surviving torso, and their glance still shone out, like stars, at the places where the surfaces had been broken. So the god could stare back at the poet across twenty-five centuries, smiling and radiant and inscrutable, and say to him, 'Du musst dein Leben ändern.' 'You have to change your life.'

That truth is, for the visionary poet Rilke as well as for the two geniuses who fashioned *Ariadne auf Naxos*, the truth spoken by both nature and art. Transformation is the law of life. Any scientist can observe it in nature. And in art, I think we've all felt, after exposure to one of the great works, that we have been lifted to a level where we re-evaluate all of living, all of experience. Great art has the cathartic power to purify, to exalt, to change our lives.

Some of us may feel that our century has produced, amid its wonderful scientific discoveries and its terrible world wars, no art that has that stature, that transforming power. Or that we've lost the sense of our proper place in the history of the development of civilization. Some of us may feel that our power-mad century really knows nothing of the greatest power of all, the transforming power of love. I suspect we haven't yet taken the full measure of *Ariadne auf Naxos*.

There are all sorts of ways to interpret it. That goes without saying. It is a complex work of art. But when I see it at this late point in our troubled century, it seems to me to look forward. Its myth and its music put me most in mind of those hopeful words of Teilhard: 'Someday, after we have mastered the ether, the winds, the tides, and gravity, we will harness for God the energies of love. And then, for a second time in the history of the world, man will have discovered fire.'

Further Reading

To the list of studies recommended in my volumes *Wagner's Ring* and *First Intermissions*, I should like to add, for in-depth discussion of the works treated in this volume, the following:

The New Grove Dictionary of Opera, edited by Stanley Sadie. 4 volumes (London: Macmillan, 1992). Almost all of the major entries in this comprehensive and beautifully produced reference work supersede those in the complete *New Grove*, a testimony to the scrupulous dedication of editor Stanley Sadie (who also edited and contributed to the earlier, fourteen-volume work) and to the rapid turnover of supposed fact and received opinion in matters operatic that has marked the last two decades. The new entries are predictably of a very high order, and adequate space has been allotted to well-produced illustrations and valuable bibliographies. A little browsing will disclose a gaffe or two, though nothing so egregious as some specimens made by contributors and printers but detected before the final printing and engagingly reported by Mr Sadie in the English magazine *Opera*: 'He emigrated to Belgium where he was heard singing in a café and encouraged to return to Italy for study' ... 'He died in a brothel after trying a very odd experiment' ... 'Massenet wrote for her the "fabliau" as an alternative for the garotte in Act 3.' One of the more pleasant aspects of the four volumes is that a good deal of intended humor made it into print, along with the uncompromising scholarship.

The Viking Opera Guide, edited by Amanda Holden, Nicholas Kenyon, and Stephen Walsh (London: Viking Press, 1993). This is now quite easily the best single-volume reference work on opera. More than eight hundred composers are represented, and more than fifteen hundred operas, from Peri's *Dafne* to Glass's *The Voyage*, are given detailed plot summaries and perceptive analyses – and that is almost as many as can be found in the four-volume *Grove*. There are concise entries by such distinguished and readable scholars as David Cairns (on Berlioz), John Deathridge (on Wagner), Philip Gossett (on Rossini), and Roger Parker (on Puccini). Yes, the print is small, the pages tend to smudge, and with 1305 of them the volume is unwieldy. But this is a volume for the desk, not the armchair, and it is indispensible.

The Oxford Illustrated History of Opera, edited by Roger Parker (London and New York: Oxford University Press, 1994). The promised illustrations are plenteous and well-produced, but eventually the reader turns the pages attending equally to the freshly considered and sometimes controversial articles by David Charlton (on nineteenth-century French opera), Paul Griffiths (on twentieth-century opera), Roger Savage (on staging), and William Ashbrook (on singing). Some of the rest of the writing is, admittedly, on the stiff side.

Cambridge Opera Handbooks (London and New York: Cambridge University Press, 1981–). A uniformly excellent series of studies of individual operas. Each volume provides a musical analysis, a fresh appreciation, an extensive bibliography, and a discography. John Whenham's *Orfeo* (Monteverdi), Patricia Howard's *Orfeo* (Gluck), Julian Rushton's *Don Giovanni*, Peter Branscombe's *Die Zauberflöte*, Paul Robinson's *Fidelio*, James A. Hepokoski's *Falstaff*, Derrick Puffett's *Salome*, and Roger Nichols and Richard Langham Smith's *Pelléas et Mélisande* all meet the high standard set by the series.

Mozart's Don Giovanni, by Hermann Abert, translated by Peter Gellhorn (London: Eulenberg Books, 1976; originally published in 1924). Though not so up to date as Rushton's volume in the Cambridge series, this classic essay, written for the sixth German edition of Otto Jahn's monumental *Life of Mozart* (and partly written by Jahn himself), has good observations on the music, on sources, and especially on the composer's penetrating insight into the psychology of his characters.

Beethoven: His Spiritual Development, by J.W.N. Sullivan (1927; currently out of print). This brief – and, to some, notorious – treatise is one of the most unusual and demanding books ever written about a composer. Sullivan, a mathematician and philosopher, argues persuasively that Beethoven's work 'will live because of the permanent value, to the human race, of the experiences it communicates.' Little attention is given to *Fidelio*, but an attentive reader will see Beethoven's only opera as part of a line of development that leads to the mature works which communicate 'experiences to which the race, in its evolutionary march, aspires.'

Wagner Handbook, edited by Ulrich Müller and Peter Wapnewski (Cambridge, Mass.: Harvard University Press, 1992). Although Wapnewski's long and ambitious first chapter seems to me sometimes to run seriously off-course, this scholarly anthology, first published in Germany, is up to date and full of interesting detail, with incisive and much-needed chapters by Dieter Borchmeyer (on Wagner's anti-Semitism), Ernst Hanisch (on Wagner's political significance), and Müller himself (on Wagner and the Greeks).

Recordings and Videos

As compact discs with remastered sound now bring performances of fifty or more years past to vivid new life, I shall not favour in these listings new recordings with state-of-the-art aural ambience where older recordings now reissued on CD are clearly better from every other point of view. My intention is to select, wherever possible, the best single recording of each work discussed in this volume. Video selections here are few; not every opera can be found on video in an outstanding performance or, more to the point, in a performance that one would want to see more than once. Some of my audio and video choices may not be available (or may be available on labels other than those here given) in Canada, the United States, or Europe.

Orfeo

With Monteverdi's operas there is always a scholarly problem to be faced: the surviving works as we have them provide only approximations of melody, recitative, tempi, and instrumentation, and we are not at all sure about many details of style. But if you feel confident with His Majesty's Sagbuts and Cornetts, the English Baroque Soloists, and the Monteverdi Choir, you might opt for John Eliot Gardiner's impressive reading on Deutsche Grammophon. The most famous Monteverdi stagings in recent years, unveiled in Zurich and seen in several other cities in Europe and America, have been those of the 'Triptych' (*Orfeo*, *Il Ritorno d'Ulisse in Patria*, and *L'Incoronazione di Poppea*) designed and directed by Jean-Pierre Ponnelle and conducted by Nikolaus Harnoncourt. These delicious productions, not always attentive to the latest scholarship, may be seen on videos from London.

Orfeo ed Euridice

Again, there are scholarly considerations: Gluck's opera, written in Italian for Vienna, revised for Parma, rewritten in French for Paris, adapted later by Berlioz, with its title role sung at various times by castrati, sopranos, mezzo-sopranos, tenors, and basses, exists in many different versions. A very professional performance, using the best of the many versions and certainly serviceable as an introduction to the opera, is Decca/London's from 1969, with Sir Georg Solti conducting Marilyn Horne, Pilar Lorengar, Helen Donath, and Covent Garden forces. I've always preferred above all recordings of this opera the 1956 performance of the Paris version, in French, with sensitive conducting by Hans Rosbaud and a superb realization of the title role by that prince of Mozart tenors, Léopold Simoneau, recently transferred to CD on Philips, but not at the time of writing available in North America. Arturo Toscanini's beautiful 1952 performance of Act II, with Nan Merriman as Orfeo, is now available in volume 46 of the Toscanini Collection from RCA. On video, the 1982 Glyndebourne production directed by Peter Hall and conducted by Raymond Leppard, on HBO, is unsatisfactory in many of its visual aspects but preserves the touching farewell performance, all Winckelmannian noble simplicity, of Janet Baker.

Don Giovanni

Of the thirty-odd recordings of the 'opera of all operas,' many of them very good indeed, there is one standout: Carlo Maria Giulini's on EMI/Angel (1959), with Elisabeth Schwarzkopf giving one of her best performances on records, and with Joan Sutherland, Graziella Sciutti, Eberhard Wächter, Giuseppe Taddei, Luigi Alva, Gottlob Frick, and Piero Cappuccilli in dramatically apt and vocally splendid form – but Giulini is the real hero of the proceedings. On video, I wish I could recommend the 1954 Salzburg performance on VAI unreservedly; any Mozartian will want more than once to see as well as hear this stellar cast – Cesare Siepi, Elisabeth Grümmer, Lisa della Casa, Erna Berger, Anton Dermota, Otto Edelmann, and (in a star turn as Masetto!) Walter Berry. But even veteran film director Paul Czinner is defeated by the old Felsenreitschule stage, and even Wilhelm Furtwängler's Significant Conducting is undone by primitive sound reproduction. And there are no subtitles.

The Magic Flute

Of the twenty-odd recordings of Mozart's Masonic opera, some of them classics, there is no clear choice. No one who grew up with Sir Thomas Beecham's idiomatic 1938 recording with Tiana Lemnitz, Erna Berger, and Gerhard Hüsch (but without the spoken dialogue) will want to be without it on its CD reissue on EMI/Angel. Otto Klemperer's monumental 1963 performance, also on EMI/Angel (and also without dialogue), has particularly fine singing from Gundula Janowitz, Lucia Popp, and, as the three ladies, Christa Ludwig, Marga Höffgen, and Elisabeth Schwarzkopf (who reportedly sang in the chorus of the Beecham version!). Solti's second recording (1990, on Decca/London) is surprisingly light-textured for this once-heavy-handed Mozartian, and has the advantage of up-to-date sound and a Sarastro with one of the most beautiful voices before the public today, Kurt Moll. The quietly commanding Moll also appears in the best available video, a well-acted and generally well-sung 1992 Deutsche Grammophon issue conducted by James Levine, with the picturesque David Hockney designs for Glyndebourne enlarged, without losing their effectiveness, for the Metropolitan Opera stage.

Fidelio

Here there is one clear choice: Klemperer's 1962 recording on EMI/Angel, based on a series of performances at Covent Garden, with Christa Ludwig (a mezzo who commands the upper reaches) and Jon Vickers (a tenor who explores his role to the depths). The seventy-six-year-old conductor, partially paralysed by an illness that would have killed most men, seems to gain strength from the music as he conducts it. Of Vickers's heroic Florestan a Covent Garden critic once said, 'The part and he have become as one, the searing diction, sung and spoken, harrowing the heart of the listener.' (It should be said that the Leonore Overture no. 3, which Ernest Newman called 'the greatest thing of its kind ever written,' but which Beethoven himself excised because it overwhelmed the rest of the opera, is not included in this recording. One of the 1941 Bruno Walter / Kirsten Flagstad perfomances at the Met, referred to in the Fidelio chapter of this volume, does include it, and much else that is historic, on a set available with a donation to the Metropolitan Opera Guild, Lincoln Center, New York, NY 10023.) On video, a 1985 Glyndebourne performance from VAI, conducted by Bernard Haitink, is small-scaled but generally effective, with a radiant performance by Elisabeth Söderström.

L'Elisir d'Amore

No one today would want a Nemorino other than Luciano Pavarotti, a loveable know-nothing at the top of the class in the 1970 Decca/London recording with Joan Sutherland, and with Richard Bonynge conducting. The performance has the additional advantage of being complete. Of the two Metropolitan Opera videos featuring Pavarotti in this work, the first, on Paramount with Judith Blegen and with Nicola Rescigno conducting, is distinctly preferable.

Lucia di Lammermoor

I suspect that Walt Whitman would have chosen Pavarotti and Sutherland here; they're marvellous on Decca/London's 1971 recording, under Richard Bonynge. But during my Met intermission feature (the basis of the chapter in this book) I found time as well for moments from other 'measureless sweet vocalists of ages': Enrico Caruso, Giuseppe De Luca, and Amelita Galli-Curci (in the 'Sextet'), Maria Callas (in the 'Mad Scene'), and John McCormack (in the 'Tomb Scene'). God bless them all!

Il Trovatore

Caruso once said that all *Il Trovatore* needed was 'the four greatest voices in the world,' and it came near to getting them in a slightly cut 1952 recording from RCA. The darker aspects of the score may not be completely realized by conductor Renato Cellini, and the rich-voiced Fedora Barbieri may be too young and unacquainted with grief as Azucena. But Leonard Warren is at his considerable best as di Luna, Jussi Björling is nothing less than superb as Manrico, and in Zinka Milanov's 'D'amor sull' ali rosee' you can hear the most beautifully sustained legati and the most delicately spun pianissimi ever put on disc. The Milanov voice, with the sumptuously, almost voluptuously beautiful timbre usually associated with earlier golden ages of song, floats effortlessly along Verdi's elegant but perilous musical line, shimmering and gleaming on the high notes, fearlessly heroic, poignant with the imminence of death, alive with a sense of wonder at what Tennyson called 'the doubtful doom of humankind.' All competition pales. On video, Bel Canto Society has rescued a 1957 RAI black-and-white film in which Barbieri's Azucena has, in the five years since the recording discussed above, grown immensely in stature. Her high-powered colleagues – Leyla Gencer, Mario del Monaco, and Ettore Bastianini – are less skilled than she at lip-synching (and by the end they almost seem to forget that the musical performance is prerecorded), but the over-the-top acting and singing of the four of them, despite musty studio sets and the absence of subtitles, give more idea of what *Il Trovatore* is all about than does any other stage or video performance I've seen. Plinio Clabassi is the authoritative Ferrando. Fernando Previtali conducts.

La Traviata

The recording that comes closest to realizing Verdi's intentions is the 1955 live recording from La Scala with Maria Callas, on EMI/Angel and other labels. Although the sound is only acceptable, even by the standards of its day, and although both Giuseppe di Stefano and Ettore Bastianini have done better work elsewere, Callas, directed by Luchino Visconti, is marvellously responsive to all aspects of the drama, and Carlo Maria Giulini conducts eloquently. The RCA Toscanini recording, drawn from two 1946 broadcasts, is notoriously fast-paced in several places, but must be heard for Licia Albanese's classic Violetta and for many moments in which the passionate conductor all but convinces us that only he has realized Verdi's intentions on record. (He also sings along, which may or may not have pleased Verdi.) Toscanini's assistant at La Scala, Ettore Panizza, preserves much of the maestro's fiery approach on a 1935 Met broadcast, but adapts his tempi often (and transposes down occasionally) in deference to the great Rosa Ponselle, whose overwhelming intensity all but bursts the bonds of Verdi's opera. This powerful performance, with a memorable Germont père from Lawrence Tibbett, is available from the Metropolitan Opera Guild (see *Fidelio* listing). On video, the photogenic Angela Gheorghiu offers a Violetta of considerable range and depth in a 1995 Solti-led performance from Covent Garden, on London.

La Forza del Destino

The original St Petersburg version of Verdi's 'opera made of ideas' can be heard in a new recording from Philips, fittingly in a performance from St Petersburg, sung with utter conviction by an all-Russian cast, and passionately conducted by Valery Gergiev. The best recording of the standard version is James Levine's vivid 1976 reading with Leontyne Price, Plácido Domingo, and Sherrill Milnes, on RCA. The famous 1928 recording of 'La Vergine degli Angeli' by Rosa Ponselle and Ezio Pinza, now available in the Nimbus Prima Voce series, belongs in every Verdian's collection. On video the choice is a remarkable black-and-white kinescope of a 1958 *Forza* from Naples's San Carlo, under Francesco Molinari-Pradelli, available from Legato Classics or, with reportedly better visual quality, from Bel

Canto Society: superb performances by Renata Tebaldi and Franco Corelli, and very good ones by Ettore Bastianini, Renato Capecchi, and Boris Christoff, crash through what might have been an insurmountable barrier of poor sound and poorer visuals. There are no subtitles.

Aida

If Toscanini's intense, beautifully detailed 1949 broadcast performance on RCA had the marvellous vocalizing that Zinka Milanov and Jussi Björling provide on the 1955 recording under Jonel Perlea, also on RCA, there would be a definite choice here. Buy both.

Falstaff

If Toscanini's mercurial 1950 broadcast performance on RCA had the marvellous vocalizing that Tito Gobbi and others provide on the 1956 recording under Herbert von Karajan on EMI/Angel, there would be a definite choice here. Buy Toscanini, but don't forget that Karajan, Solti (1963), Bernstein (1966), and Giulini (1982) have all left us estimable recordings of this conductor's opera *par excellence*. On video, Jean-Pierre Ponnelle's charming 1973 Glyndebourne production, with John Pritchard conducting and with Donald Gramm as a fine Falstaff, is available on VAI.

Les Troyens

Colin Davis's 1969 recording on Philips, using the Covent Garden forces that gave this work its first complete performance, remains one of the events of the century, phonographically speaking: a great opera emerged from a hundred years of obscurity, and two stars ascended into the operatic firmament – Davis himself, who seemed suddenly to make sense of what had baffled others in the marathon score, and Jon Vickers, who quickly established himself as the only tenor of his time with the sound (and, on stage, the look) of a Virgilian hero. A 1994 recording on Decca/London, with Charles Dutoit leading Montreal forces, is interesting for reconstructing and restoring a scene for the Greek spy Sinon, planned by Berlioz but left unorchestrated. The Metropolitan Opera's 1983 telecast, with Plácido Domingo, Jessye Norman, and Tatiana Troyanos, and with James Levine conducting, has been issued on video by Paramount and is often smashingly good.

Rienzi

The only acceptable version currently on CD (acceptable despite its dated sound) is a live 1960 performance from Vienna, under Josef Krips, with Set Svanholm, Christa Ludwig, and Paul Schöffler, on Melodram. It is, predictably, heavily cut.

Tristan und Isolde

Still regarded as one of the phonograph's greatest documents is the magisterial 1952 recording with Kirsten Flagstad and Ludwig Suthaus, conducted with great authority by Wilhelm Furtwängler, currently on EMI/Angel, but in a rather lacklustre pressing. A performance quite different in tone, fast-paced and with moments of tremendous excitement (and perhaps the best version for those coming to the work for the first time) is Karl Böhm's 1966 recording, taken directly from the Bayreuth stage, with Birgit Nilsson and Wolfgang Windgassen, now on CD from Deutsche Grammophon. Those who have seen the rock-solid Nilsson and/or the overwhelming Jon Vickers in live performances of Tristan will want to have the video of their 1973 performance, conducted by Böhm, from the stage of the outdoor Roman theatre at Orange, available on special order from Bel Canto Society. (Caution: the typically seventies painted-in-light production, with murky blacks and sometimes lurid reds, is often effective but takes some getting used to; the generally good sound is occasionally affected by audience noises and a threatening Mistral, and is sometimes out of synch with the visuals; the standard 'big cut' is made in Act II, and the subtitles are in Japanese only. But with each successive viewing I've found all of these distractions less distracting as the passion of the performance takes hold.) Finally, Wagner-lovers will want to have the Tristan excerpts recorded in the thirties by the great Lauritz Melchior with the indispensible Flagstad, as well as those Melchior sang with Frida Leider, now available on various CD reissues.

Palestrina

Deutsche Grammophon's 1973 recording under Rafael Kubelik, a fervent if somewhat studioesque reading, is a Who's Who of the tenors, baritones, and basses who sang in German houses, large and small, in what now appears to have been a golden age of male voices. Dietrich Fischer-Dieskau, Hermann Prey, Bernd Weikl, and Karl Ridderbusch are only the most famous names among the churchmen at the Council of Trent, while Nicolai Gedda sings Palestrina.

Salome

It's usually Solti vs. Karajan when it comes to recorded Strauss. Their readings – Solti's spine-tingling, with the perhaps too overwhelming Birgit Nilsson, on Decca/London (1961), and Karajan's luxuriant, with the young Hildegard Behrens, on EMI/Angel – do not disappoint. But connoisseurs may well prefer the famous 1952 Fritz Reiner broadcast from the Met, with Ljuba Welitsch, Elisabeth Höngen, Set Svanholm, and Hans Hotter, available on LP only from the Metropolitan Opera Guild (see *Fidelio* listing). The Guild should be persuaded to issue as well the Reiner/Met broadcast from three years before, when the supporting cast was less impressive but the youthful Welitsch was captured – the right word – in what might best be called innocent depravity. Finally, there is a stunningly cinematic (but pre-recorded) 1974 video performance, directed by Götz Friedrich, with the unforgettable Teresa Stratas (who never attempted the role in the theatre), with a fine supporting cast, and with Karl Böhm conducting the Vienna Philharmonic, on Deutsche Grammophon. Unless you have a hi-fi VCR, you may not hear every last orchestral detail of this performance, but you'll certainly want to see it, and more than once.

Manon Lescaut

The astonishingly vivid 1956 Metropolitan Opera broadcast mentioned in the *Manon Lescaut* chapter in this volume, with Licia Albanese and Jussi Björling, is not yet available in the Met Guild Series. But the two artists recorded their roles together earlier, for RCA under Jonel Perlea in Rome in 1954, and until the Guild realizes what a treasure it has on its hands, RCA's often very good but always studio-bound performance is the one to buy. A video of the 1980 Met telecast, with Renata Scotto and Plácido Domingo in good form, and with James Levine conducting, is available from Paramount. Strauss and Puccini remain the composers best served by close-ups and film editing, and that says something about their shrewd twentieth-century approaches to operatic composition.

Pelléas et Mélisande

I return most often to the classic recording made by Roger Désormière in Paris in 1941, now on EMI/Angel. It seems to me to be challenged, among existing recordings, only by Herbert von Karajan's quite different 1978 reading on the same label, with the limpid Mélisande of Frederica von Stade and the moving

Golaud of José van Dam. Karajan's realization of Debussy's intentions is more dramatic and much more sumptuous in sound than Désormière's, but also something of an anomaly: Conrad L. Osborne once said that Karajan was the perfect interpreter, not of Debussy at all, but of Maeterlinck. And as Herr Herbert also seems determined to make clear Debussy's debt to Wagner, I suspect that Debussy would have seconded me in choosing Désormière's performance, not least because, in its EMI reissue, it is supplemented by several Debussy *Mélodies* sung by Maggie Teyte, with Alfred Cortot at the piano, and, from 1904, by Mélisande's brief Act III aria sung by Mary Garden, with Debussy himself at the piano.

Dialogues des Carmélites

The 1958 recording on EMI/Angel has the principals of the Paris première singing under Pierre Dervaux and the personal supervision of the composer himself. The 1994 recording from the Opéra de Lyon, on Telecom, has state-of-the-art stereo, generally good singing, sensitive conducting by Kent Nagano, and the short 'Bastille scene' (spoken words over percussion effects) that is usually cut in stage performances. Neither recording is as theatrical as one is likely to encounter in most stagings today, which may or may not be a blessing. I have not seen the generally admired Australian Opera video performance, in English, with Joan Sutherland as Mme Lidoine and with Richard Bonynge conducting, on Sony video.

Porgy and Bess

The 1988 recording on EMI/Angel, a souvenir of the long-running Glyndebourne production, has the heart-rending Porgy of Willard White, remarkable ensemble sense (in the duet of superimposed prayers, 'O Doctor Jesus'), and some very impressive choral singing (in the 'Requiem'). The conducting by Simon Rattle is by turns virtuosic (the often-cut fugue for brass instruments during the Act I fight is vindicated at last!) and eccentric (a too aggressively razzle-dazzle opening segues into a 'Summertime' that threatens to collapse under its own calculated languor). Perhaps it should be said that this performance served as the soundtrack for a lip-synched and disappointingly studioesque 1993 video from EMI. *Porgy* fans will not want to be without the excerpts recorded in the thirties for Victor by Lawrence Tibbett and in the fifties for RCA by Leontyne Price, William Warfield, and John Bubbles. (And it would be churlish not to mention the jazz versions done in the sixties for Verve by Louis Armstrong and Ella Fitzgerald.)

For the compleat and authentic *Show Boat* one must have the important, not to say scholarly, 1988 reconstruction by John McGlinn on EMI/Angel. The 1938 Universal and 1950 MGM film versions, both available on video, are better than their reputations would have it: the former preserves the classic performances of Paul Robeson and Helen Morgan and the latter has William Warfield, Marge and Gower Champion in small roles, and a touching performance by Ava Gardner.

Oklahoma!

The 1943 original-cast album now on MCA is undeniably authentic but, even with remastering, fairly primitive in sound, and listeners might prefer the 1955 soundtrack album on Angel. Better still, buy the piano score and sing the songs yourself.

Ariadne auf Naxos

No *Ariadne* on disc is without merit. I learned to love the work from Karajan's elegant 1954 performance, now on EMI/Angel. But my first choice since 1968 has been and remains Rudolf Kempe's, on the same label. The singing of Gundula Janowitz, James King, Hermann Prey, and others is certainly accomplished, but it is Kempe's conducting – precise, beautifully detailed, and unfailingly right – that gives this recording an edge over all others as we face the new century.

Index

Abert, Hermann, 218
Adams, John, 206
Aeschylus, 6, 34, 88, 208
Agostini, Philippe, 172
Agrippa, 103
Albanese, Licia, 154, 157, 225, 228
Allen, Peter, 60
Alva, Luigi, 222
Andrews, Julie, 182
Angelico, Fra, 15
Antony, Mark, 90, 105–6
Apollinaire, Guillaume, 173, 204
Appia, Adolphe, 201
Argento, Dominick, 206
Aristophanes, 194
Aristotle, 152
Arlen, Harold, 185, 205
Armstrong, Louis, 229
Arnaud, François, 18
Ashbrook, William, 58, 218
Auber, Daniel, 55, 114, 153, 156
Auden, W.H., 137, 204
Augustine, Saint, 102, 137, 199
Augustus, Caesar, 90, 104–6, 198, 200

Bach, J.S., 15, 33, 40, 115, 121, 144
Baker, Janet, 222

Bakunin, Mikhail, 116
Balzac, Honoré de, 107
Barbarossa, Frederick, 116
Barber, Samuel, 206
Barbieri, Fedora, 224
Bardi, Giovanni, 5
Barrault, Jean-Louis, 173
Barrett, William, 203
Barth, Karl, 40
Bartók, Béla, 202, 204; *Bluebeard's Castle*, 204
Barzini, Luigi, 112–13
Bastianini, Ettore, 224, 225, 226
Baudelaire, Charles, 22, 132, 158, 159
Beardsley, Aubrey, 147
Beaumarchais, Caron de, 21
Beecham, Thomas, 223
Beethoven, Ludwig von, 12, 22, 23, 27, *42–53*, 98, 115, 121, 144, 218, 223; *Fidelio*, x, 12, *41–53*, 218, 223
Behrens, Hildegard, 228
Belli, Domenico, 8
Bellini, Vincenzo, 65; *Norma*, 65, 194; *La Sonnambula*, 65
Berg, Alban, 203, 205; *Lulu*, 203, 205; *Wozzeck*, 188, 203, 207
Berger, Erna, 222, 223

Bergman, Ingmar, 30, 32
Berlin, Irving, 183–4, 205; *Annie Get Your Gun*, 186
Berlioz, Hector, 10, 14, 15, *101–10*, 116, 218, 226; *Béatrice et Bénédict*, 102; *Les Troyens*, x, xi, 10, *101–10*, 226
Bernanos, Georges, 171–81, 204
Bernhardt, Sarah, 81
Bernstein, Leonard, 97, 185, 206, 226; *West Side Story*, 185
Berry, Walter, 222
Bertati, Giovanni, 21
Birtwistle, Harrison, 11, 205
Bizet, Georges, 190; *Carmen*, 132, 188, 190
Björling, Jussi, 154, 157, 224, 226, 228
Blegen, Judith, 224
Bloch, Ernst, 51
Bock, Jerry: *Fiddler on the Roof*, 186
Böhm, Karl, 46, 227, 228
Boito, Arrigo, 99, 100
Bonynge, Richard, 224, 229
Borchmeyer, Dieter, 219
Born, Ignaz von, 31–2, 39
Borromeo, Carlo, 139–40, 143
Bouilly, Jean-Nicolas, 48
Boulez, Pierre, 205
Brahms, Johannes, 27, 115
Branscombe, Peter, 218
Brasseur, Pierre, 173
Braunbehrens, Volkmar, 39
Brecht, Berthold, 86, 201, 204
Britten, Benjamin, 204, 205, 207; *Billy Budd*, 204; *Death in Venice*, 204, 205; *Owen Wingrave*, 204; *Peter Grimes*, 204, 207; *The Turn of the Screw*, 204, 205
Broch, Hermann, 202, 213
Bronte, Emily, 127

Brown, John Mason, 99
Bruckberger, Raymond, 172–3
Bubbles, John, 229
Büchner, Georg, 205
Budden, Julian, 80
Buddha, 134–5, 136
Bülow, Hans von, 115, 119
Bulwe-Lytton, Edward, 113
Burton, Richard, 182
Busoni, Ferruccio, 143–4, 204; *Doktor Faust*, 143–4, 204
Byron, Lord, 22, 102

Caccini, Guilio, 6, 7
Cage, John, 193
Cairns, David, xi, 50, 218
Callas, Maria, 224, 225
Calzabigi, Raniero de', 9, 13, 14, 17
Camerata, the, 5–8, 140, 162, 213–14
Cammarano, Salvatore, 73
Campbell, Joseph, 34
Campra, André, 8
Canticle of Canticles, 147–8
Capecchi, Renato, 226
Capek, Karel, 204
Cappuccilli, Piero, 222
Carré, Albert, 165–6
Carter, Elliott, 11
Caruso, Enrico, 170, 224
Casanova, Giovanni, 22
Casella, Alfredo, 11
Cather, Willa, 201
Catullus, 108, 134
Cavalieri, Emilio de', 6–7
Cavalli, Francesco, 193
Cavour, Camillo, 74, 86
Cellini, Renato, 224
Cervantes, Miguel de, 34
Chabrier, Emmanuel, 173

Champion, Marge and Gower, 230
Charlton, David, 218
Chekhov, Anton, 205
Cherubini, Maria Luigi, 27
Chesterton, G.K., 134
Chopin, Frédéric, 23, 41, 107, 121
Chrétien de Troyes, 132
Christoff, Boris, 226
Cicero, 103, 111
Clabassi, Plinio, 225
Clark, Kenneth, 98
Claudel, Paul, 204
Cleopatra, 105–6
Cocteau, Jean, 173, 201, 204
Colbert, Jean-Baptiste, 175
Colette, 204
Colloredo, Archbishop, 29
Congreve, William, 194
Conrad, Joseph, 187, 201, 205
Constantine, 112
Corelli, Franco, 226
Corsi, Jacopo, 5–6
Cortot, Alfred, 229
Craft, Robert, 20
Cross, Milton, 60, 84
Czinner, Paul, 222

Dahlhaus, Carl, 145
d'Albert, Eugen: *Tiefland*, 202
Dallapiccola, Luigi, 205
Dante Alighieri, 15, 78, 162
Da Ponte, Lorenzo, 20, 21, 22, 24
Davis, Colin, 130, 226
Debussy, Claude, *158–69*, 174, 201,
    202, 205, 229; *Pelléas et Mélisande*, x,
    158–69, 205, 207, 218, 229–30
de Gaulle, Charles, 172
Delacroix, Eugène, 107
della Casa, Lisa, 222
De Luca, Giuseppe, 224

del Mar, Norman, 152
Del Monaco, Mario, 195
De Mille, Agnes, 195
Dent, Edward, 24
Dermota, Anton, 222
Dervaux, Pierre, 229
Desormière, Roger, 228–9
Dexter, John, 172, 180
Diaghilev, Sergei, 201
DiMaggio, Joe, 41
di Stefano, Giuseppe, 225
Domingo, Plácido, 225, 226, 228
Donath, Helen, 222
Donington, Robert, 145
Donizetti, Gaetano, *54–65*, 99; *Anna
    Bolena*, 58; *Don Pasquale*, 54, 56;
    L'Elisir d'Amore, x, *54–9*, 99, 223–
    4; *Lucia de Lammermoor*, x, *60–5*,
    224
Dorn, Heinrich, 115
Dostoevsky, Feodor, 85, 205
Dukas, Paul, 165
Dumas, Alexandre, fils, 79–81, 83
Duplessis, Marie, 80–1
Dürrenmatt, Friedrich, 205
Duse, Eleanora, 81
Dutoit, Charles, 226
Dvořák, Antonín: *Rusalka*, 202

Eckhart, Meister, 42
Edelmann, Otto, 222
Eichendorff, Joseph, 144
Einem, Gottfried von, 205
Einstein, Albert, 213
Eliot, T.S., 120, 122, 129, 132, 137, 199,
    201, 205, 214
Ertmann, Baroness, 44
Euripides, 6, 11, 34, 205

Falla, Manuel de, 205

Faner, Robert, 66
Fauré, Gabriel, 165
Ferdinand I, 140, 142–3
Fernandel, 173
Fischer-Dieskau, Dietrich, 227
Fitzgerald, Ella, 229
Flagstad, Kirsten, 46, 49, 223, 227
Flaubert, Gustave, 60
Floyd, Carlisle, 206
Forster, E.M., 60, 201
Foster, Stephen, 182
Freud, Sigmund, 111, 118, 149, 195,
　201, 203, 212, 213
Frick, Gottlob, 222
Friedrich, Götz, 228
Friml, Rudolph: *Rose Marie*, 182
Furtwängler, Wilhelm, 46, 144, 222, 227

Gagliano, Marco da, 193
Galilei, Vincenzo, 5
Galli-Curci, Amelita, 224
Gallus, Cornelius, 105
Garbo, Greta, 81
García Lorca, Federico, 205, 214
Garden, Mary, 165–6, 229
Gardiner, John Eliot, 221
Gardner, Ava, 230
Garibaldi, Giuseppe, 86
Gautier, Théophile, 104
Gavazzeni, Gianandrea, 77
Gazzaniga, Giuseppe, 21
Gedda, Nicolai, 227
Gencer, Leyla, 224
Genghis Kahn, 198
Gergiev, Valery, 225
Gerhard, Anselm, 85
Gershwin, George, ix, 174, 182, *187–
　90*, 193, 205; *Porgy and Bess*, 41, 182,
　187–90, 193, 205, 229
Gheorghiu, Angela, 225

Gibbon, Edward, 111
Gieseking, Walter, 158
Gilson, Etienne, 197, 206
Giulini, Carlo Maria, 222, 225, 226
Glass, Philip, 193, 205, 217; *The Voyage*,
　217
Glinka, Mikhail, 58, 85; *A Life for the
　Czar*, 85
Gluck, C.W. von, 9–10, 11, *13–18*, 27,
　184, 222; *Alceste*, 13; *Orfeo ed Euri-
　dice*, x, 9–10, 11, *13–18*, 218, 222
Gobbi, Tito, 98, 226
Goethe, J.W. von, 20, 31, 36, 38, 45, 46,
　48, 101, 107, 205
Goldoni, Carlo, 21
Gonzaga, Francesco, 3
Gossett, Philip, 218
Gottfried von Strassburg, 132, 135
Gounod, Charles, 20, 65, 107, 202;
　Faust, 20, 65, 202
Goya, Francisco, 84
Gozzi, Carlo, 205
Gramm, Donald, 226
Greene, Graham, 205
Gregory XIII, 140
Griffiths, Paul, 185, 218
Grümmer, Elisabeth, 222
Guttiérrez, A. García, 67–8, 76

Haitink, Bernard, 223
Halévy, Jacques, 114
Hall, Peter, 222
Hamilton, David, 195
Hammerstein, Oscar, II, 54, 182, 183,
　184–7, 191–6
Handel, George Frideric, 9, 14, 15, 24
Hanisch, Ernst, 219
Hanslick, Eduard, 17
Hanson, Howard, *Merry Mount*, 186
Harnoncourt, Nikolaus, 221

Hart, Lorenz, 184, 192, 193
Hauptmann, Gerhart, 205
Haydn, Joseph, 10, 27; *L'Anima del Filosofo*, 10
Heine, Heinrich, 104
Henderson, Dave, 42
Henri IV, 6
Henze, Hans Werner, 205
Hepokoski, James A., 218
Herbert, Victor, 183
Herman, Jerry: *Hello Dolly!*, 186
Hess, Rudolph, 46
Highet, Gilbert, 192
Hindemith, Paul, 143–4, 204; *Mathis der Maler*, 143–4, 204
Hitler, Adolf, 45–6, 113–14, 200
Hockney, David, 223
Höffgen, Marga, 223
Hoffmann, E.T.A., 20, 23, 26
Hofmannsthal, Hugo von, 203–4, 205, 207, 209, 212–14
Holden, Amanda, 217
Hölderlin, Friedrich, 11, 136
Homer, 34, 36, 48, 106, 208
Honegger, Arthur, 204; *Jeanne d'Arc au Bûcher*, 204
Höngen, Elisabeth, 228
Horace, ix, xi, 105, 108, 194
Horne, Marilyn, 222
Hotter, Hans, 228
Howard, Patricia, 218
Hughes, Eddie, 41
Hugo, Victor, 107
Hüsch, Gerhard, 223
Huysmans, Joris Karl, 152

Ibsen, Henrik, 165
Ismail Pasha, Khedive, 120

James, Henry, 205

Jahn, Otto, 218
Janáček, Leoš, 204, 207; *Jenůfa*, 207; *The Makropoulos Case*, 204
Janowitz, Gundula, 223, 230
Jeritza, Maria, 207
Jesus, 52, 113, 116, 175, 198
John of the Cross, 138
Johnson, Samuel, 206
Joseph II, 31–2, 39
Joyce, James, 23, 111, 120, 201
Juliana of Norwich, 42
Jung, C.G., 34–5, 111, 118, 201, 204

Kafka, Franz, 205
Kant, Immanuel, 144
Karajan, Herbert von, 97, 226, 228–9, 230
Kauffmann, Stanley, 81
Kempe, Rudolf, 230
Kenyon, Nicholas, 217
Kerman, Joseph, 12, 129–30, 135
Kern, Jerome, 182–3, 184, 185, 186–7, 189, 190, 192, 193, 205; *The Girl from Utah*, 182–3; *Show Boat*, 186–7, 190, 192, 193, 230
Kierkegaard, Søren, 20, 26
King, James, 230
Klemperer, Otto, 223
Klopstock, F.G., 45
Kolbe, Maximilian, 180
Korngold, Erich W., 204; *Die Tote Stadt*, 204
Křenek, Ernst, 11
Krips, Josef, 227
Kubelik, Rafael, 145, 227
Kubrick, Stanley, 198, 212
Kurosawa, Akira, 98
Kurz, Selma, 207

Landi, Stephano, 8

Lang, Paul Henry, 7, 44
Lavery, Emmet, 172
Lawrence, D.H., 120, 201
Leblanc, Georgette, 165
le Fort, Gertrud von, 172, 174, 181
Legouvé, Ernest, 104
Lehár, Franz, *The Merry Widow*, 193, 200
Lehmann, Lotte, 49, 180, 207
Leider, Frida, 227
Lemnitz, Tiana, 223
Leoncavallo, Ruggiero, 155
Leopold II, 32
Lepidus, 90
Leppard, Raymond, 222
Lerner, Alan Jay, 54, 182
Levine, James, 223, 225, 226, 228
Lévi-Strauss, Claude, 111, 201
Liszt, Franz, 23, 80, 107, 121, 131
Livy, 105
Lloyd Webber, Andrew, 193
Loesser, Frank, 185, 205; *Guys and Dolls*, 185
Loewe, Frederick, 54, 182, 185, 190, 205; *Camelot*, 34, 182, 190, 194; *My Fair Lady*, 185, 194
Lorengar, Pilar, 222
Louis XIV, 175
Lucretius, 103
Ludwig, Christa, 223, 227
Lukács, Georg, 199
Lully, Louis, 8
Lully, Jean-Baptiste, 8
Lully, Jean-Baptiste, fils, 8
Luten, C.J., 166
Luther, Martin, 14, 144

Maecenas, 105
Maeterlinck, Maurice, 160–1, 165–9, 205, 229

Magee, Bryan, 200
Mahler, Gustav, 144, 201
Malipiero, Gian Francesco, 11
Mallarmé, Stéphane, 120, 158, 160, 164
Malory, Sir Thomas, 132
Manet, Edouard, 158
Mann, Thomas, 111, 120, 128, 132, 145, 201, 205
Mann, William, 151–2
Manzoni, Alessandro, 87
Maria Teresa, 31–2
Maritain, Jacques, 137
Martin, George, 203–4
Martinelli, Giovanni, 41
Martinů, Bohuslav, 205
Marx, Karl, 199, 213
Mascagni, Pietro, 155; *Cavalleria Rusticana*, 188
Massenet, Jules, 5, 153, 156, 217; *Don Quichotte*, 202; *Manon*, 153, 156
McCormack, John, 22, 224
McGlinn, John, 186, 230
Medici, Maria de', 6
Melchior, Lauritz, 227
Menotti, Gian Carlo, 206
Mérimée, Prosper, 22
Merriman, Nan, 222
Mesomedes of Crete, 5
Messager, André, 165
Messiaen, Olivier, 165; *St Francis of Assisi*, 165
Metastasio, Pietro, 8
Meyerbeer, Giacomo, 5, 114, 115–16; *Les Huguenots*, 65; *Le Prophète*, 65; *Robert le Diable*, 65
Meyerowitz, Jan, 155–6
Michelangelo, 47
Milanov, Zinka, 224, 226
Milhaud, Darius, 11
Miller, Arthur, 206

Milnes, Sherrill, 225
Milton, John, 36
Mitropoulos, Dimitri, 154
Molière, 21, 24, 207
Molinari-Pradelli, Francesco, 225
Moll, Kurt, 223
Monet, Claude, 158
Montemezzi, Italo: *L'Amore dei Tre Re*, 202
Monteverdi, Claudio, ix, 7–8, 11, 18, 174, 213, 221; *L'Incoronazione di Poppea*, 221; *Orfeo*, 7–8, 11, 218, 221; *Il Ritorno d'Ulisse in Patria*, 221
Moore, Douglas, 206
Moreau, Gustave, 147
Moreau, Jeanne, 173
Morgan, Helen, 230
Morgan, J.P., 151
Mörike, Eduard, 19, 23, 25, 26
Morris, Joan, 183
Moyers, Bill, 34
Mozart, Constanze, 29
Mozart, Wolfgang A., 9, 10, 12, *19–40*, 43, 54, 58, 65, 77, 78, 121, 132, 156, 180, 195, 203, 209–10, 213, 218, 222–3; *Don Giovanni*, x, *19–26*, 54, 65, 218, 222; *The Magic Flute*, x, 12, *27–40*, 195, 210, 218, 222–3; *The Marriage of Figaro*, 9, 19, 21, 27, 132, 202; *Requiem*, 28–9
Müller, Ulrich, 219
Musset, Alfred de, 22, 26
Mussolini, Benito, 113, 114
Mussorgsky, Modest, 77, 85, 163, 174; *Boris Godunov*, 85, 163, 188

Nagano, Kent, 229
Napoleon Bonaparte, 45, 113, 114
Napoleon III, 104
Newman, Ernest, 53, 223

Nichols, Roger, 218
Nietzsche, Friedrich, 3, 30, 120, 137, 197, 200, 206, 212–13
Nilsson, Birgit, 119, 227, 228
Nisbet, Robert, 200
Norman, Jessye, 226
Novalis, 11, 136

Offenbach, Jacques, 10, 22; *Orphée aux Enfers*, 10; *The Tales of Hoffman*, 22
O'Neill, Eugene, 206
Orff, Carl, 11, 205
Osborne, Conrad L., 172, 229
Ovid, 4, 6, 105, 208, 212, 213

Palestrina, Giovanni, 5, 16–17, 139–40
Panizza, Ettore, 225
Parker, Horatio: *Mona*, 186
Parker, Roger, 218
Pasternak, Boris, 85
Pavarotti, Luciano, 223–4
Pedro II of Brazil, 120
Penderecki, Krzysztof, 205
Pergolesi, Giovanni Battista, 121
Peri, Jacopo, 6–7, 11, 18, 217; *Dafne*, 6, 217; *Euridice*, 6–7, 11
Perlea, Jonel, 226, 228
Petrarch, 112
Pfitzner, Hans, *139–46*, 204; *Palestrina*, x, *139–46*, 204, 227
Philips-Matz, Mary Jane, 82
Piave, Francesco Maria, 79
Piffl, Archbishop, 151
Pinza, Ezio, 84, 225
Pirandello, Luigi, 205
Pius IV, 140, 142–3
Plato, 206
Plautus, 20, 55, 56
Poe, E.A., 205

Politian, 3–5, 6, 7, 11
Ponnelle, Jean-Pierre, 221, 226
Ponselle, Rosa, 225
Popp, Lucia, 223
Porter, Andrew, 24
Porter, Cole, 183, 185, 190, 205; *Kiss Me, Kate*, 186, 190, 194
Poulenc, Francis, 5, 165, *170–81*, 202, 204, 229; *Dialogues des Carmélites*, x, 165, *170–81*, 204, 229; *Les Mamelles de Tirésias*, 173, 204; *La Voix Humaine*, 173
Previtali, Fernando, 225
Prévost, Abbé, 156
Prey, Hermann, 227, 230
Price, Leontyne, 225, 229
Pritchard, John, 226
Prokofiev, Sergei, 204, 206; *The Fiery Angel*, 204; *Semyon Kotko*, 206; *The Story of a Real Man*, 206
Proust, Marcel, 103, 111, 120, 130, 158, 201
Puccini, Giacomo, 10, 54, *153–7*, 165, 168, 202, 204, 206, 218, 228; *La Bohème*, 132, 156; *Edgar*, 154; *La Fanciulla del West*, 165; *Gianni Schicchi*, 156; *Madama Butterfly*, 54, 156, 191, 204, 206; *Manon Lescaut*, x, *153–7*, 228; *Tosca*, 156, 204, 206; *Turandot*, 155, 156, 204; *Le Villi*, 154
Puffett, Derrick, 218
Pushkin, Alexander, 22

Rather, L.J., 111
Rattle, Simon, 229
Ravel, Maurice, 173, 174, 204; *L'Enfant et les Sortilèges*, 204
Reimann, Aribert, 205
Reiner, Fritz, 228

Reinhardt, Max, 207
Renoir, Jean, 202
Rescigno, Nicola, 224
Reynolds, Herbert, 182
Ricordi, Giulio, 153
Ridderbusch, Karl, 227
Rienzo, Cola di, 111–17
Riggs, Lynn, 195
Rilke, Rainer Maria, 17, 18, 214
Rimsky-Korsakov, Nicolai, *Le Coq d'Or*, 202
Rinuccini, Ottavio, 6
Rivas, Duque de, 84
Robbins Landon, H.C., 39
Robeson, Paul, 230
Robespierre, Maximilien, 171
Robinson, Paul, 218
Röckel, August, 116
Rodgers, Richard, 54, 184–5, 190, *191–6*, 205; *Allegro*, 186; *Carousel*, 54, 185, 190, 193; *I Married an Angel*, 184; *The King and I*, 54, 193; *Oklahoma!*, x, 54, 186, *191–6*, 230; *Pal Joey*, 193; *The Sound of Music*, 186, 193, 195; *South Pacific*, 54, 193
Romani, Felice, 55, 59
Romberg, Sigmund: *The New Moon*, 182
Roosevelt, Franklin D., 174
Rosbaud, Hans, 222
Rossi, Luigi, 8
Rossini, Gioachino, 20, 26, 54, 57, 65, 85, 99, 218; *The Barber of Seville*, 54; *La Gazza Ladra*, 85; *William Tell*, 65
Rostropovich, Mstislav, 46
Rougement, Denis de, 135–6
Rousseau, Jean-Jacques, 9
Rubini, Giovanni Battista, 22

Rudolph, Archduke, 45
Ruffo, Vincenzo, 140
Rushton, Julian, 218
Russell, John, 98

Sadie, Stanley, 217
Sallust, 111
Sanderson, Julia, 182, 183
Sappho, 137, 199
Sargeant, Winthrop, 22
Sartre, Jean-Paul, 89, 197, 206
Satie, Eric, 173
Savage, Roger, 218
Schikaneder, Emanuel, 31, 48
Schiller, Friedrich, 45, 53, 86
Schlegel, A.W., 85
Schnorr von Carolsfeld, Ludwig, 119
Schnorr von Carolsfeld, Malvina, 119
Schöffler, Paul, 227
Schönber, Arnold, 25, 120, 143, 158,
    165, 201, 202–3, 204; *Erwartung*,
    204; *Die Glückliche Hand*, 204; *Moses
    und Aron*, 143, 203, 207
Schopenhauer, Arthur, 128, 135, 136,
    138, 144
Schubert, Franz, 27
Schumann, Robert, 144
Schwarzkopf, Elisabeth, 222, 223
Sciutti, Graziella, 222
Scott, Walter, 60
Scotto, Renata, 228
Scribe, Augustin, 55, 59
Shadwell, Thomas, 21
Shakespeare, William, 20, 26, 36, 86,
    90–6, 101, 107, 108, 134, 137, 170,
    199, 205
Shaw, G.B. 20, 22, 32, 155, 201
Sheean, Vincent, 74
Shostakovich, Dimitri, 200, 205
Sibelius, Jean, 165

Siepi, Cesare, 222
Simoneau, Léopold, 23, 222
Smith, Richard Langham, 218
Söderström, Elisabeth, 223
Solti, Georg, 97, 222, 223, 225, 226, 228
Sondheim, Stephen, 193, 206; *Pacific
    Overtures*, 206
Sonnleithner, Joseph, 48
Sophocles, 6, 10, 34, 88, 98
Spengler, Oswald, 136–7, 201
Spontini, Gasparo, 114
Stalin, Joseph, 46, 200
Starr, Lawrence, 189
Stein, Gertrude, 206
Steinbeck, John, 206
Steiner, George, 213
Stockhausen, Karlheinz, 205
Stratas, Teresa, 178, 228
Strauss, Johann, Sr, 27
Strauss, Johann, Jr, 27
Strauss, Richard, 10, 25, 97, 120,
    143, 144, *147–52*, 165, 201, 202,
    203–5, *207–14*, 228; *Die Aegyptische
    Helena*, 203–4; *Ariadne auf Naxos*,
    207–14, 230; *Capriccio*, 143, 207;
    Elektra, 165, 205, 207; *Die Frau
    ohne Schatten*, 206; *Intermezzo*, 143;
    Der Rosenkavalier, 205, 206–7;
    Salome, x, *147–52*, 165, 205, 207,
    218, 228
Stravinsky, Igor, 11, 174, 201, 202, 204;
    Oedipus Rex, 204; *The Rake's
    Progress*, 204
Strepponi, Giuseppina, 74, 81–2, 88
Striggio, Alessandro, 8
Strindberg, August, 205
Sullivan, Arthur: *HMS Pinafore*, 193
Sullivan, J.W.N., 51, 218
Suthaus, Ludwig, 227
Sutherland, Joan, 222, 224, 229

Svanholm, Set, 227, 228
Swanston, Hamish F., 51
Swinburne, Algernon, 132
Synge, J.M., 205
Szymanowski, Karol, 205

Taddei, Giuseppe, 222
Tauber, Richard, 23
Tchaikovsky, Pyotr, 20; *The Queen of Spades*, 200
Tebaldi, Renata, 226
Teilhard de Chardin, Pierre, 212, 215
Tennyson, Alfred Lord, 1–3, 103, 224
Teresa, Mother, 178
Terrasson, Jean, 31
Teyte, Maggie, 166, 229
Thayer, A.W., 44
Thérèse of Lisieux, 179
Thomas, Ambroise, 107
Thomas à Kempis, 45
Thomson, Virgil, 202, 206; *Four Saints in Three Acts*, 206; *The Mother of Us All*, 206
Tibbett, Lawrence, 41, 225, 229
Tippett, Michael, 204; *The Midsummer Marriage*, 204
Tirso de Molina, 21
Tolstoy, Leo, 22, 60, 85, 86
Toscanini, Arturo, 45, 90, 97, 100, 222, 225, 226
Tovey, Donald, 14
Toye, Francis, 77
Treitschke, G.F., 48
Troyanos, Tatiana, 226
Twain, Mark, 34, 187

Upanishads, the, 137, 199
Updike, John, 38

Valéry, Paul, 214

Valli, Alida, 173
van Dam, José, 229
Vasselli, Virginia, 59
Vaughan Williams, Ralph, 205; *Riders to the Sea*, 205
Velázquez, Diego de, 84
Verdi, Giuseppe, 10, 14, 15, 30, 49, 54, 58, 65, *67–100*, 114, 154, 155, 174, 180, 202, 203, 224–5; *Aida*, x, *90–6*, 97, 226; *Ernani*, 65; *Falstaff*, x, 90, *97–100*, 218, 226; *La Forza del Destino*, *84–9*, 225–6; *Otello*, 74, 88, 90, 202; *Requiem*, 88, 115; *Rigoletto*, 49, 76, 81; *Te Deum*, 88; *La Traviata*, x, 58, 76, *78–83*, 97, 100, 225; *Il Trovatore*, x, 30, *67–77*, 81, 87, 97, 98, 100, 142, 224–5
Verlaine, Paul, 158, 159
Viardot, Pauline, 20
Vickers, Jon, 223, 226, 227
Virgil, 4, 10, 17, 33, 36, 101–10, 141, 198, 200, 202, 208, 212
Visconti, Luchino, 225
Vishnevskaya, Galina, 46
von Stade, Frederica, 228

Wächter, Eberhard, 222
Wagner, Cosima, 119
Wagner, Minna, 115, 119
Wagner, Richard, x, 5, 10, 11–12, 13, 14, 20, 22, 25, 38–9, 54, 61, 72, 77, 88–9, 99, 102, *111–38*, 141, 143–4, 145, 154, 155, 159–60, 161–2, 190, 191, 200–2, 203, 204, 210, 211, 213, 218, 219, 227, 229; *The Flying Dutchman*, 115; *Lohengrin*, 11, 115, 116, 134, 202; *Die Meistersinger*, 11–12, 99, 115, 132, 141–2, 143–4, 188–9, 190, 191, 201; *Parsifal*, 22, 115, 128, 145, 155, 159–60, 162, 201;

Rienzi, 111–17, 227; *Der Ring des Nibelungen*, 38, 115, 201, 210; *Tannhäuser*, 11, 54, 72, 115, 134; *Tristan und Isolde*, x, 11, 20, 115, *118–38*, 155, 159, 201, *202–3*, 211, 213, 227
Wagner, Wieland, 201
Walter, Bruno, 20, 45–6, 49–50, 144, 223
Walsh, Stephen, 217
Wapnewski, Peter, 219
Warfield, William, 229
Warren, Leonard, 224
Weber, C.M. von, 144
Wedekind, Frank, 205
Weikl, Bernd, 227
Weill, Kurt, 185, 195, 204; *Mahagonny*, 185, 204
Welitsch, Ljuba, 228
Welles, Orson, 99

Wells, H.G., 197, 212
Wesendonck, Mathilde, 118–19, 122, 128, 132
Whenham, John, 218
White, Willard, 229
Whitman, Walt, 60–6, 224
Wieland, C.M., 31
Wilde, Oscar, 23, 147–8, 152, 165, 205
Wilhelm II, Kaiser, 151
Williams, Tennessee, 206
Winckelmann, Johann J., 9, 17–18, 222
Windgassen, Wolfgang, 227
Woolf, Virginia, 201

Yeats, W.B., 199–200, 205, 212, 214

Zimmermann, Bernd Alois, 204; *Die Soldaten*, 204
Zuckerman, Elliott, 137